MURDERED

IN

JERSEY

MURDERED
IN
JERSEY

GERALD TOMLINSON

RUTGERS UNIVERSITY PRESS • NEW BRUNSWICK, NEW JERSEY

Library of Congress Cataloging-in-Publication Data

Tomlinson, Gerald, 1933–
    Murdered in Jersey / Gerald Tomlinson.
       p. cm.
    Includes bibliographical references and index.
    ISBN 0-8135-2077-0 — ISBN 0-8135-2078-9 (pbk.)
    1. Murder—New Jersey—Case studies.   2. Crime—New Jersey—Case
studies.   I. Title.
HV6533.N3T66   1994
364.1'523'09749—dc20   93-35007
                                                               CIP

British Cataloging-in-Publication information available

Design by John Romer

DEDICATED TO

— *the police, who investigated*
— *the journalists, who reported*
— *the victims, who died*

Contents

Acknowledgments

Since this book is based primarily on newspaper accounts of the sixty murder cases, I am greatly indebted to the reporters who, with or without bylines, covered the cases in the daily, and occasionally, the weekly newspapers. As the bibliography at the end of the book indicates, the reporters for the *New York Times* and Newark *Star-Ledger* deserve special thanks, since, with rare exceptions, their articles were used as the main sources of factual information.

A number of librarians, archivists, and historians furnished valuable assistance, including, at the institutional level, the reference staffs of the Morris County Free Library; Newark Public Library, New Jersey Division; Alexander Library, Rutgers University, Special Collections and Archives; and the Free Public Library of the City of Trenton. Among the many individuals who responded helpfully to requests for information are the following: Constance Brewer, Kemper Chambers, Peggy Davis, Susan R. Feibush, William Frolich, Olga Griminger, Edith Hoelle, Laura C. Mahoney, Harold Q. Masur, James Stuart Osbourn, Donald A. Sinclair, Dian Spitler, Cathy Stout, John Walz, and Charles Webster.

Several members of the New Jersey State Police have been generous with their time and expertise in helping to correct misinterpretations of fact or inference. They are August Wistner III, Michael Langan, Robert M. Scott, and Tom DeFeo, historian and curator of the New Jersey State Police Museum and Learning Center in West Trenton. For cases in which the state police were involved, their assistance was most helpful.

As time passed and the book developed, several other people with specific interests and knowledge read all or parts of the manuscript and made suggestions concerning it. These readings resulted in additions, corrections, deletions, and qualifications, and, with them, improvements in the final text. Special thanks on this score are due to Alexis, Matt, and Eli Tomlinson—all of them in the family and all astute editors—as well as to Timothy B. Benford, Carol Wistner, Brian Doherty, and Willa Speiser.

Note

The date shown after the introductory headline for each case is, unless otherwise indicated, the date, or the presumed date, of the murder, murders, or abduction. It is not the date of the discovery of the body or bodies, nor is it the date of the first newspaper reports, which nearly always will be one day later than the events being covered. (The Source Notes at the end of the book show the actual key newspaper dates.) When more than one murder or set of murders occurred, the date used is that of the first murder.

MURDERED
IN
JERSEY

Introduction

There were 397 murders in New Jersey in 1992, down from 410 in 1991 and 432 in 1990. These figures suggest that the Garden State is not the murder hub of the nation. Indeed, in 1990 New Jersey's murder rate of 5.6 per 100,000 inhabitants was less than half as high as those of New York, California, Texas, and four states in the Deep South: Alabama, Georgia, Louisiana, and Mississippi. In the District of Columbia the murder rate in 1990 was nearly 14 times as high as New Jersey's.

Still, New Jersey, if not exactly the Homicide State, has had many highly publicized murders since that fateful September night in 1922 when the Reverend Edward Wheeler Hall and his choir-singer mistress, Mrs. Eleanor Mills, were murdered in a lovers' lane near New Brunswick. Few homicides have attracted as much press attention as that celebrated case. The Hall-Mills affair had virtually every element of a front-page news story—steamy sex, an unknown killer or killers, prominent participants, more than one victim, shameful treatment of the deceased, and a shocking surprise or two as the case developed.

Most of the murders in this book have one or more of those elements, which is what sets them apart from the thousands of other cases between 1922 and 1992. A separate but important category of front-page homicide, however, often lacking any of those elements, is that in which a police officer is the victim. The press and public understandably take these murders very seriously. Robbery and domestic violence, on the other hand, even when they result in murder, are seldom unusual enough to attract media attention. Editors may not care much about the taxonomy of sensationalism, but they have a sure feel for newsworthiness. If the story has the right elements, disturbs and maybe also titillates, it gets coverage.

One consequence of choosing cases for their media appeal is that the geographical distribution of the cases, while broad, does not match the actual incidence of murders in New Jersey. For example, the three counties with the most murders in 1990 were Essex (133), Camden (43), and Hudson (42). Of the 60 murders in this book, however, only 5 occurred in Essex County, 4 in Hudson County, and 3 in Camden County. By contrast, 4 of the 60 murders took place in Morris County and 4 in Somerset County. In 1990 these affluent and mainly suburban counties registered only 7 and 2 murders respectively.

Nor does the racial distribution of murders in the book match current New Jersey percentages. Sixty-six percent of the persons arrested for murder in 1990 were black and 34 percent were white. Of the 60 cases in the book, however, only 12 murders, or 20 percent, were committed by blacks. (A few cases are unsolved, none of them with likely black killers.) The murders involving black perpetrators are quite evenly spread in time, with 2 in the 1920s, 3 in the 1940s, 1 each in the 1950s and 1960s, 3 in the 1970s, and 2 in the 1980s.

In the golden age of detective fiction, the puzzle element was paramount. There are occasionally such puzzles in real-life murders. The Hall-Mills case surely qualifies, as do the two bombings in this book, the Hyland and Puskas slayings. Several murders, including those of the Lindbergh baby and Exxon executive Sidney J. Reso, both kidnappings, remained unsolved for weeks, months, or even years. The two most famous physician-as-killer cases in New Jersey (Drs. Coppolino and Jascalevich) generated mystery, controversy—and acquittals. Mob hits typically, but not always, go unpunished.

Often, however, the motive and the culprit in a murder are known within days, hours, or minutes. The interest lies elsewhere—in the mad homicidal spree of Howard Unruh; the pen-pal support of a respected columnist for convicted murderer Edgar Smith; the radical and violent politics of Joanne Chesimard; the celebrity status of boxer Rubin (Hurricane) Carter; the mass killing and well-planned flight of churchly John List. These cases all have one or more of the elements that make for bold headlines.

A familiar observation, sometimes in the form of a complaint, is that the murder of a wealthy socialite in Highland Park is big news, whereas the apparently similar murder of a blue-collar worker in Irvington is a nonstory. The statement is accurate. Many of the cases in this book—and on the front pages of New Jersey's daily newspapers—would not be there if the victims, or killers, or both were people without money or social status. If Margaret McDade, murdered in Haddon Heights on V-J Day, had been the daughter of an ex-governor and a DAR dowager, people might be talking about her demise to this day. As it is, the slain waitress gets only a few paragraphs in the book, and those only because of the inscription on the party hat she was wearing.

Not every case that wows the daily press has a long shelf life. The kidnapping and murder of Mary Daly are all but forgotten today, yet when it occurred in Montclair in the mid-1920s the *New York Times* gave it front-page coverage day after day. The case of the "Trenton Six" in the late 1940s was a *cause célèbre* that faded as fast as it bloomed. Some cases, of course, are kept alive by true-crime books. Insurance broker Robert Marshall's bungled murder-for-hire of his wife in a picnic area on the Garden State Parkway might have slipped into obscurity except for the publication of Joe McGinniss's *Blind Faith*. The lunatic actions in Leonia of Joseph Kallinger, pursuing, as he thought, a "mission of global massacre," were preserved in book form by Flora Rheta Schreiber in *The Shoemaker*. Even the well-known rub-out of mobster Dutch Schultz probably gained a shade more notoriety with the appearance of Paul Sann's *Kill the Dutchman!* and the fictionalized account of Schultz's life and times in E. L. Doctorow's *Billy Bathgate: A Novel*.

It is unfortunate, in a way, that a few sensational New Jersey cases have overwhelmed the rest. The Lindbergh case is fascinating, true, but how many more Hauptmann-didn't-do-it theories are really needed? There are other noteworthy New Jersey murder cases, some equally absorbing, and the aim of this book is to present concise accounts of many of them. These cases provide a capsule history of homicide in New Jersey through seven decades. In addition to the familiar cases, the book presents a number of lesser-known murders, about which Sherlock Holmes might have said, "There are decidedly points of interest."

Choosing the cases was inevitably subjective. All sixty murders were front-page news, not only locally but sometimes nationally and even internationally. Still, there have been hundreds of front-page murders over the years, and not all of them appear in this book. Not even all the murders that appear in books of their own have made the list of sixty.

With a single exception—the three murders in 1942 at Fort Dix—the accounts in this book are based on newspaper reports and any relevant secondary sources (see pages 213–227). All the facts presented are part of the public record, and any interpretations, correct or incorrect, are based on my reading of that record. Where journalistic accounts differ, I have tried to judge fairly between them, comparing articles in different papers or checking later articles that may contain corrections or clarifications, and eliminating details that cannot be accurately determined. Even so, the nature of newspaper reporting makes it probable that some errors of fact will have been made by the journalists of the day and will be repeated in this book.

Here, then, are sixty memorable New Jersey murders, headlined and summarized. They offer a revealing glimpse of homicide in the Garden State from the days of Prohibition to the present, from the unsolved but probably quite rational slayings of the Reverend Hall and Mrs. Mills in 1922 to the solved but morally inexplicable murder of Sidney J. Reso in 1992.

PART ONE

FROM HALL-MILLS
TO
LINDBERGH

Under a Crab Apple Tree

FRANKLIN TOWNSHIP

Rector and Woman Choir Singer Found Murdered in Lovers' Lane

SEPTEMBER 16, 1922

"You are a true priest. You see in me merely your physical inspiration."

Thus begins one of the handwritten notes found in the pocket of the slain Reverend Edward Wheeler Hall, forty-one, rector of Saint John the Evangelist Episcopal Church in New Brunswick. The note had been written by the woman who now lay dead beside him—Mrs. Eleanor Mills, thirty-four, a choir singer at Saint John's and, it seemed evident enough, the lover of the corpulent, asthmatic minister.

The two bodies had been carefully arranged under a crab apple tree. Both lay on their backs, with the rector's right hand placed partially (lovingly, it would appear) under Mrs. Mills's shoulder and neck. Their clothing was neatly in place, as if for burial. A Panama hat partially covered the rector's face. A scarf concealed the choir singer's face and neck. One bullet hole in the Reverend Mr. Hall's head and three in Mrs. Mills's head left little doubt about the cause of death. As a finishing touch, Mrs. Mills's throat had been cut from ear to ear, and maggots filled the gaping wound. Letters, notes, and cards lay scattered between the bodies. A calling card propped up jauntily against the minister's left foot identified him to his discoverers—although they, a fifteen-year-old girl and her much older boyfriend, soon fled from their gruesome find.

Even the staid *New York Times* quoted such lines as these from the scrawled love missives that the choir singer had written to the rector: "I know there are girls with more shapely bodies, but I do not care what they have. I have the greatest of all blessings, a noble man, deep, true, and eternal love."

Not anymore. The love affair had ended. Where it ended was at first in dispute. Some thought the murders had been committed elsewhere, not in the secluded lovers' lane, just off De Russey's Lane, where the bodies were found. Territoriality proved to be a problem from the outset. New Brunswick police were the first to respond, but the actual site of the victims' bodies was out of their bailiwick, for the killer or killers had staged their grimly accusatory scene roughly 350 feet beyond the Middlesex County line in Somerset County. Thus, New Brunswick's premier murder case fell under the jurisdiction of Somerville.

The bodies had lain under the crab apple tree for thirty-six hours before being discovered at about ten o'clock on a Saturday morning. And, indeed, the Reverend Mr. Hall and Mrs. Mills had been unaccountably missing from their homes since Thursday night. When Frances Hall, the rector's wife, met James Mills, the choir singer's husband, on Friday morning at the church—James was the sexton there—Mrs. Hall greeted him and said, "Mr. Hall did not come home all night."

To which James said he responded, "My wife did not come home all night." He added, "Do you think they eloped?"

Mrs. Hall replied, "God knows. I think they are dead and can't come home."

Those are curious statements in view of what the sexton and the widow were presumed to know. Jim Mills, a laconic and evidently purblind handyman, supposed that his wife and the rector met only to discuss "church matters" and that robbers probably killed Hall "for his gold watch and his money." Thin, sad-faced Jim Mills claimed (untruthfully, as it turned out) to have been perhaps the only person connected with Saint John the Evangelist who had no inkling that the minister and the choir singer were carrying on an affair. "I care more for Mr. Hall's little finger than I do for your whole body!" Eleanor once told Jim angrily. But the sexton saw nothing seriously amiss in his marriage—except, of course, that Mr. Hall and Mrs. Mills might have eloped.

Mrs. Hall, for her part, far from dismissing the elopement idea, jumped to the dire conclusion that their spouses, having vanished on the same night, were both dead.

The local and state authorities made a hash of the investigation. A patently innocent man was quickly charged with the murder and just as quickly cleared. A Somerset County grand jury listened to a fanciful story from a widow, Jane Gibson, a fiftyish local pig farmer (immortalized in the annals of American crime as the Pig Woman), who claimed—a bit too late in the inquiry for credibility—to have observed a great deal of activity on the night of the murder while riding her mule, Jenny. The Pig Woman, who lived at one end of De Russey's Lane, had seen, among other things, two men and two women arguing bitterly near a crab apple tree. On a later jaunt on her mule, the observant Pig Woman, having lost a moccasin the first time out and hoping to recover it, saw Mrs. Hall kneeling beside her husband's corpse and sobbing. An easily convinced special prosecutor sought an indictment. He didn't get it.

Weeks dragged into months, months into years. "The case is not dead," a Middlesex County detective insisted in September 1923. But it was.

And then, suddenly, it wasn't. In July 1926 the New York *Daily Mirror* reported the appearance of what it said was important new evidence. The power of blaring headlines persuaded the authorities to look into the case again, and before you could say "crab apple tree," a grand jury handed down four indictments. The most important one named Mrs. Edward Wheeler Hall, last seen by the Pig Woman nearly four years earlier, crying morosely in the moonlight over her husband's lifeless body near De Russey's Lane.

Mrs. Hall's accomplices, said Alexander Simpson, the special prosecutor—an energetic but erratic state senator brought in from Hudson County to try the case—were her brothers Henry Stevens and William Stevens (always called Willie), along with the elegantly named Henry de la Bruyre Carpender, a first cousin. Carpender received a severance and was to be tried separately, but the indictment against him was later dismissed.

The star witness for the state would be . . . not the man who had inspired the *Daily Mirror* to challenge the *Daily News* for circulation supremacy. No. The state's star witness would be the Pig Woman. And so, dying of cancer at fifty-six years of age, she belatedly told her story. She testified from an iron hospital bed in the Somerset County courthouse, while her seventy-six-year-old mother, Mrs. Salome Cerenner, sat in a front-row seat, muttering, "She's a liar."

The Pig Woman's story had become a bit more vivid and detailed over the years. She placed Mrs. Hall and Henry and Willie Stevens at the scene of the crime—it was now generally conceded that the murders took place where the bodies were found. She had heard a "rumbling of voices," she said, followed by a woman's angry shout, "Explain those letters!" She saw Henry Stevens (her identifications were emphatic) wrestling with another man. Mrs. Gibson's natural curiosity turned to fear when a gunshot rang out, sending her running for her mule. Then she heard

"Bang! Bang! Bang!" The Pig Woman's testimony matched the newspaper accounts quite neatly, and if the jury believed her, Mrs. Hall and the Stevenses were on their way to the Big House.

As the Pig Woman was transferred from her iron bed to a stretcher, she fixed a baleful eye on the defendants and pointed a trembling finger. "I've told the truth, so help me God, and you know I've told the truth."

The jury was of a different opinion. After five hours of deliberation, the jurors, whom prosecutor Simpson regarded as openly hostile, returned three verdicts of not guilty. Said one juror, "I would remain here for 30 years rather than vote a verdict of guilty on such evidence." Most people who had followed the case agreed, but Charlotte Mills, the outspoken daughter of Jim Mills and a self-proclaimed flapper, wailed, "Money can buy anything."

The case was over, the mystery unsolved, the millions of words of journalistic speculation wasted. The question remained: Who killed the Reverend Edward Wheeler Hall and Mrs. Eleanor Mills in their trysting place? Who knows?

One person who thought he could give a better answer than prosecutor Simpson had offered was lawyer William M. Kunstler, the noted civil rights attorney. In his 1964 book, *The Minister and the Choir Singer*, he blamed the 1922 murders on one of the then-active New Jersey branches of the Ku Klux Klan. This proposed solution is less startling than some reviewers have suggested, because Klan involvement was rumored from the start. But it is not a wholly satisfying explanation, as Kunstler admits in his book. The Klan itself made no claim, then or later, to having struck this sanguinary blow for sexual morality in New Brunswick. Nor were the two victims the Klan's usual kinds of targets, despite Kunstler's citations of vaguely similar cases.

Donald W. Sinclair, coauthor with John T. Cunningham of *Murder Did Pay*, is inclined to think that Mrs. Hall, despite her easy acquittal and successful libel suit against the *Daily Mirror* and *Evening Journal*, may have had a hand in the murders. She was, after all, the only one (except for the passive James Mills) who had a glaringly evident motive. She was a proud woman disgraced.

Others continued to suspect the Stevenses. Former Judge Arthur Meredith of Flemington, who presided for seventeen years in the Somerville courtroom where the Hall-Mills trial was held, said in a 1992 interview with *Star-Ledger* reporter Jonathan Jaffe, "I'm confident that the Stevens family were responsible for the murders. The reason the prosecution couldn't win the trial was because the case wasn't well tried. They had lousy witnesses, and the defense was excellent."

Support for both these views came a few years after the publication of Kunstler's book, when a retired gas station owner, thinking he was about to die, told a New Brunswick patrolman a story that, if true, should have been told forty-eight years earlier. The man, Julius Bolyog, claimed that he and Willie Stevens were old friends and that Stevens had recruited him to act as a cash-carrying delivery man between Mrs. Hall and two unidentified men.

Bolyog said Stevens told him that Mrs. Hall knew about the affair between the minister and the choir singer (no surprise there) and that she despised her husband (as she very possibly did). On the day after the murder, according to Bolyog, Willie Stevens led the gullible gas station owner down George Street to a place where Mrs. Hall was waiting in a parked car. Stevens told Bolyog to take some envelopes from Mrs. Hall and give them to two young men who were waiting in an alley nearby. He did so. The envelopes, said Bolyog, contained six thousand dollars.

This somewhat improbable story passed two lie detector tests, but, beyond that, there was no way to confirm it. Who were the two men in the alley? Were they the killers? If so, how did Mrs. Hall recruit them? Why had Bolyog, a mere dupe and a seemingly superfluous one at that, remained silent all those years? Bolyog's sensational but belated testimony, the polygraph tests notwithstanding, was too vague and peculiar to attract much support.

To this day no fully persuasive case has been made against any person or persons in the scandalous Hall-Mills affair that titillated the nation in the Roaring Twenties.

The Brigham Murder

ORANGE

Youth Confesses to Rape, Murder; His Mother Accuses Her Husband

DECEMBER 27, 1922

The rape and murder of Mrs. Eleanor L. Brigham, thirty-four, at 266 Fuller Terrace, Orange, brought fear, but only briefly, to the then-fashionable residential area where Mrs. Brigham lived with her husband and their three children. The husband, Charles F. Brigham, was a New York City businessman, sales manager of the Charles R. Debevois Company, a brassiere manufacturer.

Within hours a suspect was in custody. He was William E. Battle, a youthful black handyman who, along with his father, had been taking care of the furnace in the Brigham home.

Mrs. Brigham's body was discovered by the Orange police at about midnight in a preserve closet in the cellar of her house. Her husband had searched in vain for her in every other room of the large house. According to the examining physician, Mrs. Brigham had been dead for approximately seven hours. She had been strangled, and, judging by the appearance of her body, she had put up a terrific fight.

Battle's undoing was the noise of the attack. It awakened one of the Brigham children, Virginia, seven, who appeared suddenly at the top of the cellar stairs and asked, "What is all that noise down there?" Battle, according to his confession, responded that he had fallen down the stairs.

"Where is Mama?" the little girl asked.

"She's gone for a loaf of bread."

According to Battle's statement, he then went up the stairs, where he saw and talked with Virginia and her younger brother, Bobbie. Apparently he took the opportunity to lift some money from a purse on the living room mantel before starting for home. He made a few other mistakes, too. He took Mrs. Brigham's watch after killing her, and later that day, in the company of a friend, dropped it off at a local jewelry store to have it repaired. He also left his cap behind at the Brighams' house, and the police found incriminating fingerprints.

It looked like an open-and-shut case, and it was. Virginia, dressed all in white, took the witness stand and identified Battle as "the colored man" in the house on the day her mother "went away."

Mrs. Carrie Battle, the mother of William, tried vainly to pin the murder on her husband, James, claiming he was at the Brigham house at 5:00 P.M. on the day of the murder, and reminding everyone that he was an ex-convict who had served fourteen years of a twenty-year sentence for raping a white woman in Orange. Mrs. Battle knew that her son faced a likely sentence of death if convicted. By accusing her husband, she apparently hoped to cast doubt on the accuracy of seven-year-old Virginia Brigham's identification.

But Virginia's calm testimony, plus the rest of the evidence, including William's confession, carried the day. On January 6, 1923, ten days after the murder, a jury in the Court of Oyer and Terminer in Newark found William E. Battle, nineteen, guilty of murder in the first degree, declining to recommend mercy. When a court attendant asked Battle if he had had a fair trial, he answered, "Yep, I'm satisfied."

Two days later he was sentenced to die in Trenton's electric chair.

Battle quickly repudiated his confession, saying it was all a lie. He also denied admitting the murder to Dr. Walter S. Washington, a psychiatrist (called an alienist in those days) who had examined him for the state and found him sane. Then he had another change of heart and confessed again, saying, "It was a just verdict."

When William P. Brandon, Battle's lawyer, asked for a post-trial psychiatric opinion, Judge Fred G. Stickel, who had tried the case, said okay. Brandon hired two physicians of his own choosing, who, probably to no one's surprise, found Battle "suffering from a form of insanity." Brandon opined, "Battle is just a poor boob who would sign any confession put before him."

Judge Stickel thought otherwise.

On February 13, 1923, a month and a half after the murder of Mrs. Brigham, William Battle was electrocuted.

Not long after the execution Judge Stickel was in Atlantic City and went to a barber shop for a shave. The black barber lathered the judge's face, poised his razor to begin his task, and murmured, "You sentenced my cousin, Bill Battle, to the chair."

Judge Stickel shrank from the barber's threatening leer and wished he had chosen a different shop. But the barber wasn't out for homicide. He cut no more than the judge's whiskers, declaring, "He wasn't any good, anyhow."

Trooper Coyle
at the Quarry

BOUND BROOK

Thugs Kill Trooper in Revenge for Thwarting Payroll Holdup

DECEMBER 18, 1924

The Bound Brook Crushed Stone Company operated a quarry in a sparsely settled area near Somerville. Once a week the manager of the quarry, Charles B. Higgins, would drive to a bank in Bound Brook to pick up money for the payroll. On this particular Thursday he was going to bring back about six thousand dollars.

It looked like an easy heist—just grab Higgins on his way from the bank. The little-used Chimney Rock Road would in all likelihood be deserted. But the two men who planned the holdup were none too clever. They stopped Higgins going *to* the bank and asked him a number of suspicious-sounding questions.

Higgins, who was no fool, telephoned Troop B of the New Jersey State Police at Pluckemin. He asked for an escort back to the quarry, and the state police obliged, dispatching Troopers Robert Coyle and John Gregovesir to meet the manager at the bank. Their trip back with the payroll passed without incident, although on the way they did see one of the men who had questioned Higgins.

With the payroll safely delivered to the quarry, Coyle and Gregovesir got into their car to return to Pluckemin. But as bad luck or ill fate would have it, the suspicious stranger was still skulking about the unfrequented road. The troopers decided to stop and question him. When they did, his answers proved so evasive that Coyle, after searching him perfunctorily, ordered him into the car for further questioning back in Pluckemin. He got in, and the car started off.

The two troopers were in the front seat. The man, unattended in the back, shouted, "Hands up!" When Coyle turned, reaching for his own revolver, the man fired a blank directly into his face, blackening it. Gregovesir, who was driving, hit the brakes, drew his service revolver, and fired over his shoulder at the man, but missed.

The troopers' car struck a pole. The suspect—he was certainly a suspect by now—wrestled away Gregovesir's revolver, and the trooper, to avoid being shot, opened the car door and rolled out. The suspect shot Coyle two more times, this time without blanks. He then leapt from the police car and ran off, to be picked up moments later by a man driving a Buick touring car, which sped away while Gregovesir watched.

Disarmed and dismayed, Gregovesir headed for the nearest hospital, where Robert Coyle, his partner, was pronounced dead on arrival. The license number that Gregovesir reported turned out to be wrong, and there was little for the surviving trooper to do but to pore over 25,000 mug shots. Happily, to the extent that there was anything happy in this incident, he made an identification of number 1,076 in Hoboken: Daniel Genese, twenty-three, of West New York. Genese had previously been arrested in New York, Philadelphia, Bayonne, and Hoboken, always for the theft of Buick automobiles.

Governor George Silzer asked the Jersey City police to help the state police find Genese, who was understandably trying to lie low. Two Jersey City lieutenants, Harry Walsh and Charles Wilson, were assigned to the case. They succeeded, tracing the culprit's mother-in-law to Plainfield, and then, posing as census takers, getting an exact address from her.

The police, who were looking for Genese already in connection with a river pirating caper at Communipaw, set up an ambush for him at his brother-in-law's isolated farmhouse in Mount Horeb, where Genese's wife and two children were found holed up. After two and a half days of waiting, the police arrested Genese the moment he arrived in yet another stolen Buick. After his arrest he confessed and implicated his accomplice, John Anderson of Jersey City, who was brought in the next morning.

Their cases were tried separately, Genese's first. On the witness stand the defendant implied that Trooper Gregovesir had shot Coyle by mistake while trying to subdue Genese. Three days earlier Gregovesir had vigorously denied this suggestion when it was made by defense counsel during cross-examination. The jury believed the testimony of Gregovesir. On April 2, 1925, Daniel Genese was found guilty of murder in the first degree, with no recommendation for mercy. That left Supreme Court Justice Charles W. Parker only one option. He sentenced Genese to die in the electric chair at Trenton.

The sentence was carried out on December 15, 1925. Anderson, tried later, received a lighter sentence.

Sea Isle's
Indiscreet Squire

SEA ISLE CITY

Young Mom Wins Public Sympathy, Acquittal, After Shooting Randy JP

JULY 3, 1925

Noel Pappalardo, fifty-two, owner of the Iolanda Hotel in Sea Isle City, had roving hands. They were especially prone to rove when he was in the company of pretty Mrs. Mary Mattia, twenty-two, who was staying directly across the hall from him in Room 7. She was the mother of two children, one eighteen months old, the other three months old. Pappalardo lived in Room 6. His wife and children lived apart from him in Room 5.

Mary Mattia was married to Pappalardo's stepson, Joseph Mattia, a barber who had recently taken a summer job at a barbershop in town. Before that, Mary, Joseph, and the children had lived in Washington, D.C.

Pappalardo, a justice of the peace as well as a hotel owner, not only "was always wanting to caress me and kiss me," according to the young woman, he also was jealous of what he perceived to be the attentions of other men. He accused Mary of being intimate with Joseph's brother Teddy as well as unnamed others. (At the trial a Washington policeman who knew the Mattia family testified that Mary was "as pure as the flakes of snow that fall.")

The night before the shooting there had been a flare-up between Noel Pappalardo and Mrs. Mattia. She had gone walking on the boardwalk with a friend, Mrs. Margaret Saliba of Philadelphia, who was vacationing for a week at the Iolanda Hotel. Pappalardo berated Joseph for letting his wife go out late at night. He confronted Mary when she returned from her walk at about 11:30, accusing her of infidelity. Mrs. Saliba explained that they had merely been strolling together, that Mary had bought an ice cream cone, and that nothing improper had happened. Pappalardo called them both liars.

Next morning, July 3, Pappalardo followed Mary to her room. Joseph, the barber, had left for work. The Squire, as the *Cape May County Gazette* called him, began pressing his attentions on her once again. When she fought back, kicking viciously, he left the room. A few moments later he came in again and began choking her. She fought furiously, once more driving him back into the hall. (All this was according to Mrs. Mattia, since the Squire was not around to offer his version of the set-to.)

Mary had had enough. She ran into Room 5 to tell Mrs. Pappalardo what was going on. Outside in the hall she heard noises and, fearing it was the randy old gent ready for another go, she rummaged around in a drawer and found a gun (although in her earlier signed confession she claimed to have gotten the gun from a trunk in Room 6, Noel Pappalardo's room). Wherever she got it, she took the Squire's loaded gun to her own room, Room 7, and laid it on the bed. When she heard new noises in the hall, she flung open the door and there stood not the lustful Squire but Mrs. Pappalardo.

Mary wailed, "Why does your husband call me names and treat me the way he does?" (Mrs. Pappalardo testified that Mary's words were, "Where is your [expletive deleted] husband?")

At this instant Pappalardo barged up the steps and into view. Mary said he was yelling, "It's a lie! It's a lie!" Mrs. Pappalardo could recall no such final words.

Whatever the Squire said or failed to say, he charged toward Mary, his hands aloft. She waved the gun at him and fired a single shot. The bullet tore into Pappalardo's heart, killing him. The prosecution argued that the sequence of events spelled first-degree murder. The defense claimed that Mrs. Mattia acted in self-defense.

The jury sided with the defense. A not guilty verdict came in after one hour and fifty-five minutes of deliberation. The reporter for the *Cape May County Gazette*, a partisan of the young mother, wrote, "There was shouting, cheering, stamping of feet, and hand-clapping. Seeing the futility of any attempt to stop the demonstration, Justice Luther A. Campbell, who presided at the trial, adjourned court."

"It was all like a dream. I want to forget," said Mary Mattia after the acquittal. "I wish we could move to a new place." In fact, the Mattia family moved back to Washington, D.C., where they presumably enjoyed a more serene life than they had found in Sea Isle City.

A Crazy Rich Kid

Mary Daly, the six-year-old daughter of a Manhattan hardware company president, was playing on the front lawn of a neighbor's home at 136 Upper Mountain Avenue, Montclair. With her were three playmates—her brother David, four, and two other neighborhood children. The house belonged to Joseph A. Bower, a vice president of the New York Trust Company.

A black sedan turned into the street, according to eyewitnesses, and stopped just past where the children were playing. An athletic-looking young man, clean-shaven, with blond, curly hair jumped out of the car, grabbed six-year-old Mary Daly, carried her under his arm to the car—she was kicking and screaming—tossed her onto the front seat, slammed the passenger's door, ran to the driver's side, got in, and sped off.

(Police at first identified the abductor as "a Negro taxi driver from Newark," in spite of eyewitness accounts to the contrary, because the car the kidnapper was driving [New Jersey license plate number 0722] had that morning been in the possession of Raymond Pierce, a black cabbie.)

As luck would have it, Miss Phyllis Bower, twenty, the daughter of Joseph A. Bower, was just returning in her chauffeur-driven Buick from a shopping trip to downtown Montclair. She leapt out, crying to her driver, "Follow that man, John." While she ran to the house to telephone the police, John Santine, the chauffeur, backed his Buick out of the driveway and took off after the speeding black sedan, careening around the corner at Claremont Road in hot pursuit. The fugitive held Mary with one hand, the steering wheel with the other, as he floored the accelerator on the road out of Montclair toward Little Falls. Santine, spotting two friends along the highway, stopped to pick them up, figuring he might need help. He almost lost the other car as it roared through Little Falls, the fugitive ignoring several traffic cops, but he regained the lost ground on Little Notch Road heading toward West Paterson. Santine swerved left to get alongside the black sedan and try to cut it off. As he gained on the other car, the kidnapper turned toward him and fired one shot. It crashed through the windshield, hit Santine in the face, and sent his pursuing Buick zigzagging wildly until one of the chauffeur's friends managed to climb over the front seat, grab the wheel, and bring it to a stop. Santine, gravely but not fatally injured, was rushed to Mountainside Hospital by his game but frightened passengers. The kidnapper got away.

A check on license number 0722 led quickly to the fleeing car's owner, James Scanlon, owner of a taxi company in Verona. The man supposed to be driving the cab, Scanlon said, was Raymond Pierce of Newark. The cab itself soon turned up, abandoned in a blind road off Van Gelsen's Gap. Blood on the front cushions suggested the worst, but a plethora of fingerprints in the car offered hope of an early solution. Pierce's body was found hidden among bushes on the bank of Peckham Creek near West Paterson.

The non-Pierce fingerprints in the black sedan belonged to Harrison Noel, twenty, son of a wealthy New York lawyer, Dix W. Noel, of 295 North Mountain Avenue, Upper Montclair. Young Noel, it appeared, was as mad as a March hare. He had once been a brilliant student at Montclair High School, but something had snapped, and he had been confined for a time at the Essex County Insane Asylum at Overbrook, diagnosed as having "catatonic dementia praecox."

Brought in for questioning, young Noel refused to talk. His mother pleaded with him to tell anything he knew about the affair. The father of Mary Daly, at first calmly, then emotionally and on his knees, implored Noel to speak. The good-looking, six-foot-tall young man would say nothing. Only after much more questioning did he admit to the kidnapping. He insisted that the Daly girl was alive in Little Falls, and he would reveal her whereabouts for four thousand dollars. They wrote him a check. He said, sorry, no checks. A detective scurried about in the small hours of the morning to get four thousand dollars in cash. Noel then said he had changed his mind.

At last he confessed. He led the police to a wooded area near the

Osborn & Marcellus stone quarry on Preakness Mountain, Little Falls, and showed them where Mary's body was lying. Still neatly dressed, she looked as if she might be sleeping.

"I put two bullets into her," Noel said with what seemed to be a touch of pride.

"I killed Pierce, too," he added.

He told how he had bought a gun in New York City for $9.20, practiced with it, and then went out looking for a kidnap victim. He admitted he was familiar with the recent Chicago thrill-killing of Bobby Franks by Nathan Leopold and Richard Loeb. Noel needed transportation for his plan, so he summoned a cab from a drugstore telephone on Valley Road, Montclair. The driver was Raymond Pierce. Noel waited for a convenient moment to shoot Pierce in the head. He ditched the cabbie's body and proceeded with his scheme. After snatching Mary Daly, shooting the determined pursuer, and murdering the little girl at the quarry, he searched in the phone book for the name of the person living at 136 Upper Mountain Road. He phoned the Bowerses and demanded $4,000 in cash, but when the woman who answered asked his name, he hung up. He made no more ransom demands until the police interrogated him.

Noel had a history of bizarre behavior. He had once tried to kill his father with a hatchet. Committed to the Craig Sanitarium at Beacon, New York, he attacked and severely beat an attendant there. Later, while working as a seaman aboard the steamship *George Washington*, he tried to murder a cook. Clearly, he belonged in an institution—and he was supposed to be in one. Voluntarily admitted to the Essex County Insane Asylum at Overbrook, he had escaped. Five days later his mother tried to return him, but the institution would not accept him. Subsequently, a doctor at Overbrook tried to have Noel recommitted, but the young man's father refused, saying he would take responsibility for his son's actions.

Alienists (as psychiatrists were then called) argued long and bitterly over whether Harrison Noel was legally insane. No one doubted that he acted like a maniac. But he also made statements such as, "It is wrong to kill any human being," suggesting he knew right from wrong, which legally was all that mattered. Tried and convicted of first degree murder, Noel was sentenced to death. But the Court of Errors and Appeals at Trenton, after reviewing the case, concluded by a twelve to one vote that the killer had indeed been crazy, legally as well as self-evidently, on the day of the murder. New Jersey's Attorney General advised the Essex County prosecutor that Harrison Noel should be committed to the State Asylum at Greystone Park in Morris County, and he was.

Shootout at the French Hill Inn

Prohibition, which was launched to curb the evils of drink, greatly increased those evils and added others. The casual lawlessness of the Roaring Twenties was symbolized by speakeasies in the cities and roadhouses outside of town. These watering holes could be quite elaborate places, often catering to more appetites than just a thirst for illegal liquor.

One such place was the French Hill Inn in Wayne Township. A small gatehouse with a guard, a watchtower on the roof, and an internal buzzer warning system provided security. For the owners and staff there were secret doors, panels, and passageways. For the paying customers there were drinks, gambling, and "much-painted young women," in the cautious journalese of the day. The French Hill Inn was owned by Samuel and Anthony Alessi, late of Scranton and Wilkes-Barre, Pennsylvania.

On the night of February 17, 1926, Troopers Charles Ullrich and Charles McManus were sent from the Morristown barracks to investigate the twice-raided roadhouse. Wearing civilian clothes, the troopers drove to the three-story stucco building, which was set back among trees a hundred feet or so from the road. Trooper McManus had participated in one of the prior raids, but the risk he might be recognized was considered slight. He and Trooper Ullrich got past the gatehouse guard easily. They ordered beer and food, observed card games in progress, were propositioned now and again, and, all in all, in the few hours they spent there found the French Hill Inn to be exactly what they expected.

Before they reported back, however, one of the shady ladies whispered to the group at her table, "That's him. I know it. He's a trooper. It's the one who got us before." Someone summoned the bouncer, James (Slam Bang) DeLuccia, and told him the bad news. DeLuccia approached the table where Ullrich and McManus were sitting. The troopers stood up and identified themselves.

Pandemonium erupted. Patrons scrambled for the exit. McManus tried to detain them. Ullrich dashed for a public telephone in the downstairs bar. On the way he met the owner, Sam Alessi, armed with a pistol. Ullrich grabbed for the gun. Alessi fired. The bullet hit the trooper in the mouth, but Ullrich managed to fire three times through the pocket of his jacket. All three bullets struck Alessi, but the roadhouse owner got off two more shots of his own, one of which hit Ullrich in the head, wounding him mortally.

McManus, hearing the shots, headed in their direction. He was stopped by DeLuccia, wielding a baseball bat. Slam Bang began slam-banging the trooper with his bat. McManus fell, unconscious.

When Trooper McManus regained consciousness, he found the roadhouse dark and deserted. He saw Ullrich lying in a pool of blood. Dazed, he staggered to the phone booth, called the barracks, and collapsed. Sergeant Carl Fuchs and others sped to the French Hill Inn. They found no one there except the two troopers. Ullrich, rushed in a troop car to Saint Joseph's Hospital in Paterson, was pronounced dead on arrival. McManus was taken to All Souls Hospital in Morristown. His injuries, although grave, were not life-threatening, and he would later fill in the details of what had happened.

Sam Alessi, needing medical attention, showed up at Saint Joseph's Hospital, Paterson, where he was arrested and put under guard. Slam Bang DeLuccia, more loyal than prudent, tried to visit his boss and ended up under arrest, too. Both were tried, convicted, and sentenced to prison terms.

That left only Tony Alessi, who seemed to have made a clean escape. But the state police were not inclined to let Tony get away so easily. They put Detective Nick DeGaetano on the case, working undercover. DeGaetano eventually spotted the fugitive, evidently by accident, in Newark, but an uncooperative traffic cop refused to detain Alessi, which blew DeGaetano's cover.

The state police needed a new operative. They found him in Detective Andrew Zapolsky, formerly a Pennsylvania state trooper. Since the Alessis were originally from the anthracite region, Zapolsky centered his search there, seeking friends, enemies, relatives, or acquaintances of the fugitive. It took a long time—five years, in fact, from the date of the French Hill Inn affair—but on May 23, 1931, Zapolsky caught up with Tony Alessi in Berwick, Pennsylvania. The fugitive, masquerading as James Noble, worked at Fitch Culver's garage in Berwick. He had established himself as one of the town's best auto mechanics. Eight months after starting his search, Detective Zapolsky arrested the second Alessi.

But there was no real case against him. Trooper McManus, the key witness, had long since retired, mentally impaired as a result of the brutal beating he had taken on that fateful February night in 1926. Tony Alessi went free.

7 The Mail Truck Blitz

ELIZABETH

Bandits Wielding Submachine Gun Rob U.S. Mail Truck, Kill Driver

OCTOBER 14, 1926

It was a clear, quiet October morning in Elizabeth. Then suddenly, for a few wild minutes, the intersection of Elizabeth Avenue and Sixth Street looked like a scene from a Chicago crime movie. When it was over, one man was dead and two others were seriously wounded.

John P. Enz, the driver of a small U.S. mail truck, was on his way to the Elizabethport Banking Company with $151,700 in cash for the payroll of the Singer Manufacturing Company. As he drove south on Elizabeth Avenue and turned onto Sixth Street, a stolen blue Packard sedan with separately stolen license plates pulled out from the curb and cut off his Ford truck. Enz braked to a stop. No sooner had he done so than a man in the sedan leveled a Thompson submachine gun at the windshield of the mail truck and began spraying bullets. Two bullets hit Enz in the head, killing him instantly.

A stolen silver-gray Packard touring car, also with stolen plates, had been following the mail truck. It, too, screeched to a stop. Men leaped from the open touring car and, using a large bolt cutter, snapped off the padlock on the rear doors of the truck. Others from the blue sedan joined in the heist. They quickly loaded six mail sacks from the truck into the two cars and sped off.

In the attack that killed Enz, mail guard John Quinn, Enz's companion in the truck, was struck by three bullets, wounding him seriously but not fatally. Jacob Christman, a motorcycle policeman following the truck, was shot at and deliberately run over by the driver of the Packard. Witnesses, of whom there were many, agreed that seven men in all had taken part in the bold daylight robbery. On this point they were right. On certain other points they were wrong. The sedan that cut off the mail truck, for example, they misidentified as a Studebaker, and later they would make other, more serious mistakes.

The bandits' escape route soon seemed clear—but like so much else in this case the reports on it proved to be misinformation supplied by eager but unreliable witnesses. Excited descriptions of two speeding autos that ignored traffic signals and waving patrolmen came in from Millburn, Livingston, Summit, and Madison. State troopers and local police rushed toward the Orange Mountains and Watchung Mountains, trying to locate the fleeing perpetrators in this sparsely settled region of "mountains, forest, lakes, rivers, valleys, and towns." One speeding car was flagged down and found to carry four hunters and a pile of dead rabbits. The bandits got away.

Still, there were all those witnesses. And they soon picked out, correctly, one of the desperadoes from a rogues' gallery of photographs. He was James J. (Killer) Cunniffe of the notorious Bum Rodgers gang, a group of West Side New York thugs believed responsible for a recent series of robberies and at least four murders in Newark, Rahway, Perth Amboy, and New Brunswick. A warrant had been issued for Killer Cunniffe's arrest, charging him with the murder of a man and his son near New Brunswick as Cunniffe made a frantic getaway following a failed airmail truck holdup.

The Watchung Mountains yielded none of the seven fugitives. Two of them came to grief within two weeks anyway, though not in New Jersey, or even in New York, but in suburban Detroit. Killer Cunniffe and a man first identified as William James Olsen were ensconced in an apartment in Highland Park, Michigan. They had been drinking champagne and whiskey as they divvied up a sizable sum of cash. There may have been a fight over the money, or "William James Olsen"—soon identified as William (Ice Wagon) Crowley, like Cunniffe a member of the Bum Rodgers gang—may have decided to keep all the cash for himself. Whatever the specifics, Crowley shot Cunniffe seven times and shot Cunniffe's girlfriend, Frances Harris of Elizabeth, twice.

Highland Park police, responding to urgent phone calls from the apartment building, raced to the scene. Patrolmen Ernest Jones and Ephraim Rancour knocked on the door of Apartment 20. Ice Wagon Crowley, dressed in underwear and a bathrobe, opened the door.

"What's all this shooting about?" Jones asked.

"It's about this," snapped Crowley, whipping a pistol from behind his back and shooting Jones in the forehead, killing him. Crowley then shot Rancour in the right shoulder. The startled Rancour, injured and enraged, pumped six shots into Ice Wagon Crowley, icing him.

Two of the seven bandits were now accounted for. Witnesses in Elizabeth made positive identifications of Crowley as one of the holdup men. Unhappily, they proceeded to make two other positive identifications— James Sweeney, twenty-four, of the Bronx, and Edward Purtell, thirty-six, of Manhattan—that were flatly wrong. True, both men were well acquainted with Cunniffe and Crowley, but neither had participated in the holdup. Nonetheless, Sweeney was tried, convicted, and sentenced to life imprisonment. Purtell was jailed for eleven months awaiting trial. Both men were saved, not by astute investigation, but by an anonymous tip.

The tipster wrote a persuasive letter in which he named Benjamin Haas, thirty-five, of Manhattan as the driver of the silver-gray Packard touring car. The tipster was right. Haas began to sing. Sweeney and Purtell, wrongly identified, were released. But another Bum Rodgers protégé, Frank ("The Ghost") Kiekart, was fingered by Haas as one of the seven men in on the holdup. Kiekart, no stand-up guy, decided to join Haas in turning state's evidence. Separately tried, Haas and Kiekart drew ten years each for mail theft, a federal crime, and were sentenced to serve their time at the federal penitentiary in Atlanta, Georgia. Before their trial, they identified the other three mail-truck bandits: Canice Neary, William Fanning, and Daniel Grosso. Neary and Fanning were soon picked up and charged, but Grosso was nowhere to be found. Neary and Fanning, with no real defense, were tried, convicted, and given life terms at Newark State Prison. They could not find it in their hearts to forgive Haas and Kiekart for singing. When they were led from the courtroom after sentencing, Fanning sneered, "I hope the two dogs who testified against us are satisfied now."

But, finally, where was Daniel Grosso, the seventh bandit, and, if the other six men were telling the truth, the one who had killed Enz? The *New York Times* reported that Grosso "is believed to be in South America." Who believed this is not specified. But Benjamin Haas was more than willing to tell what he did know.

Killer Cunniffe, Haas said, had been living in an apartment on Clinton Place, Newark. Haas met him there one day after Canice Neary suggested that he might want to get in on the big heist being planned. Frances Harris shared the apartment with Cunniffe, but he shooed her out of the room. Killer then explained the scheme to Haas. A few days later all seven participants met again at the apartment. Haas was to drive the touring car, Neary the sedan. Cunniffe rode with Haas. Grosso, the man with the submachine gun, rode with Neary. As Neary cut off the mail truck, Grosso opened fire with the deadly Thompson, killing Enz. Haas ran down Patrolman Christman, while Cunniffe fired the shots at the fallen motorcycle cop. Cunniffe was also the man who cut the lock on the mail truck.

The bandits made their way not into the sheltering Watchung Mountains but straight back to Cunniffe's apartment in Newark, where Haas got his cut for driving, twenty thousand dollars. Haas then went home to New York via the Hudson Tubes. He saw Neary not long afterward, and the other driver was unhappy, complaining that Fanning was "cabareting and talking too much."

The nagging question remained: What about Grosso, the killer of Enz? Did Haas have any information he would like to impart? Haas answered curtly, "He's out, I'm in."

In fact, Daniel Grosso was "in," too. On July 5, 1929, police in New York City arrested Grosso as a material witness in the murder of Frank Marlow, a Broadway racketeer. Three months later New Jersey authorities learned that the man they wanted for Enz's murder was already in custody. He was extradited to New Jersey, tried in the Elizabeth Court of Oyer and Terminer, found guilty of killing John P. Enz in the Elizabeth mail-truck holdup, and sentenced to die in Trenton's electric chair.

Sympathy for him came from an unusual quarter, the widow of John P. Enz, who doubted that Grosso had fired the fatal shot. She had heard too many self-serving stories about the events of that bloodstained morning. But Supreme Court Justice Clarence E. Case saw no compelling reason to order a new trial, and Governor Morgan F. Larson found no good excuse to grant clemency. Shortly before 10:00 P.M. on April 10, 1931, Daniel Grosso was led to the electric chair, and on the hour the executioner pulled the switch.

Dr. Lilliendahl's Death

HAMMONTON

Elderly Doctor Slain on Lonely Road;
His Wife Claims "2 Negroes" Did It

SEPTEMBER 15, 1927

Dr. A. William Lilliendahl, seventy, was a man of some substance. Scion of a distinguished New York family, he had earned a law degree from the University of Pennsylvania but soon turned his attention to studying medicine and became a physician. Upon graduation from medical school, he joined two of his brothers in Mexico, where the family ran a large mining and smelting company employing seven thousand workers. Dr. Lilliendahl served as staff physician for eight years, then returned to the United States, practicing medicine in New York and Pennsylvania before establishing an office in Mountain Lakes, New Jersey. He retired to his estate between Millville and Vineland after an unpleasant run-in with federal authorities involving the overprescription of drugs to narcotics addicts.

But the salient point in this case had nothing to do with Dr. Lilliendahl's transgressions. Instead it had to do with those of his second wife, Margaret, forty, who, tiring of her aging spouse, began, as secretively as possible, an affair with a fifty-seven-year-old South Vineland poultry dealer. The affair led to a plot, and the plot led to big trouble for Mrs. Lilliendahl and her married lover, the affable Willis Beach.

The story began (for the police and the newspapers) when Mrs. Margaret Lilliendahl stumbled, disheveled and bleeding, from a side road off the main Hammonton-Atsion road, screaming for help. The men who responded found the Lilliendahl car a hundred feet back, where the pine scrub was thick. Dr. Lilliendahl was slumped over the wheel, dead, his neck perforated by three bullets. Margaret told an incoherent story—which became more coherent as the occasion demanded—of two black ruffians who had jumped on the running board of the slow-moving Lilliendahl car, brandishing pistols. They had forced Mrs. Lilliendahl, the driver, to turn down a little-used byroad, where they had made her leave the car, but not before grabbing her rings, necklace, and purse. The old doctor, belatedly responding to this outrage, lunged toward the assailants. They shot him dead.

So said Margaret Lilliendahl. The police, not wholly convinced, questioned her at length. They noticed contradictions in her story. They learned that Willis Beach was her more-than-casual friend. When they tried to question Beach, he went into hiding. That made them even more suspicious. They put Mrs. Lilliendahl's home under twenty-four-hour surveillance. The press, correctly sensing not just a garden-variety murder but a much more newsworthy sex scandal, sent reporters scurrying to the scene.

One news photographer found Mrs. Lilliendahl mowing her front lawn. He approached her. "Would you shoot me," he asked with a smile, "if I tried to take your picture?"

To his surprise, she bristled, "I never shot anybody in my life!"

He explained that he was only joking. Regaining her composure, she said: "I have nothing on my conscience. People have been kind, especially to my eight-year-old son, Alfred. He is not aware of this tragedy, and I try to shield him as much as I can. Neighbors take him to school every day. I sleep well; one must go on, you know."

Four days later the Atlantic County prosecutor decided to present the case to a grand jury in Mays Landing. Indictments would be sought against two persons: Willis Beach, still on the lam, and Mrs. Margaret Lilliendahl, widow of the deceased. Three witnesses, it seemed, had observed Beach jump into his car on the lonely side road not fifty feet from the scene of the murder at the very hour of the crime and take off toward Hammonton. So much for the phantom black attackers.

More evidence came to light. In Philadelphia a man resembling Beach had pawned a $1,200 ring belonging to Mrs. Lilliendahl. And a witness in Vineland discredited Margaret Lilliendahl's account of her movements on the morning of the murder. Atlantic County Prosecutor Louis Repetto, now convinced he had the goods on the two perpetrators, announced he would seek the death penalty for the cheerful widow and the brash poultryman.

The prosecution relied heavily on circumstantial evidence and fairly obvious inference. It was not an airtight case, and the defense pressed hard to show reasonable doubt. The judge, Luther A. Campbell, offered the jury four options: first-degree murder, second-degree murder, manslaughter, or acquittal. On the first ballot the jury voted nine to three for acquittal—not because they believed the defendants were innocent but because they felt the state had not proved its case. The three jurors who favored conviction argued that it would be a travesty of justice to let the guilty go free—all twelve jurors agreed on the guilt of the accused—just because the prosecution was unable to nail down the case in all respects.

After many ballots, more than anyone counted, the jury reached what it admitted was a compromise. It found both defendants guilty of voluntary manslaughter, a verdict that showed common sense to an uncommon degree but took the courtroom spectators by surprise. "They either murdered the old doctor or they didn't," objected the onlookers. But the prosecutor knew right away what had happened, and he moved for an immediate maximum sentence "in consideration of the mercy shown by the jury toward the defendants, I ask that no mercy be extended in the matter of sentence." Justice Campbell refused to be pressured. He delayed passing sentence, but when he did, it was the maximum, ten years for each defendant.

Mrs. Carrie L. Calkins, foreman of the jury, tried to explain the widely questioned decision: "We felt our responsibility very keenly. We did the very best we could, and we feel we gave the best service we knew how to the county and the state." She could not accept the either-or demands of the critics. "We tried to eliminate all personal feeling in considering the evidence," she said, "and felt, after deliberate consideration, that the verdict was just and proper."

It probably was. A jury more legalistically inclined would have had to acquit. But this particular jury, striving for justice in a flawed prosecution, convicted—reluctantly.

 # An Arrest Gone Bad

David Ware, a West Indian in his late forties, had a history of roughing up Pansy Keaton, the woman in his life. She had complained before, but this time she decided to take action. On her complaint, State Trooper Peter W. Gladys of the Hightstown Barracks arrested the burly, six-foot Ware and prepared to drive him from Allentown to Hightstown for arraignment. Trooper Gladys directed Ware to ride beside him in the front seat of the patrol car and Pansy Keaton to ride in the back seat.

As they drove along the Robbinsville-Windsor Road, Ware began to argue with Mrs. Keaton. Trooper Gladys ordered him to keep quiet. Apparently the same violent temper that had gotten him into this minor scrape in the first place rose up again. Ware drew a razor and slashed the trooper's throat. He then took Gladys's service revolver from its holster and fired one shot into the trooper's body. Having thus lurched headlong into real trouble, he jumped from the car, taking with him the revolver and Gladys's cartridge belt, and disappeared into the densely wooded marshland.

Passing motorists discovered Gladys's body, and within a few hours scores of troopers and volunteers were scouring the area. A U.S. Navy J-3 airship joined in the search. But David Ware, having hidden in a swamp near the Camden and Amboy railroad tracks, caught a freight train and made his way to Carteret. Even though he still had on the bloodstained shirt he was wearing when he killed Trooper Gladys, Ware asked two Carteret policemen for directions to the boardinghouse he was seeking.

Twelve hours later Lieutenant Ray J. Dowling of the Carteret Police learned by chance that a tall black man, unknown to the locals, had been seen entering the boardinghouse. Dowling went there immediately and, pistol in hand, burst into Ware's upstairs room. The fugitive surrendered without a fight. Gladys's pistol was found in the room, as were the burned remains of Ware's bloodstained shirt.

This time Ware was taken to Trenton, not Hightstown, for arraignment. And this time he was charged with murder, not disorderly conduct.

Meanwhile, the family of Peter W. Gladys made funeral arrangements. Only twenty-two years old when he died, Gladys had been a state trooper for just six months. A native of Stanhope and a popular high school athlete, he was buried in Union Cemetery there on Monday, December 31, 1928. That day the Morristown *Daily Record* carried a banner headline in Old English type, reading, "Happy New Year to All."

David Ware went on trial in early February in the Criminal Court of Mercer County. Judge Erwin E. Marshall halted the trial pending a sanity test when Ware began acting strangely in court. Doctors at the Trenton State Hospital for the Insane examined him, declared him mentally fit, and he was returned for trial. Convicted and sentenced to death, Ware went to the electric chair at Trenton on May 5, 1929.

10 Murder of a Prohibition Agent

ELIZABETH

Federal Raid on Rising Sun Brewery
Ends in Murder of Prohibition Agent

SEPTEMBER 19, 1930

John G. Finiello, forty-four, worked out of the office of John D. Pennington, U.S. Prohibition Administrator in Philadelphia. National Prohibition had been in effect for more than a decade, and raids like this one were just part of a day's work, although Finiello had not previously been involved in a foray outside Pennsylvania.

Six federal agents drove up from Philadelphia in a single car after their other car was involved in a collision before reaching the Philadelphia city limits. Since the collision had appeared to be intentional, the agents figured that someone had tipped off the New Jersey beer interests about their plans. They went ahead with the raid anyway. Their destination was the Rising Sun Brewery, whose plant was a bleak red-brick building in the Union Square section of central Elizabeth.

Evidently a number of gangsters had hidden in the office of the brewery, across the street from the plant, anticipating the agents' arrival. No sooner had the feds swarmed into the brewery, rounded up eleven employees, and herded them into the boiler room than a dozen men arrived from the brewery office, guns drawn. They burst through the doorway, taking the feds by surprise.

While the gangsters were collecting the agents' pistols, John Finiello, unaware of the situation, walked in on them. He had been inspecting another part of the plant. One of the gangsters shouted, "There's Finiello— give it to him!" A volley of shots cut down the veteran agent.

The gang immediately took off through the doorway on Marshall Street, raced across the street into the brewery offices, exited through a rear doorway, ran across an open lot into Franklin Street, and escaped, presumably in automobiles. Eight of the eleven nabbed brewery workers escaped in the confusion. The other three were booked.

Curiously, neither the Elizabeth police nor the Newark deputy administrator of Prohibition had been told in advance of the Philadelphia agents' raid. But now they knew, and a call was also put in for state troopers from the Metuchen barracks. The local police and troopers stood guard outside the brewery that night as federal agents dumped one hundred thousand gallons of beer inside. Agents had raided the Rising Sun Brewery four times before. All four cases had been dismissed. (Prohibition was not especially popular in urban New Jersey.) But the authorities, whether federal, state, or local, could hardly ignore the cold-blooded murder of an agent of the United States government.

Union County Prosecutor Abe J. David announced the next day that the identities of the slayers were known and that arrests were just a matter of time. He released the name of one man who was wanted for questioning in the incident, Nicholas Delmore, proprietor of the Maple Grove Inn in Berkeley Heights. The prosecutor also revealed the probable reason for the targeting of Finiello. It seemed that Finiello had recently accepted a ten-thousand-dollar bribe intended to forestall a raid on a South Jersey brewery. The agent immediately turned the money over to his superior, the raid took place as planned, and the double-crossed brewers (it was assumed) decided to take their revenge.

The investigation did not go smoothly. Nicholas Delmore, the most-wanted suspect, disappeared. Other culprits, those who were picked up, were mostly employees of the illegal brewery—the frightened workers who had been rounded up by the Prohibition agents, not the gangsters who had stormed in and shot Finiello. Twenty-one indictments were handed down for conspiracy in operating the Rising Sun Brewery, but the job descriptions of the indicted workers—barrel washer, engineer, boiler fireman—hardly suggested that the killers were among those in custody.

In fact, the gangsters had scattered. They were reported as having come from Philadelphia, Camden, and New York, but when a break in the case finally came, nearly two years later, it arrived by way of Saint Paul, Minnesota. On July 25, 1932, two hit men shot down a couple of bootleggers, Abie Loeb and Al Gordon, near a speakeasy in downtown Saint Paul. Police caught up with the hit men a couple of blocks away. Under arrest the two gunmen admitted to nothing at all except to being Joe Schaeffer and George Young, whom they were not. When their aliases were sorted out, they were identified as John Newman (otherwise known as Jeff Newman and Jacob Newman) and Albert I. Silverberg. The fingerprints on their discarded but recovered pistols gave them away. As it happened, these thugs were two of the crew wanted in Elizabeth for the murder of John G. Finiello.

The two were convicted and sentenced to life terms in Minnesota. No doubt they deserved their fate, but it is hard to escape the conclusion that the lawlessness of the Prohibition era, the collusion of law enforcers and law breakers, and the impossibility of sorting out the good guys, the bad guys, and the bystanders made a neat and satisfactory wrap-up to this case all but impossible.

Oh, yes. Nicholas Delmore, the first suspect named, an alleged co-owner of the Rising Sun Brewery and former Republican leader of Berkeley Heights, was finally located—at his home in New Providence. Delmore's arrest came more than three years after the shooting of Finiello and less than two months before the repeal of Prohibition. Delmore was acquitted of any involvement in the murder. In a later trial, he beat a charge of interfering with federal officers in the raid on the Rising Sun Brewery, despite the courtroom testimony of three witnesses who placed him at the scene.

One of the other principal witnesses for the state, August Gobel, a boiler fireman who witnessed the murder, had been shot to death on November 8, 1932, while stoking the boilers of the brewery.

11 America's Crime of the Century

"This is Charles Lindbergh," the voice on the telephone said. "My son has just been kidnapped."

This anguished call to the state police barracks at Wilburtha launched the most intensive and at times emotional criminal investigation in the history of New Jersey. No wonder. Charles Lindbergh was a national hero like no other, then or now. A daredevil aviator, young and handsome, he had flown solo across the Atlantic Ocean in his *Spirit of Saint Louis*. He had married the beautiful, talented, and moneyed Anne Morrow of Englewood. He had fathered a much-photographed towheaded son, upon whose birth journalist Heywood Broun said, "I am already moved with compassion. He cannot possibly realize yet the price he must pay for being a front-page boy."

He never did realize it, for the price he paid was death at the age of twenty months.

On the blustery night of Tuesday, March 1, 1932, the large fieldstone house at the secluded Lindbergh estate, Highfields, seemed a quiet and safe haven to Colonel Lindbergh, just as he had intended it to be—a private enclave where he, Anne, and the baby could avoid the celebrity-obsessed public and its media representatives. Two middle-aged servants of the Lindberghs, Oliver and Elsie Whately, were in the house with them. So was pretty young Betty Gow, the baby's nurse, who had been summoned from the Morrow estate in Englewood to care for young Charles, who had a slight cold.

A few minutes after 9:00 P.M. Lindbergh, sitting in the living room with his wife, heard a sound like that of "a crate breaking." He commented on it to Anne, who had not heard it. Shortly thereafter, Mrs. Lindbergh went to bed, and the Colonel went to his study, directly below the baby's second-floor nursery. At about 10:00 P.M. Betty Gow went to the baby's room to make her usual check. She found the crib empty. At first she assumed that either his mother or his father had taken the baby. When her questioning proved otherwise, Lindbergh bounded up the stairs to the nursery. The realization hit him like a jolting downdraft. "Anne," he cried, "they've stolen our baby."

Clues were by no means lacking at the scene of the crime. The most obvious clue was the ransom note, contained in a small, white envelope on top of the windowsill in the nursery. The note, crudely written in blue ink, demanded fifty thousand dollars for the child's safe return. Phonetic spellings in the message suggested that the writer might be German. A symbol consisting of two interlocking symbols with three small, punched holes would serve to identify further messages from the kidnapper.

Another important item of evidence was a three-piece homemade wooden extension ladder the police found abandoned about seventy-five feet from the house. Its ingenious design, though not its slapdash construction, suggested that its designer understood carpentry. The bottom section of the ladder had broken about five feet above the ground, apparently as the kidnapper came down with the baby. The police also found footprints and tire tracks, but failed to record them in a satisfactory manner.

Lindbergh had built his Highfields retreat specifically to escape the invasive attention of the press and the nation. What he got now was a media carnival coupled with an investigation that turned personal tragedy into farce. And, sadly enough, the Colonel's own judgment often proved less than sound as he tried to sort out the hoaxers and charlatans from the serious investigators. For two and a half months the search was fueled by a frantic desire to save the baby. Money was no object to Colonel Lindbergh, although he was not really a wealthy man. The ransom would be paid.

Then on May 12, 1932, a baby's body was discovered in a shallow grave on Mount Rose Hill, about two miles from Hopewell. The corpse was wearing the flannel nightshirt Betty Gow had made for the child on the very night he disappeared.

By that time, alas, the ransom had been paid—but to whom? The bizarre sequence of events that led to the payoff began in the home of Dr.

John F. Condon at 2974 Decatur Avenue in the Bronx. Condon, a kindly seventy-two-year-old retired elementary school principal, wanted to help Colonel Lindbergh, whom he idolized, to find his baby. About a week after the kidnapping Condon penned a letter to the *Bronx Home News* in which he offered one thousand dollars of his own money (in addition to the fifty thousand dollars Lindbergh was prepared to pay) and promised to "go anywhere, alone, to give the kidnapper the extra money and . . . never to utter his name to any person."

Condon's three grown children were mortified at the silliness of the offer. But, *mirabile dictu*, the day after the letter appeared in the limited-circulation local newspaper, an envelope arrived at the Condon house. "Dear Sir," it began. "If you are willing to act as go-between in Lindbergh cace please follow stricly instruction." A note within the letter was ad-dressed to Colonel Lindbergh. Excitedly, Condon phoned Lindbergh, was put through, and read the letter. Lindbergh asked him also to read the note addressed to him personally. Condon finished reading, then remarked, almost as an afterthought, that a strange symbol appeared on the note—two interlocking circles with three holes punched in them. That did it.

Colonel Lindbergh approved a code name suggested by Condon, his new intermediary: "Jafsie," from the three initials of Condon's name. With ransom negotiations under way, the kidnapper asked for a meeting with the elderly schoolmaster. It took place in Woodlawn Cemetery near Jerome Avenue and 233rd Street. "Did you gottit my note?" asked the man, who identified himself as John (thus "Cemetery John" in later jour-nalistic accounts). The two men carried on an extensive conversation, recounted in detail at the trial.

But Jafsie did not yet have the ransom money for Cemetery John, and a second meeting had to be arranged. This one took place at another graveyard, Saint Raymond's in the East Bronx. Over Lindbergh's objec-tions—for the Colonel, unaccountably, had great faith in the kidnapper or kidnappers (considerably more than he had in the police) and was con-vinced his child was still alive—twenty thousand dollars of the ransom money was readied in gold notes, a variety of currency soon to be with-drawn from circulation. Every serial number was recorded.

"Have you gottit the money?" asked Cemetery John on the evening of Saturday, April 2. Condon had it, and soon John had it in exchange for a note supposedly revealing the whereabouts of the Lindbergh baby. "The boy is on the Boad Nelly," said the note. "It is a small boad 28 feet long."

Young Charles Augustus Lindbergh, Jr., was not on the boat *Nelly* off Martha's Vineyard, as John had said he would be. No. The baby was in a shallow grave on Mount Rose Hill, New Jersey, and had been there since the night of the abduction. The Colonel had been conned. And the best hope now for bringing the culprit to justice lay in the fact that, against Lindbergh's wishes, part of the ransom had been paid in gold certificates with recorded serial numbers. It was a long shot, to be sure, and almost two and a half years passed before the police got their crucial break.

Ransom money began turning up in New York City almost immediately at the rate of about forty dollars a week. A Loew's Sheridan Theater cashier in Greenwich Village even managed to match a Condon-prompted police portrait of Cemetery John with the man who, speaking in a heavy German accent, had given her one of the damning five-dollar gold notes. She described him as a man in his mid-thirties with a German accent, a prominent nose, a small mouth, and a pointed chin. But the trail could not be tracked.

Still the bills appeared, and still Cemetery John remained at large. Radio commentator Walter Winchell ridiculed the investigators: "Boys, if you weren't such a bunch of saps and yaps, you'd have already captured the Lindbergh kidnappers." But finally the saps and yaps got lucky. Almost a year after the Loew's cashier had described the suspect and identified his picture, a bank teller at the Corn Exchange Bank in the Bronx came across a listed ten-dollar gold certificate. The investigators noticed "4U-13-14 N.Y." penciled on the margin of the bill. Since it looked very much like a car license number, Lieutenant James Finn and his men scoured the local gas stations. Sure enough, they found a gas station attendant who remembered taking the bill—and remembered jotting down the car's license number because he thought the gold certificate might be counterfeit. He also recalled that the driver had a German accent.

This looked like the big break at last. When Finn called the Motor Vehicle Bureau, he learned that the car—a blue 1930 Dodge sedan—was registered to one Richard Hauptmann, 1279 East 222nd Street, the Bronx. According to the registration, Hauptmann was a thirty-four-year-old German-born carpenter. The search was over. The arrest came on the morning of September 19, 1934. Hauptmann steadfastly denied any connection with the Lindbergh case, but did admit he had stopped working as a carpenter in the spring of 1932 to devote his time to stock market investing.

A search of Hauptmann's garage revealed a possible reason for his early retirement. Nearly twelve thousand dollars of the ransom money had been stashed there. Next the police found Dr. Condon's telephone number and street address scrawled on the inside door trim of a closet in Hauptmann's house. If that weren't enough, a wood expert matched one of the rungs of the kidnap ladder to a sawed-off floorboard in the Hauptmanns' attic. The carpenter-turned-investor continued to deny all. But by now there was more than enough evidence to extradite him to New Jersey to be tried for murder.

The trial of Bruno Richard Hauptmann took place in the Hunterdon County Courthouse, Flemington, with Judge Thomas W. Trenchard presiding. (Headline writers quickly fastened on "Bruno," the defendant's first name, even though Hauptmann and his wife, Anna, always used "Richard.") Well-known writers and journalists, including H. L. Mencken, Edna Ferber, Damon Runyon, and Fannie Hurst, swarmed to Flemington and invaded the Union Hotel across the street from the courthouse. Eager spectators waited overnight for courtroom seats. Hawkers prospered, one selling models of the kidnap ladder, another (less honestly) golden locks of "the Lindbergh baby's hair." Prosecutor David T. Wilentz, the attorney general of New Jersey, presented a solid, if circumstantial, case.

Handwriting experts left little doubt as to who had written the ransom notes—the matchups between the kidnapper's notes and the prisoner's writing samples were well-nigh perfect. The wood expert tied the ladder and its construction convincingly to ex-carpenter Hauptmann. Although the defense attorney, Edward J. Reilly of Brooklyn, did his best, he had neither a persuasive theory of the crime nor any credible witnesses. The jury convicted Hauptmann of first-degree murder, and Judge Trenchard sentenced him to die in the electric chair. Hauptmann went to his death on April 3, 1936, proclaiming his innocence to the end. His widow, Anna, demanded Richard's vindication for the next half-century.

Was he innocent? Not likely. Did Hauptmann have an accomplice? Perhaps, but probably not. Attempts to prove he was a scapegoat have been unconvincing. His widow's long-standing loyalty was heartfelt and touching. But to believe that Hauptmann was guiltless of the Lindbergh kidnapping (and of the child's conceivably accidental death) is to believe in the kind of intricate juridical conspiracy that Agatha Christie presents as fictional froth in *Murder on the Orient Express*, in which a whole menagerie of Highfields servants ritually dispatch a quasi-Bruno Richard Hauptmann.

No. Hauptmann was not a cynically framed dupe. He was the man on the ladder.

PART TWO

GANG WARS
AND
WORLD WAR II

12

The Greenberg– Hassel Rubout

Beer Wars Claim 2 Bootleggers in Elizabeth-Carteret Hotel Suite

APRIL 12, 1933

First of all, there was some confusion about the identity of the two victims. Although the *New York Times* listed the dead as James Feldman, thirty-three, of Elizabeth and Joseph Greenberg, about thirty, of Reading, Pennsylvania, it added that "Feldman's true name was Mendel Gassel and that he had also used the alias Max Hassell." Greenberg's first name, it turned out, was Max.

When the *Times*'s reporters finally sorted out the aliases and the spellings, they decided that the two men shot dead in an elaborate suite occupying most of the eighth floor of the Elizabeth-Carteret Hotel were Max Greenberg and Max Hassel. Both men had an interest in the Harrison Beverage Company, which brewed Old Heidelberg beer.

Not slain in the affray was beer baron Irving Wexler, better known as Waxey Gordon, who had been in Room 804, opposite the Greenberg-Hassel suite, at the time of the murders. Gordon left in a hurry at about 4:15 P.M. when he heard "breaking glass" or something like that. If he had been in the suite, he admitted, "I'd have got the works, same as they did. They was both good friends of mine."

Investigators discovered that all three apparently had connections in Asbury Park, where they had been issued pistol permits. The police chief there, when asked about it, promised to be "more careful" with permits in the future.

What happened in the bloodstained eighth-floor suite was obvious enough. Greenberg sat slumped in a chair facing a roll-top desk, one hand clutching a fully loaded Asbury Park–approved pistol, which he had been unable to draw from the pocket of his jacket. He had been shot five times in the head. Hassel lay sprawled face down between the living room of the suite and a room that had been furnished as an office. He had been shot three times in the back of the head.

The suite contained eight partially filled highball glasses, some bottles of liquor, a keg of beer, eight sets of golf clubs, and nary a witness to the shootings. The manager of the Elizabeth-Carteret Hotel claimed not even to know which room Waxey Gordon occupied. Furthermore, he could not connect a "Mr. Rogers," who was registered in the hotel, with any of the long-term residents whose photographs he was shown. Hotel employees seemed to know even less than their manager about the various gentlemen on the eighth floor. No one at the scene—bodyguards, hotel employees, or guests—had observed anything out of the ordinary that afternoon.

Nevertheless, nearly three years later New York City police picked up thirty-one-year-old Frankie Carbo outside Madison Square Garden as a fugitive from justice, wanted in Union County, New Jersey, where he had just been indicted for the murders of Max Greenberg and Max Hassel. This Frankie Carbo was well known to the police, being a reputed triggerman for Louis Buchalter, better known as Louis Lepke of Murder Inc.

At the age of twenty Carbo had been sentenced to a two- to four-year prison term for manslaughter, after claiming self-defense in the fatal shooting of a cabbie he was allegedly shaking down. He served twenty-three months. In 1931 he was indicted for the murder of Mickey Duffy, a Philadelphia gangster shot in Atlantic City, but he was later released. In his life of crime, Carbo would be arrested five times for murder. He beat the rap every time.

The case against him in the Greenberg-Hassel killings fell apart because of the customary lack of witnesses. There was no trial. Frankie Carbo was always lucky that way. In 1941, informer Abe ("Kid Twist") Reles was about to testify that Carbo had murdered Harry ("Big Greenie") Greenberg in front of his Hollywood, California, apartment on Thanksgiving Eve, 1939. Reles, although guarded by six men, somehow managed to fall from a sixth-floor window at the Half Moon Hotel in Coney Island. With Kid Twist out of the way, Frankie Carbo once again walked free.

It should be remarked that the way Frankie Carbo gained the reputation that earned him a three-column obituary with photo in the *New York Times* of November 11, 1976, was not so much by purportedly shooting big-time hoods as by becoming in his mature years New York City's underworld "czar of boxing." His machinations in that line of work eventually brought him a twenty-five-year prison sentence—only the second prison term ever for this quiet, conservatively dressed mobster who was aptly described as "one of the nicest killers you could ever meet."

Did Murder Inc.'s Frankie Carbo shoot Max Greenberg and Max Hassel at the Elizabeth-Carteret Hotel on that April afternoon in 1933? Probably. But why? In his book *Gangster #2: Longy Zwillman*, journalist Mark A. Stuart suggests that the double hit may have stemmed from a failed Greenberg-Hassel plot to murder Zwillman, whom the two bootleggers regarded as an interloper in the northern New Jersey beer business. The price of such a failed plot was death. Whatever the motive, Longy Zwillman took over the dead partners' brewery operations.

13 Killing the Dutchman

Dutch Schultz Shot in Men's Room at Palace Chop House and Tavern

OCTOBER 23, 1935

Born Arthur Flegenheimer in the Bronx, he took the name of Dutch Schultz because "it was short enough to fit in the headlines. If I'd kept the name of Flegenheimer, nobody would have heard of me." As it was, plenty of people heard of him. While still in his early twenties, he moved in on the lucrative Bronx beer trade. Shortly thereafter, allying himself with a mathematical wizard named Otto ("Abbadabba") Berman, he took over the Harlem numbers racket from previously independent black operators.

When he tangled with the notorious chiseler Jack ("Legs") Diamond and the rampaging Vincent ("Mad Dog") Coll, both of whom had business interests that conflicted with his own, the Dutchman came out on top. The other two came out dead. With that, his reputation soared, although he wasn't really liked, just respected.

He might have remained respected if he hadn't lost his aplomb. In 1935 New York's Governor Herbert H. Lehman named Thomas E. Dewey as a special prosecutor to investigate racketeering and vice. The investigation soon focused on Dutch Schultz, who enjoyed publicity, but not that kind. Schultz decided that Dewey should be terminated. He presented his proposal to the mob's national board.

The three L's—Luciano, Lansky, and Lepke—and Frank Costello nixed the idea. They thought the Dutchman had gone slightly bananas. He didn't convince them otherwise when he stormed out of the meeting, saying, "I still say he ought to be hit. And if nobody else is gonna do it, I'm gonna hit him myself."

Syndicate leaders could see right away that their colleague was more dangerous to them than even Tom Dewey was. They decided that the guy who ought to be hit was named Dutch Schultz.

The scene then shifted to New Jersey, to the Palace Chop House and Tavern, 12 East Park Street, Newark, a couple of blocks away from the busy intersection of Broad and Market streets. At 6:00 P.M. on October 23, 1935, Schultz, flanked by bodyguards Bernard ("Lulu") Rosenkrantz and Abe Landau, strode into the one-time speakeasy and walked straight to a round table in the dining room at the back. Sometime during the evening Abbadabba Berman joined the gathering. Abbadabba was Damon Runyon's inspiration for the lovable horseplayer named Regret. In fact, Berman wasn't lovable.

At about 10:15 P.M. the front door of the Chop House and Tavern opened and in walked a short, heavy-set man who barked, "Don't move, lay down." The bartender and others dropped down, but not before they saw a second man enter, taller, older, with an unbuttoned overcoat drawn about him. Both men headed for the back dining room.

Public Enemy Number One on J. Edgar Hoover's private list—for Dutch Schultz had achieved that status—was not at his table. But Berman, Rosenkrantz, and Landau were. Within seconds the three men were staggering around the room, all fatally wounded in a burst of gunfire. Berman was hit six times, Rosenkrantz seven, Landau three.

But where was the Dutchman? As luck would have it, he had donned his light topcoat and gray fedora and stepped into the men's room just seconds before the two assailants arrived. Schultz was standing at one of the two urinals when a killer kicked open the men's room door and fired two shots, one that found its mark, one that missed.

The thirty-three-year-old Dutchman did not die right away. With a perforated large intestine, gall bladder, and liver, he hung on, raving incoherently for two days at Newark City Hospital, a half-century-old institution on Fairmount Avenue. His most quoted dying line was "A boy has never wept . . . nor dashed a thousand kim." It sounds poetic, but has no apparent meaning. His final words added nothing concrete to the picture: "Shut up, you got a big mouth! Please help me up, Henny. Max, come over here . . . French Canadian bean soup . . . I want to pay, let them leave me alone."

Then he lapsed into a deep coma and expired about two and a half hours later. Although asked repeatedly, the Dutchman could not (or would not) reveal the names of the killers. One of them, identified many years later, was Charles ("The Bug") Workman, a Murder Inc. gunslinger from Manhattan's Lower East Side. Workman drew a twenty-three-year sentence.

14 Willful Gladys Took an Ax

BAYONNE

Daughter and Boyfriend Arrested In Axing of "Old-fashioned" Mom

JULY 31, 1936

Mrs. Helen MacKnight of 826 Avenue A, Bayonne, told her daughter, Gladys, that if she wanted an early dinner, she would have to get it herself. That did it. Seventeen-year-old Gladys had had enough. She grabbed a hatchet from the top of the refrigerator and brought it down on her mother's head.

But to go back to the beginning: Gladys, a short, none-too-svelte blue-eyed blonde, had been dating Donald Wightman, eighteen, a strapping six-foot redhead who lived at 97 East 24th Street, Bayonne. On the day of the murder, the two of them went to a local beer garden at about four in the afternoon, where each of them polished off three or four glasses of beer. They walked to the MacKnight home an hour or so later. Mrs. MacKnight sat rocking on the front porch. Gladys greeted her with what a neighbor viewed as typical insolence.

The daughter then went to the basement and got a hatchet, intending, she said, to tack down some loose carpet. Instead she put the hatchet on top of the refrigerator in the kitchen, and asked her mother, who had since come into the house, if she and her boyfriend could have an early dinner, because they were planning to play tennis at six o'clock. Her mother said, "Yes, if you get it yourself."

Fair enough, you may think. But a quarrel broke out at this point, and, according to Gladys's confession, Wightman (for a reason never clarified) pinned Mrs. MacKnight's arms while Gladys grabbed the hatchet from atop the refrigerator and advanced menacingly. Mrs. MacKnight began to scream.

A point of contention at the trial: Mrs. MacKnight, then or later, may or may not have had a butcher knife in her hand. She may or may not have been wielding it in a threatening manner. Both Donald and Gladys depicted the indulgent, mild-mannered, forty-year-old mother poised (for reasons unknown) like an attack dog, an image at which the prosecution naturally scoffed. Mrs. MacKnight was no longer around to explain the incident from her perspective.

Anyway, Gladys—as she later admitted—struck six times with the hatchet, leaving five deep gashes on the top of her mother's head and one across the forehead. Mrs. MacKnight suffered a general compound skull fracture and died quickly.

A neighbor, hearing the commotion, ran into the MacKnights' yard and yelled, "What's the matter? She was screaming."

"Oh, go away, Mrs. Feury," Gladys said impatiently, "Mother cut her finger a little bit, that's all."

Whereupon Donald and Gladys bolted, locking up the house and speeding off in the family car. Gladys's father, Edgar W. MacKnight, a superintendent at the General Cable Company in Bayonne, came home shortly thereafter to find his wife murdered. He phoned the police. The two culprits, driving aimlessly around in the MacKnight automobile, were apprehended four hours later in Jersey City.

At first Donald claimed to be the killer, with Gladys chiming in piously, "I didn't do it. I couldn't do anything to stop it. It took such a short time. My mother was old-fashioned in a great many ways."

That odd non sequitur about the "old-fashioned" Mrs. MacKnight came up again and again. Evidently old-fashionedness was a basic motive for the murder. Wightman, in talking with Gladys about the outmoded ways of her mother, had once remarked casually, "We ought to kill her."

Gladys remained calm throughout the questioning. A Bayonne detective said, "She was the coolest thing I ever saw. All the time she talked she sat with one leg thrown over the arm of the chair. She smoked one cigarette after another. She weighed every word before she replied to questions."

Wightman seemed a lot more bothered, but the two were in equally deep trouble. The prosecution claimed they had discussed the murder the night before, although the confessions they signed made the killing sound spontaneous. The pair would admit only that they had sometimes "jokingly" discussed murdering Mrs. MacKnight.

The jury, less amused by the crime than Gladys had occasionally seemed, found her and Donald Wightman guilty of second-degree murder. Judge Thomas F. Meaney of the Court of Oyer and Terminer sentenced them to twenty-nine to thirty years each at hard labor, the maximum term he could impose. Gladys showed no emotion, but Donald looked a bit upset, perhaps remembering the words he had shouted at her the day the jury returned its guilty verdict: "You—you made a murderer out of me!"

Death of a Union Boss

When it comes to name recognition, he wasn't Jimmy Hoffa or even Jock Yablonski, but labor leader Norman Redwood was a union notable in his day—and unpopular enough with somebody to end up suddenly dead.

It's a poignant story. At about 7:30 P.M. on February 19, 1937, Redwood, fifty-two, the business agent of Local 102 of the International Hod Carriers, Building and Common Laborers of America, was returning to his home at 1130 Laurelton Parkway, Teaneck. In his car he had a box of strawberries, a gift for his wife, who was preparing dinner. She and others heard noises that sounded like a series of backfires followed by the sound of a car speeding away.

The backfires were in fact gunshots, four of which struck their target, ripping away the left side of Redwood's face. Ten minutes later, a doctor who had been summoned to the scene pronounced the union leader dead.

By 1:00 A.M. John J. Breslin, the prosecutor for Bergen County, announced that a warrant "for questioning" would be issued for two men: Samuel Rosoff, a New York City subway contractor, and Joseph Fay, president of the Hoisting Engineers Union, an outfit that had little use for Redwood's sandhogs. Rosoff's Sand and Gravel Company was locked in a bitter and costly strike with Redwood's local. Fay had long disliked, perhaps hated, Redwood as a union rival, opposing him as a man too cozy with the upstart CIO, the Committee (later Congress) of Industrial

Organizations which, amid much dissension, was splitting off from the old, relatively staid American Federation of Labor (AFL).

Breslin never wavered in his belief that Rosoff and Fay were involved in the sudden leave-taking of Norman Redwood. Breslin produced witnesses' statements in which Samuel Rosoff, in a face-to-face confrontation with Redwood, virtually promised the union leader he would kill him. The problem was that Rosoff himself *didn't* kill Redwood. Hired gunmen did the job. But how to link those hired gunmen to Messrs. Rosoff and Fay? How indeed.

The Bergen County prosecutor could point to some seemingly strong evidence. He had obtained testimony from a man who should know, a delegate of Local 102 who had attended a meeting with Redwood in Rosoff's office on Friday, February 5, two weeks before the murder. During the meeting the union boss threatened a strike against Rosoff's subway and sewer jobs. The powerful contractor, a stocky, self-made man with a booming voice, jumped up from his desk, waved a fist under Redwood's nose, gave him a shove, and snarled, "I will kill you stone dead." When Redwood seemed less than terrified, Rosoff, according to Breslin's witness, went on, "I have two guns. If I don't use them, I will get the men who will use them." And if that weren't enough, he added later in this stormy meeting, "There is no man that ever pulled a strike on me and got away with it, and remember, Redwood, if you do anything like that you will be a dead man, and you can tell the police if you want to."

Meanwhile, Rosoff had been working with Joseph Fay to sidestep Redwood altogether. Redwood learned of the treachery, and in an angry session at the offices of Local 102 he put his cards on the table, accusing Fay, in essence, of strikebreaking. Fay countered by accusing Redwood of being in bed with the upstart CIO, a charge Redwood refused to deny. The two of them were talking at cross-purposes, and the meeting ended with bitterness on both sides.

When the prosecutor asked Mrs. Redwood if she had any idea who killed her husband, she told a story about a man, a mysterious figure, who refused to identify himself after coming to her house on the Sunday after the murder.

"Mrs. Redwood, do you know who killed your husband?" the man asked.

"No."

The stranger supplied the information: "Joe Fay and the Big Six. Joe Fay, the Big Six, and Sam Rosoff were in a hall on 14th Street waiting for the news to tell them Norman was done away with."

Maybe so. The Big Six were presumably mobsters.

But Rosoff refused to come to New Jersey to answer the prosecutor's questions, and he made his refusal stick. Fay never bothered to deny the allegations at all. And nothing happened. Breslin, having laid out his case in an eleven-page statement to the press, evidently decided it wouldn't stand the scrutiny of a grand jury.

The prosecutor next turned his attention to the actual killers, not the presumed masterminds. This approach also came to naught, although the police did arrest Moe ("Luger Mike") Saraga, a jowly character who had once supplied mobster Dutch Schultz with pistols, shotguns, rifles, bullets, and bulletproof vests. Saraga, arrested on board the *Queen Mary* after returning from Europe, admitted that he had dealt in mob artillery once upon a time, but disclaimed any direct connection with the pistols used in Redwood's murder.

The investigation dragged on and finally died out. Neither the instigators of the murder nor the execution squad in Teaneck ever came to trial. The death of Norman Redwood, who by all accounts was a decent, honest labor leader, remained unavenged.

Perhaps not, though—at least not entirely. Three days after Redwood's murder, Samuel Rosoff's 263-foot freight-and-passenger steamer, the *Benjamin B. Odell*, named after a former governor of New York, burned to the water line in its winter berth at Marlboro, New York, on the Hudson River. The New York State Police said the fire had "all the earmarks of having been set."

16 Who Murdered the Littlefields?

NORTH ARLINGTON

Incestuous Sheriff Gets Boy, 18, to Take Rap for Double Slaying

OCTOBER 16, 1937

Two North Arlington police officers noticed an expensive car with Maine license plates parked behind a gas station. A shabbily dressed but good-looking young man was asleep behind the wheel. When the cops asked him for his license and registration, they learned that he was Paul N. Dwyer, eighteen, of South Paris, Maine, and that the car belonged to James G. Littlefield, also of South Paris. Dissatisfied at the discrepancy between the name on the driver's license and that of the car's owner, they trundled the youngster off to the police station.

An officer remained behind to search the car. A few moments later he raced back to police headquarters and burst into the room where Dwyer was being questioned.

"You're a murderer!" he shouted.

"I didn't kill them!" said the kid.

"What do you mean—'them'?"

"What did you find?"

The cop seemed taken aback. "A woman's body in the back seat."

"Well," said Dwyer, "if you look in the trunk, you'll find a man's body there. But I didn't kill them."

Sure enough, the trunk yielded a second body. The victims were Dr. James G. Littlefield, sixty-seven, a general practitioner, and his wife, Lydia Littlefield, sixty-three. Both had been strangled and beaten to death.

The police searched for a motive. Even if Dwyer hadn't killed them, he might know why they were killed.

Under further questioning, the young man changed his story, saying he *had* killed them, but offering two such bizarre motives for the brutal crimes that the North Arlington police remained perplexed. Young Dwyer claimed that the murder of Dr. Littlefield in the doctor's South Paris home stemmed from "senseless rage," while the murder of Mrs. Littlefield in her car near the village of New Gloucester, Maine, resulted from her growing doubts about a silly story Dwyer said he had concocted to lure her (for no apparent reason) away from her house.

Okay, Paul, now what really happened?

Why did you bring along in the car a box of love letters to you from various girls back in Maine? Quite a hometown Lothario, were you? Any connection between those steamy letters and those two stiffs you were taxiing around the Northeast?

Since *l'affaire* Littlefield was a Maine murder case rather than a New Jersey crime, it seems reasonable to jump right to the denouement.

On December 2, 1937, Dwyer pleaded guilty in South Paris, Maine, to both murders and was sentenced to life imprisonment. But the Oxford County sheriff found his story hard to believe, especially when Dwyer suddenly changed it, declaring that the motive had been robbery, not rage. The investigation continued even after the confessed killer had taken up residence in Thomaston State Prison.

On June 24, 1938, the Oxford County grand jury indicted Francis M. Carroll, forty-three, a former deputy sheriff, for the already-solved murder of Dr. James G. Littlefield. Carroll had been under arrest for several weeks in South Paris on a morals charge involving his eighteen-year-old daughter, Barbara.

Incest. Therein lay the key to the whole affair. Not only had Paul Dwyer had sexual relations with Barbara, but so had her father, Francis Carroll. Barbara, in her letters to Paul, told him how she had been seduced by her father. This was explosive information, of course, and while Paul was being examined at his home for possible venereal disease, he conveyed the news to Dr. Littlefield. The doctor, outraged, phoned Carroll, who sped over to the Dwyer house. An altercation followed, with the usually kindly "Dr. Jim" telling Carroll that he knew "all about you and Barbara" and vowing to put him in prison.

Carroll had heard enough. He began kicking the doctor, then slugged him with the butt of his pistol, and finally strangled him with his belt. Dwyer claimed that Carroll later killed Mrs. Littlefield, too, though not in New Gloucester, as his first story had it, but outside Carroll's home— after Dwyer had driven around for some time with the confused Lydia

Littlefield in the front seat and the dead doctor, unbeknownst to her, in the car's trunk.

Young Dwyer, terrified, he said, of the savagely rampaging and threatening deputy sheriff, embarked on a frantic six-state tour that ended in North Arlington.

The jury found the prosecution's case convincing and pronounced Francis M. Carroll guilty of murder. Carroll, sentenced to life imprisonment, joined Paul N. Dwyer in the same cell block at Thomaston State Prison, both men serving time for the same murder. Astonishingly, Carroll, the actual killer, was released after serving twelve years of his sentence, while Dwyer remained in prison.

17 The Duck Island Murders

The fifth and sixth murders did not occur at Duck Island, strictly speaking, but in a car parked off Cypress Lane, a few miles away, though still in Hamilton Township. But an eyewitness description of the killer matched a description provided by one of the first two victims. The first couple, like this one, died of shotgun blasts. And the Cypress Lane murders, like the other two pairs, took place in a trysting place for lovers. The two latest bodies were those of Ludovicum Kovacs, twenty-five, and Mrs. Carolina Morconi, twenty-four. A fingerprint on Kovacs's car supplied one clue. Ludovicum's missing watch might in time help nail the killer.

Duck Island, a desolate filled-in area along the Delaware River near Trenton, was in those days a favorite parking place for lovers.

On the night of November 8, 1938, Vincenzo Tonzello, twenty, drove his girlfriend, Mary Mytovich, sixteen, to a secluded spot at Duck Island and parked. After a while they were interrupted by a man who yanked open the door on the driver's side and demanded money. Before Tonzello could respond, the man shot him at point-blank range with a shotgun.

Mary Mytovich jumped from the car and ran. The assailant shot her in the back with a second shotgun blast. She died less than a day later in Saint Francis Hospital, Trenton, but she was able to give detectives a vague description of the killer. At the scene of the shooting, police also found two twelve-gauge shotgun shells and a palm print on Tonzello's car that belonged to neither victim.

On the night of September 30, 1939, about a year later, Frank Casper, twenty-eight, an automobile mechanic, drove Mrs. Katherine Werner, thirty-six, his inamorata, to a place at Duck Island not far from the site of the Tonzello-Mytovich murders. Almost exactly the same sequence of events ensued. Casper died in the car from a shotgun blast. Part of Katherine Werner's right arm was blown off, apparently as she was running away from the car. Both died at the scene. A scavenging junk dealer discovered their bodies.

One shotgun shell was found nearby. Marks on its brass matched those on the two shells found in the earlier killings. Watches and jewelry had been taken from both victims, and descriptions of the items were sent out to jewelers and pawnshops in the region. Hamilton Township police and the New Jersey State Police were convinced they were on the trail of a serial killer, but the trail led nowhere.

Less than a year later two incidents of attempted robbery with a shotgun were reported from towns in Pennsylvania—Morrisville and Bristol, across the Delaware River. The surviving couples' descriptions of the gunman bore some similarity to Mary Mytovich's deathbed recollection. But still there was no specific suspect.

Then came the Kovacs-Morconi murders—two more in the Duck Island sequence, for a total of six. The investigation continued into 1941 and 1942 without results. After Pearl Harbor some of the men who were under suspicion left for the military, and the prospects for an arrest seemed dim.

But, in fact, the murderer was still in the area—and still active. On March 7, 1942, he finally met his Waterloo on a lonely lovers' lane in Tullytown, Pennsylvania, northeast of Philadelphia. He approached a soldier parked with his girlfriend and demanded money. When the soldier resisted, a shotgun blast tore into his left arm and side. In a repeat of past events, the girl tumbled out of the car and began to run. The shooter chased her and hit her over the head with the stock of his shotgun. The soldier, wounded but conscious, and intent on retaliating, started his car, gunned it toward the would-be killer, and forced him, scrambling for his life, into the adjoining woods. The soldier then picked up his girl and went for medical aid. This time clues abounded. A clear description of the assailant now existed, and, as expected, it pointed to the same person as before, a young black man in his late twenties or early thirties. There was a fingerprint on the door of the car. It, too, matched earlier evidence. Most important of all, part of the shotgun had broken off during the attack on the girl, and the stamp "A-639" on it led to an identification of the weapon as a Harrington & Richardson single-barrel shotgun.

Police pursued a long and tortuous path in trying to tie the shotgun to its owner or user. An expired pawn ticket that the presumed owner of the gun had casually given to a WPA (Work Projects Administration) co-worker years earlier, during the Depression, yielded the name "Hill." A description of this Hill, a one-time WPA worker, suggested that at long last the search might be leading somewhere. Hamilton Township police knew the Hill family, and the family member who most nearly fit the various descriptions was Clarence Hill, thirty-three, a soldier for the last eighteen months, now stationed in the South.

Astonishingly, Private Clarence Hill recognized his old WPA buddy among the viewers when, as a suspect, he was standing in a police lineup of soldiers. The picture of affability, or perhaps gullibility, he hailed his friend by name. At that, the army transferred Private Hill to Fort Dix, and Fort Dix immediately turned him over to Hamilton Township civil authorities to await action by the Mercer County grand jury.

Hill confessed to all the assaults that bore his trademark, saying that his motive was more sexual, or voyeuristic, than larcenous, and that robbery was of no real importance to him. He was tried for the murder of Mary Mytovich, whose vague deathbed description of the killer matched Hill's appearance. Convicted after five hours of jury deliberation, he was sentenced to life imprisonment.

18 Ambush at Fort Dix

FORT DIX

3 Enlisted Men Shot and Killed in Racial Brawl Near Barracks

APRIL 2, 1942

Fort Dix, like any army post, has had its share of violence through the years. Between the world wars, however, the military reservation near Wrightstown (then called Camp Dix) saw little violence or anything else. The historians of the Federal Writers Project, reporting on it in 1939, observed only "rows of deserted barracks, huge parade grounds overgrown with grass, and an occasional concrete gun emplacement." But after the Japanese bombed Pearl Harbor in December 1941, the 8,700 acres of low, piney hills changed almost overnight. Within weeks Camp Dix (suddenly transformed into Fort Dix) swarmed with men and activity.

A popular off-base recreation center, the Military Sports Palace, stood just opposite the fort's old barracks in what was then the tiny community of Pointsville. The center, containing a bar and liquor store, had only one public telephone, which was much in demand. At about 9:00 P.M. on April 2, 1942, a soldier stepped out of the telephone booth, and two other soldiers—one black, one white—bolted from the waiting line and made a rush for it. Words led to blows, and some of the other waiting callers jumped into the fray.

The U.S. Army, it should be noted, was segregated in 1942, but the privately owned Military Sports Palace was not. Integration had not produced conflicts. There had been no serious incidents at the center, racial or otherwise, prior to this one.

On this night in early April, the mood seemed unaccountably ugly, as a number of witnesses would later testify. A white soldier approached two military policemen who were on duty in the building, privates first class Manie W. Strouth and Alfred L. H. Hayhoe. The white soldier complained about the actions of a black soldier at the phone booth, who, he said, was trying to jump the line. The MPs went to investigate and found an angry and combative group of blacks near the phone booth, one of whom was Private Isaac W. Brown of Henderson, Tennessee. Apparently the MPs tried to arrest Brown, who had been drinking heavily, when another black soldier, Private Joe Gray, also intoxicated, broke into the tussle. Gray lunged for Strouth's .45-caliber pistol but failed to get it, and Brown took the opportunity to bolt from the building. Other black soldiers, caught up in the dispute, became involved in the scuffle.

The mood of the crowd was becoming increasingly quarrelsome when two military police motor patrolmen, on a routine visit, came into the Sports Palace. They were Private First Class Merrill Immerman and Private James P. Mildenberger. When these additional MPs arrived, Private Gray and others broke loose and fled from the "amusement enterprise," as the army called it. All four MPs went after them, and Strouth, Hayhoe, and Immerman caught one of the fleeing soldiers a short distance from the building. As they fought to subdue him, another group of black soldiers came out of the Sports Palace, intending, the MPs believed, to try to free the prisoner from custody.

Immerman fired a warning shot in the air. So did a black sentry who was posted nearby. At that moment Private Isaac W. Brown, the first to break away from the MPs, returned with a rifle. He strode toward the four military policemen, and when he was eight or ten feet away, raised his rifle and fired. Private First Class Manie Strouth of Honey Camp, Virginia, fell to the ground, mortally wounded.

Immerman and Mildenberger immediately returned the fire with their pistols, and Private Brown fell dead.

The three surviving MPs, leaving their unidentified prisoner outside, retreated into the Sports Palace, where Private Mildenberger placed an urgent phone call to the post provost marshal for help. Some of the black soldiers returned to their barracks, directly opposite the Sports Palace. Rifles (which were properly there) and ammunition (which should not have been) came into play. Sporadic gunfire erupted from the direction of the barracks, wounding five soldiers, all black.

As additional military police, exterior guard, and volunteers arrived at the center, they were ordered to advance toward the barracks, stopping everyone they met and using whatever force was necessary to restore order. During this operation, a black soldier, Corporal George W. Hall of Conyers, Georgia, was shot and killed for allegedly refusing to halt on command, bringing the number of dead to three.

A Summary Court investigation of the incident found, not surprisingly, that a considerable cache of unauthorized ammunition had been in the hands of the unruly and unhappy soldiers. The court said that more care should be taken in the future to keep track of the dispensing, handling, and collecting of ammunition.

The court also asked for "proper military action" against a single participant in the affray, Private Joe Gray. The only undisputed murderer—Private Isaac W. Brown—had himself been shot dead, and no charges other than "interference," "escape and assistance in escape," "intoxication," and "refusal to obey the proper and lawful order of Military Policemen" were recommended in regard to Private Joe Gray.

First His Wife, Then a Trooper

BRAINARDS

Man Sought for Axing His Wife Shoots 2 Troopers, Killing 1

JULY 15, 1945

Ernest Rittenhouse, thirty, of Orange was a man with problems. Troopers Cornelius O'Donnell and Frank C. Perry of the New Jersey State Police already knew something about his problems, because a while back he had escaped from a mental institution and fled to the home of his parents in Brainards, a town on the Delaware River north of Phillipsburg. Trooper O'Donnell, forty-three, commander of the Washington barracks, and Trooper Perry found him hiding out there and returned him to custody.

Rittenhouse, the father of three, was now in more serious trouble. A domestic quarrel at his family's home in Orange had ended with him seizing an ax and striking his twenty-eight-year-old wife, Angeline, with it, killing her. Police in Essex County, trying to track him down, realized that he might have headed once again for his parents' home in Brainards. Troopers O'Donnell and Perry set out on his trail and learned that Rittenhouse was indeed in the area, but he had crossed the Delaware and was hiding out in a cabin in Martins Creek, Pennsylvania.

Phone lines were down in the area because of a severe storm, making it impossible for the pursuing troopers to contact Pennsylvania authorities. Instead, they decided to bring Rittenhouse back to New Jersey immediately, walking across a railroad bridge over the Delaware. Trooper O'Donnell led the way. Behind him were Rittenhouse and Trooper Perry, and behind them a small group of local residents. As they approached the middle of the bridge, Rittenhouse bolted, as if to jump off the bridge. O'Donnell whirled and grabbed him. As the two of them scuffled,

Rittenhouse managed to wrest O'Donnell's revolver from its holster and fire two shots into the trooper's stomach. The killer then turned and fired at Perry, hitting him in the chest. Trooper Perry got off three shots at Rittenhouse as the fugitive leapt from the trestle and began swimming furiously back toward the Pennsylvania side.

Horrified onlookers dashed the rest of the way across the railroad bridge and used the troopers' car radio to alert the Washington barracks. Both troopers were taken to the Warren Hospital in Phillipsburg, where O'Donnell died a few hours later. An intensive manhunt ensued, and at about seven the next morning searchers found Rittenhouse asleep in a shack near the river. Surrendering without a struggle, he was incoherent at first, unkempt, suffering from gunshot wounds to the face. He waived extradition to New Jersey, saying, "I've done it and I'm ready to face it." He was taken to the Warren Hospital for treatment, then held without bail in the Warren County jail.

The Essex County prosecutor indicated a willingness to let Warren County try Rittenhouse first for the murder of Trooper O'Donnell. It was an open-and-shut case, for there were several eyewitnesses to the shooting. Rittenhouse's lawyer saw the futility of mounting a defense and entered a plea of guilty. The killer of two received a life sentence.

20 "It's All Over"

HADDON HEIGHTS

Cistern Near Black Horse Pike Yields Body After V-J Day Bash

AUGUST 15, 1945

Two fifteen-year-old boys, noticing confetti scattered near a twenty-foot well, looked into it, saw a corpse, and notified police. Camden County detectives identified the nude, battered body as that of Margaret McDade, twenty-three, a Philadelphia waitress known as Rita. She had last been seen at a victory celebration the night before, toasting V-J Day, the day the Japanese surrendered to the Allies, ending World War II. The man with her that night, witnesses said, was Howard Auld, twenty-two, a medically discharged two-hundred-pound ex-paratrooper.

The mayor of Mount Ephraim, J. Herbert Phillips, accompanied by two policemen, caught up with Howard Auld as the suspect was walking along the Black Horse Pike. He claimed to be "George Jackson," but army discharge papers in his pocket showed his true identity. Although Auld said, "I didn't do it," he later signed a confession admitting that in fact he did.

It was a brutal crime. The autopsy showed that Rita McDade had been stripped and assaulted, then tossed, still alive, into the well, where she drowned. In addition to the confetti on the ground near the well, police found a pair of orchid evening slippers, bloodstained underclothing, and a red V-J Day party cap bearing the words, "It's all over."

It was indeed all over, not only for Rita McDade and the war in the Pacific, but for Howard Auld as well. Six years later, on May 27, 1951, he was put to death by electrocution at Trenton State Prison.

PART THREE

SILENT-GENERATION MURDERS

21

The Keyport Trunk Murder

KEYPORT

Motorist Finds Body of Woman Stuffed in Trunk Blocking Road

APRIL 19, 1947

Identifying the victim, not finding the murderer, sparked most of the excitement in this bizarre case. When the police finally learned who the victim was, they had little difficulty in getting a confession from the killer.

But attaching a name to the corpse was no cinch. Indeed, it took nearly three months.

The notorious Keyport Trunk Murder case began shortly after 9:00 P.M. on April 19, 1947, when James S. Van Mater, an elderly resident of Hazlet, was driving along Bethany Road, about two hundred yards off Route 35, in Monmouth County's pleasant farming country. He came upon a steamer trunk in the middle of the narrow highway. Since it was blocking his path, he had no choice but to get out of the car and drag it to the side of the road.

Naturally, he wondered what such a heavy trunk was doing on the highway, and what might be in it. Since it was unlocked, he decided to take a look.

He wished he hadn't. What was in it was the nude body of a woman, her body contorted to fit the container. Later examination determined that she was about five feet two inches tall, weighing 145 pounds, with hazel eyes and light brown hair streaked with gray. Scars suggested that she had borne one or two children. A leather dog leash circled her neck tightly. There were no other marks of violence on the body.

Mr. Van Mater did not linger. He jumped in his car and hied off to the state police barracks at Keyport.

Clues were few. There were no tire tracks, no witnesses, no identifying marks on the trunk or the woman. Two shoulder straps from a nightgown were found in the trunk, suggesting that the gown had been ripped from her body before the murderer stuffed the corpse in the trunk. The troopers traced the trunk and dog leash to their manufacturers, but the trail ended there. A fragment of a shipping label, however, was removed from the lid of the trunk, photographically enlarged, and found to begin with the three letters *SCH,* which might prove helpful.

The state police made and distributed dental charts and photographs. Responses of "maybe she's—" ran into the hundreds. When four people identified the body as that of Mrs. Flora Gracy, a former Wrightstown waitress, the mystery appeared to be solved. But Mrs. Gracy phoned from Cambridge, Ohio, disputing the accuracy of the findings.

Another seemingly positive indentification followed. The body was thought to be that of the long-missing New Jersey–bound Miss Mattie Workman of Lawrence County, Tennessee. A number of her relatives journeyed north to view the remains. They took a brief look, said no, and went home.

No fewer than 3,400 fliers with dental charts of the corpse were distributed by the state police. They led to a few possible identifications, but none proved correct. The photograph in newspapers, on the other hand, yielded one tenuous lead that turned out to be on the money.

It came from a union official who thought the victim resembled the wife of a man he had met casually in a Plainfield bar. When the union man saw the husband again after the murder, he asked him about his wife's whereabouts. "She's visiting relatives in Chicago," the man said. Many weeks later the two met again in the same tavern—and the man's wife was purportedly *still* visiting her folks in Chicago.

With some reservations, the union official reported his suspicions to the Keyport troopers. They followed up, questioning first the son of the man named. The son agreed that the woman in the photo did indeed resemble his mother, Mrs. Anna Katherine Schreil, fifty. But it couldn't possibly be, he said, because she was visiting relatives in Chicago.

The son provided the names and phone number of his family's relatives in Illinois. These relatives told the troopers that, yes, Mrs. Schreil had been expected to come for a visit some time ago, but she had never arrived.

A Newark dentist confirmed that the dental charts in the flier matched those of Mrs. Schreil's X-rays.

Confronted with the accumulating evidence against him, Philip A. Schreil, fifty-seven, a New York City photoengraver who lived in Plainfield, confessed to the murder. There was nothing mysterious about the deed. He had strangled his wife at home with the dog leash, he said, then ripped off her nightgown, stuffed her body in the steamer trunk, and driven to the lonely stretch of road near Keyport to dispose of it.

A compassionate jury, swayed by Schreil's story that his wife had nagged him constantly and persisted in running up unpayable debts, found him guilty of manslaughter. He served a short prison term.

22 Drowning His Sorrow

KEARNY

Truck Driver Admits Drowning Captious Wife in Passaic River

JULY 24, 1947

Louis Eliops, twenty-four, was an unemployed truck driver with a few too many beers under his belt. He and his wife, Jean, twenty-three, a waitress at a Newark luncheonette, had been quarreling for several days, and Louis came up with an unusual way to end the acrimony (and the matrimony). At about 10:45 on the night of July 24, 1947, he told her that her younger brother had phoned with the news that he had broken his ankle on a barge in the Passaic River in Kearny. He wanted Louis and Jean to come for him. Although Louis, according to his first confession, had been drinking steadily for eight hours in two Newark taverns and must have been a bit the worse for it, Jean agreed to go, and the two of them took a taxi (they did not own a car) from their home at 27 Grant Street, Newark, to the Kearny side of the Bridge Street bridge over the Passaic River.

They got out of the taxi at about 11:00 P.M., walked a short distance to the Kearny abutment of the long-abandoned bridge for the Lincoln Highway, and scrambled down to the water's edge. Jean, seeing no sign of her brother or anyone else, asked Louis where he was. Without further ado, her husband grabbed her, dragged her into the shallow water near the bank, and repeatedly tried to hold her head under. Mrs. Eliops screamed and struggled, trying desperately to escape. But Louis finally succeeded in drowning her. He felt her body go limp. Then, for some reason, he ripped off her clothes, removed his own clothing, and began to swim.

Meanwhile, two workers at a nearby factory had heard the screams from the river and called the Kearny police. They responded and found Mrs. Eliops's nude, lifeless body in the water. Shortly thereafter they found Mr. Eliops, naked and shivering, some distance away on the river bank. He explained that he had been swimming for quite a while, trying to find the courage to drown himself. Not finding it, he waded ashore and waited for the police to find him. He was taken to the Hudson County jail.

Eliops, a U.S. Army veteran who had served in the South Pacific, had not found steady employment after his discharge. On the morning of the murder he had gone to the Lehigh Transportation Company garage in Newark to see if any drivers were needed. Learning that the answer was no, he repaired to a tavern to nurse his grievances (most of the time in the company of a nameless twenty-two-year-old blonde, according to his second confession) and, apparently, to work out the details of his murder plot.

 # Case of the Trenton Six

At about 10:30 on the morning of January 27, 1948, William Horner, a seventy-two-year-old dealer in used furniture at 213 North Broad Street, Trenton, was found bludgeoned to death in the back room of his small, cluttered store. His common-law wife of thirty years was severely beaten.

It may sound like a grungy, commonplace case. But when arrests were made and penetrating questions asked, the murder and ensuing trials (there were three) became not a throwaway news item but the celebrated case of the Trenton Six, exploited by the U.S. Communist party and the focus of media attention from Paris to Honolulu to New Delhi.

A newspaper in London (not a Communist paper) ran a headline reading "THEY MUST DIE FOR BEING BLACK."

Shakeups in the Trenton Police Department before and after the murder raised questions about the soundness of the investigation. The director of public safety, no friend of the police chief, said darkly, "There has been some bungling in the Horner case." He was partisan but right.

Yet everything seemed simple at first. Fifteen days after the crime, on February 11, five men confessed to the murder (or so it was said—they signed statements to that effect) and fingered a sixth man as an accomplice. Three of the six were unemployed: Collis English, twenty-three, a navy veteran; Ralph Cooper, twenty-three, a farm laborer; and James Thorpe, twenty-four, who had recently lost an arm in an auto accident.

The three with jobs were McKinley Forrest, thirty-five, a laborer in a wire factory; Horace Wilson, thirty-seven, a migrant worker; and John McKenzie, twenty-four, who worked in a poultry store. Only Collis English had a police record. He had once been charged with stealing chickens.

Horace Wilson, the man implicated by the others, did not confess. He had, or thought he had, an alibi. He was working on a potato farm in Robbinsville at the time of the murder. His foreman swore to it. His time sheet showed it.

In a Mercer County trial that lasted nine weeks, the five confessions were the essential evidence, but they were inconsistent. Beyond them lay a mass of muddled and often contradictory testimony. Eyewitness accounts varied wildly; none matched the confessions. No one had seen more than four men, including an alleged getaway driver, at the scene of the crime. Robbery was the supposed motive, but the murdered William Horner still had $1,642 in his pocket, while the badly injured Mrs. Horner had $900 in her stocking, untouched. Mrs. Horner's vehement accusations seemed to lack credibility.

Nevertheless, an all-white jury, after deliberating for seven and a half hours, brought in a verdict of guilty against all six defendants. Even though the jury failed to specify first-degree murder (a glaring basis for appeal), the judge assumed it and sentenced the men to die in the electric chair.

Enter Bessie Mitchell, Collis English's sister, who worked in the New York garment district. She had been trying hard from the beginning to get able legal counsel for her brother but had been rebuffed, first by the Veterans Administration, then by the NAACP.

After the verdict, she tried once more, this time approaching the Civil Rights Congress (CRC), in those days the legal arm of the U.S. Communist party. The CRC lawyers found the case made to order. They were sure they saw blatant injustice based on racial prejudice. Almost overnight, the iffy conviction of six black men on murder charges became the internationally known judicial travesty of the Trenton Six.

Of course, it wasn't really that simple, that cut and dried, or, if you will, that black and white. The state did have a case against them, albeit botched. The trial judge had made errors. The U.S. Supreme Court ordered a new trial.

This second trial began on February 5, 1949, but the prosecutor was stricken with appendicitis early on, and the judge declared a mistrial. A new trial began on March 5, 1951, once again with an all-white jury. The question now as before was, would those five questionable confessions hold up? If they did, the verdict would be guilty. If they didn't, could the state back up its allegations with enough evidence to convict? The answers were ambiguous.

The members of the jury, after deliberating for almost twenty hours without a break, found themselves hopelessly divided on the basic questions of guilt or innocence, but they were determined to return a verdict anyway. And so they did—an obvious trade-off and a rather strange compromise. The jury found two of the defendants, Collis English and Ralph Cooper, guilty of first-degree murder and recommended life imprisonment. They acquitted the other four.

By this time a whole host of supporters had lined up behind the Trenton Six (now Two), including a group of Princeton educators, the American Civil Liberties Union, and, somewhat belatedly, the NAACP. The CRC, having been declared a subversive organization by the U.S. Attorney General, no longer participated.

After the split verdict, it appeared to be an easy thing to get the two convictions overturned, and, indeed, the New Jersey Supreme Court ordered a new trial for Collis English and Ralph Cooper. But fate intervened. Another courtroom drama was not in the cards. English, though only in his late twenties, suffered a heart attack in prison and died. Cooper, facing trial alone, entered a plea of no defense and was sentenced to six to ten years in a New Jersey state prison.

This unexpected plea caused quite an uproar, because the judge, upon demanding that Cooper answer a number of questions about the puzzling case, got essentially the old original answers. Cooper placed all six men at the scene of the murder, just as the state had charged. Collis English, of course, was beyond the reach of earthly laws, but the prosecutors thought about charging the acquitted Trenton Four with perjury. Nothing came of the idea. The case soon receded into a criminological gloss on the pro- and anti-Communist hysteria of the time.

No doubt there are lessons to be learned from this *cause célèbre*. But what are they? If you believe Ralph Cooper's final account—when he had no apparent incentive to lie—one lesson is surely this: Even if the police work is sloppy, the eyewitnesses unreliable, the prosecution inept, the testimony ludicrous, and the judge napping, the defendants may still conceivably be guilty.

Unruh's Bloody Rampage

CAMDEN

"I'm No Psycho," Declares Unruh After Killing 13 in Shooting Spree

SEPTEMBER 5, 1949

Howard Unruh, twenty-eight, of 3202 River Road, Camden, thought his neighbors were talking about him behind his back. They were making fun of him. That would never do.

Unruh, an only child, had served as a tank gunner in World War II. While in the army, he had developed a liking for guns. His favorite was a nine-millimeter German Luger, but his civilian arsenal contained other pistols, too, as well as a large hunting knife and a razor-edged machete.

At his home in Camden, he lived reclusively and read the Bible. To ensure privacy, he built a high wooden fence around the backyard. He kept a diary listing all the insults he felt his neighbors were inflicting on him. After each one he wrote "retal," meaning retaliate.

Unruh's bitterness came to a head on September 5, 1949, when he returned home to find that someone had stolen a large gate he had installed for his fence. That did it. His neighbors must die.

At 9:20 A.M. the seething veteran, dressed in a brown tropical-worsted suit with a white shirt and striped bow tie, walked into John Pilarchik's nearby shoe repair shop. Unruh looked eminently respectable as he pulled out his Luger and pumped two shots into the cobbler's chest. Pilarchik died instantly.

Within the next few minutes Howard Unruh gained revenge, in his own troubled mind, not only for the theft of the gate but also for all those years of being mocked and slighted. He shot and killed twelve more people, his final victim being three-year-old Donald Hamilton, who was gazing out a window at the carnage. Unruh, a sharpshooter who often practiced target shooting in his basement, killed the child with a single bullet through the glass.

Running low on ammunition, Unruh trotted home, jumped the backyard fence, climbed the steps to his second-floor room, barricaded the door, and began to reload.

By now the police were arriving, laying siege. A few shots were exchanged before they decided to lob tear gas canisters through the windows of his small room. Not long afterward, Unruh, with fifty guns trained on him, walked out of the house with his hands up.

Was he sorry? Not a bit. When questioned later by a psychiatrist, he said, "I'd have killed a thousand if I'd had bullets enough."

Howard Unruh's postshooting enemies included the psychiatrists who questioned his claim that he "had a good mind." Diagnosing him as a paranoid-schizophrenic, they sent him off to the New Jersey Hospital for the Insane in Trenton.

A mass murder with thirteen victims sounds almost commonplace today, but in 1949 it was sensational news. As H. Paul Jeffers says in *Who Killed Precious?,* "Before Unruh, wholesale homicide had been noted in America, but rarely. After Unruh, there's hardly been a year unstained by it."

R.I.P.
Willie Moretti

CLIFFSIDE PARK
Willie Moretti Terminated in Gangland-Style Slaying
OCTOBER 4, 1951

A reporter once asked Willie Moretti if he wasn't afraid he'd be shot for talking too much to the Kefauver Committee, to a New Jersey grand jury, or to the host of a network radio talk show. Moretti snorted, "This ain't Chicago."

So Willie went about his business, which was gambling and racketeering, with a profitable laundry business thrown in for respectability. The day before gunfire erupted in Cliffside Park he had bet and lost a large sum of money on the World Series opener between the New York Giants and Brooklyn Dodgers. The morning of the shooting he had placed a five-hundred-dollar bet on a horse called Auditing to show in the third race at Belmont. Auditing finished fourth, out of the money.

By then Willie didn't care.

At about 11:00 A.M. two men walked into Joe's Restaurant at 793 Palisade Avenue, Cliffside Park. They ordered orange juice, coffee, and cake at the counter. Mrs. Dorothy Novack, the waitress, thought perhaps she had seen them before, but her memory proved Reaganesque.

A few minutes later, two more men entered the restaurant, and the four of them took a table near the front, about eight feet from the window. When they spotted Moretti's cream-colored convertible pulling up, one of the men went out to greet the balding, affable, loose-talking mobster. Back at the table, according to Mrs. Novack (who was the only other person in the dining area), all five men were laughing and conversing in Italian.

She departed for the kitchen to get the day's menu.

Almost immediately, a series of shots rang out. When Mrs. Novack, chef Joe Amento, and co-owner Mrs. Jenny (Mom) Cravotta arrived from the kitchen, Willie Moretti was still there, but the others had left. Moretti, fifty-seven, lay face up on the tiled floor, dead from gunshot wounds to the head. The police found more than two thousand dollars in cash in his pockets.

This wasn't just another mob rubout. It was big news, a front-page story even in the staid *New York Times.* Moretti, who lived in Hasbrouck Heights and had a five-acre estate in Deal, where he raised prize ducks, was on good terms (or had been) with Joe Adonis, Albert Anastasia, Lucky Luciano, and, in particular, Frank Costello, who was a boyhood friend and the best man at Willie's wedding.

Vito Genovese, on the other hand, regarded Moretti as a liability, a loose cannon. He evidently convinced the others to sanction an early funeral for Willie.

The four assassins never answered for their crime. Mrs. Novack couldn't quite get her descriptions straight, and no one on the street noticed anything useful.

From the police chief of Cliffside Park, Frank Borrell, no one expected much. He had served in that position since 1924, yet he had never made a local gambling arrest because, as he had recently explained to the Kefauver Committee—while also attempting to explain his sizable income—"I was not aware of any gambling going on in my town."

Borrell could not deny Willie Moretti's murder, of course. But neither he nor anyone else could ever solve it.

 # Bayonne's *Morro Castle* Killer

BAYONNE

Hero of "Morro Castle" Fire
Arrested in Double Murder

JULY 2, 1953

In 1934 the Bayonne City Council had awarded George White Rogers a two-hundred-dollar gold medal for heroism. A radio operators' organization named him maritime hero of the year. Rogers, a native of Bayonne, was the chief radio operator aboard the Ward Line's cruise ship *Morro Castle* in the early morning hours of September 8, 1934, when the liner caught fire off Sea Girt on its return voyage from Havana. He had acted heroically by staying at his radio and calling for help.

The ship's captain, Robert R. Wilmott, fifty-five, had died of a presumed heart attack at 7:30 P.M. the previous evening. Chief Officer William F. Warms thereupon assumed command.

A minute or two before 2:50 A.M. a fire broke out in the passengers' library. It spread rapidly. Chief Officer Warms kept the liner plowing forward, the wind on deck fanning the flames. Finally, at 3:23 A.M., with the fire raging out of control, the portly, imperturbable Rogers, having received Warms's okay, sent the SOS that brought needed but belated help. One hundred and thirty-four people perished.

After that shining moment (if it was a shining moment—some people later wondered), George W. Rogers could not stay out of trouble. A mysterious fire destroyed his radio shop in Bayonne. Rogers moved on to become a patrolman in Bayonne, assisting Lieutenant Vincent J. Doyle, who operated the first two-way police radio system in the nation.

One day in 1938 a bomb in a package addressed to "Lt. Doyle" went off in the police radio room. Rogers had just stepped out "to mail a letter." The bomb blew three fingers off Doyle's left hand. Circumstantial evidence made it clear who had constructed the bomb: George W. Rogers. The *Morro Castle* hero drew twelve to twenty years, but served only three years and ten months at the New Jersey State Prison at Trenton before being paroled.

Although Rogers had a few run-ins with the law over the next few years, he stayed out of jail until 1953, when the murder of two of his neighbors once again drew attention to him. Rogers, it seemed, had befriended the victims—eighty-three-year-old William Hummel and his fifty-eight-year-old spinster daughter—and had acquired money from them in one way or another. Their bludgeoned bodies were discovered on July 2, 1953. Police determined the probable date of death as June 19.

Here, too, the evidence was circumstantial but overwhelming. The state charged Rogers with first-degree murder. The jury deliberated for three hours before finding him guilty and recommending life imprisonment. On September 24, 1954, Judge Paul J. Duffy gave the fifty-three-year-old radioman two life sentences. This proved to be a shorter term than expected. Rogers died of a stroke in state prison on January 10, 1958.

Meanwhile Lieutenant Vincent J. Doyle had slowly and laboriously been assembling evidence to prove a theory he firmly believed, that George W. Rogers had set the *Morro Castle* fire. The arson device, Doyle said, was an incendiary fountain pen that Rogers had described to him at some length when the two of them were working together. But what was his motive? According to the lieutenant, Rogers was an all-around ne'er-do-well and perhaps a pyromaniac.

Most of the time Rogers was indeed bad news for all concerned, but during the hours of the *Morro Castle* fire he acted with real courage. Eyewitnesses swore to it. And the 250-pound blob in the radio room was not a man easily misidentified.

Still, the strange coincidence of the captain dropping dead of a heart attack and a fatal fire starting by spontaneous combustion less than eight hours later struck many (not just Doyle) as highly unlikely. Armchair detectives offered various theories of murder and arson. None was ever proved.

Hal Burton, in his 1973 book on the disaster, concluded that the shipboard doctors and the insurance companies were probably correct in their judgments. Captain Wilmott died of natural causes, and the fire on the *Morro Castle* was "an act of God."

The case seems closed. But you never know. Perhaps someone can yet show that George W. Rogers killed not only the 2 Hummels of Bayonne but 134 (or maybe 135) others.

The Avenging Motel Owner

Motel Owner Kills Fugitive Who Murdered State Trooper

NOVEMBER 1, 1955

Just after 10:30 on the night of November 1, 1955, Trooper John Anderson, thirty-six, patrolling the Holmdel section of the Garden State Parkway, spotted a new green-and-cream Pontiac sedan that had been reported stolen in Brooklyn the day before. Apparently the Pontiac was parked off the Parkway in the "official-use" U-turn lane at the 112-mile marker, which is where Trooper Anderson's car was located after his "Help! Holmdel!" radio message brought other troopers racing to the scene.

The troopers found Anderson lying on his back on the front seat, mortally wounded. His service revolver and six cartridges were missing. Anderson's holster was torn, suggesting a struggle for the gun. Before Anderson lost consciousness, he gave Troopers Anthony Scalzone and Henry Kalinowski a New York license-plate number for the vehicle, 7L 9335, and said that the driver was headed south.

Kalinowski accompanied the ambulance to Riverview Hospital. When it got there, Kalinowski called the Holmdel Station with the bad news. The revised radio and teletype message became "WANTED FOR MURDER."

While Trooper Scalzone searched the U-turn area for evidence, others were on the lookout for the killer's car. Trooper Ed Wilke, from the Shrewsbury station, was one. While patrolling Route 35 near Asbury Park, he saw a green-and-cream Pontiac, New York license plate 5L 7935, pass him going south.

The match was too close to ignore. Trooper Wilke gave chase, radioed his location and a description of the car, and motioned the driver to pull over. The Pontiac stopped, Wilke braked in behind it, and told the driver to get out.

Instead the Pontiac roared off, spraying dirt and gravel. As Wilke gave chase, the driver veered off the main highway and careened through residential side streets before being trapped in a dead end. By the time Trooper Wilke reached the car, it was empty. Neighborhood residents pointed excitedly toward a trail into a small wooded area where they said the fugitive had run. Wilke radioed for help.

Meanwhile, at the Fernwood Motel in Neptune, Edward Whritenour, forty-eight, and his wife, Patricia, forty-five, heard the doorbell ring in their office-apartment at about 11:45 P.M. When Whritenour answered it, a disheveled, out-of-breath young man brandishing a revolver shoved him back into the office. At first Whritenour assumed it was a robbery, but when the man kept pacing to the window and looking outside, the motel owner began to get a different and scarier picture.

The intruder ordered Mrs. Whritenour to tie up her husband, which she did. He then forced Whritenour into a bedroom closet and returned to his nervous vigil.

Mrs. Whritenour hadn't done a thorough job of tying up her husband. The intruder wasn't paying close enough attention, and this oversight—not to mention the fact that there were two loaded rifles in the closet—proved fatal to him. Edward Whritenour worked free of his bonds and grasped a .30-caliber Savage hunting rifle.

The intruder, having by then bound Patricia Whritenour, still kept a wary watch at the window. Hearing noises from the closet, he moved toward it and told Whritenour to quiet down.

That was his last request, for as he approached the closet, Whritenour stepped out and fired one well-aimed shot at the man's head, killing him instantly. "I stepped over this fellow who wasn't going to do anybody any harm," said the motel owner matter-of-factly, "and told the police what had happened." The public hailed Whritenour as a hero.

At 1:59 A.M. a message went out from the state police station at Trenton, canceling the wanted-for-murder notice. "Subject shot and killed in Neptune Township, N.J.," it said.

Following this citizen homicide, it remained for the investigators to learn who the murderous but careless young intruder was and why he had killed Trooper Anderson.

The murderer, it turned out, was Sammy Alvarez, twenty-seven, of

Brooklyn. Alvarez had borrowed the Pontiac from a friend, William Patterson of 455 Classon Avenue, Brooklyn, the day before the murder. When Alvarez failed to return it, Patterson reported the car stolen.

Using the borrowed car, Sammy Alvarez and a companion robbed a service station in New Jersey on the fatal night. Alvarez then drove his companion back to Brooklyn and returned alone to the Shore area. For some reason he stopped in the U-turn lane at the 112-mile marker, where Trooper Anderson noticed him.

Almost certainly Alvarez was not in the car when Anderson approached it. Police theorize that the trooper was attacked from behind when he leaned over to look into the empty Pontiac. A scuffle occurred, during which Alvarez gained possession of the trooper's service revolver and fired three deadly shots.

28 Death Row's Edgar Smith

This is the case in which columnist William F. Buckley, Jr., learned to his embarrassment that one may write, and write, and be a villain, to paraphrase the Bard. The good-looking and articulate sociopath Edgar Herbert Smith wrote three best-selling books about his legal battle to escape New Jersey's electric chair and, at the same time, to convince readers of his innocence in the brutal murder of Victoria Zielinski, fifteen, a sophomore at Ramsey High School.

While on death row, Smith persuaded Buckley, the noted conservative columnist and editor of *The National Review,* that he was the victim of a bum rap, that the many judges who denied his appeals for a new trial were either ignorant or misinformed, and that his first book, *Brief Against Death,* published by Alfred A. Knopf, should, in Buckley's words, "worry the jurors" who returned the first-degree murder verdict against him.

The thus-scolded jurors, ten men and two women, had reached their decision in slightly less than two hours—so quickly that Guy W. Calissi, the Bergen County prosecutor, was absent from the courtroom. He was out to lunch, literally. (Buckley was later out to lunch figuratively.)

Despite the hubbub the murder engendered, there was nothing very mysterious or complicated about it. Police in Mahwah and Ramsey solved the crime with relative ease and efficiency. The Bergen County prosecutor's office built what appeared to be, and in fact was, a damning case against twenty-three-year-old Edgar Smith.

The facts make it clear enough why the jurors had so little difficulty in reaching their decision. At about 8:30 P.M. on Monday, March 4, 1957, Victoria Zielinski left the home of her friend Barbara Nixon to walk home along Wyckoff Avenue. She was to meet her younger sister, Myrna, about halfway to the Zielinski house, and they would walk the rest of the way together. Myrna, starting ten minutes late from her home, walked all the way to the Nixons, but never saw Victoria.

Victoria's mother, Mary, woke her husband, Anthony, at about 12:30 A.M. to say that their daughter was missing. The Zielinskis searched in vain that night, then reported Victoria's disappearance to the Ramsey police early the next morning.

At about 9:00 A.M. on March 5, Anthony Zielinski, while cruising the streets of the neighborhood with his wife, spotted a black shoe, a loafer, at the corner of Fardale Avenue and Chapel Road, Mahwah. Stopping, he noticed a bloodstained scarf a few yards away. Mrs. Zielinski drove off to alert the Ramsey police.

In the meantime, Chief Edmund Wickham of the Mahwah Police Department arrived and joined Mr. Zielinski in the search. Within minutes the two of them discovered Victoria's body lying face down in a sand pit. Her skull had been crushed, her brains splattered about, her left eye destroyed, her nose and jaw fractured, and her teeth were loose in her mouth.

Victoria's sweater had been pulled up to her neck and her brassiere pulled down to her waist. Her dungarees appeared untouched, though spattered with blood and tissue. A blue Ramsey High School jacket lay beside her. The autopsy would show no rape and indeed an intact hymen.

The first break in the case was not long in coming. A young man named Joseph Gilroy had lent his 1950 blue Mercury convertible to his friend Edgar Smith on the night of the murder. The next day, when Gilroy saw "a spot" on one seat cover and another on the floor mat, he talked to his friends about the possible implications. They advised him to go to the police.

Edgar Smith, thus fingered, proved cooperative at first. He admitted picking up Victoria Zielinski on Wyckoff Road, admitted driving her to the sand pit, admitted having a violent argument with her, admitted that he "swung at her . . . I swung pretty hard—as hard as I could."

He admitted driving away without her, admitted returning to retrieve a shoe he had somehow lost. In fact, he admitted virtually everything except having any recollection of killing her.

It hardly mattered. Lab tests showed type O bloodstains on Smith's shoes, socks, and khaki trousers. (Victoria Zielinski's blood type was O;

Smith's was A.) Smith, no fool, had disposed of both the shoes and the trousers on the night of the murder, but later he cooperatively led police to the shoes. The police found the trousers on their own.

With type O blood on his clothes and bloodstains in the car he was driving, Edgar Smith did not have a strong defense—so he concocted a weak and shabby one that implicated, unconvincingly, though in the prosecutor's view, quite viciously, a supposedly good friend of Smith's, Donald R. Hommell. Smith had half-jokingly suggested Hommell as a "fall guy" in his first remarks to police, but then dropped the idea until the time of the trial.

What exactly did happen on the night of March 4? Why did poor Victoria Zielinski, a pleasant, likable girl, end up dead "with a decerebration traumatic" (in the medical examiner's technical but gruesome description) in a sand pit near Bogert's Trailer Camp, home of Edgar Smith and his nineteen-year-old wife and two-month-old son?

In his opening statement and later in his summation prosecutor Guy W. Calissi previewed and then explained the gist of what Edgar Herbert Smith admitted (nineteen years later) to having done.

Smith knew Victoria Zielinski. He had driven her home before without incident. She trusted him. On the night of March 4 he picked her up in the borrowed Mercury, but instead of taking her home, as he had offered, he drove her to the sand pit, a local lovers' lane, and made sexual advances, which (judging by the autopsy findings) culminated in his lifting her sweater, ripping down her brassiere, and biting her right breast. She warned him, probably in commingled anger and fright, "I'm going to tell my father."

This set off the volatile Smith, who, according to one psychiatrist, was "prone to act on impulse with little regard for the rights of others and little respect for constituted authority." His impulse on this occasion was to beat Victoria Zielinski's head to a bloody pulp, which he did with a baseball bat from the back of the car and some large rocks from the edge of the sand pit. The murder occurred about 9:00 P.M.

The time of the murder assumed great importance in the trial because the medical examiner, Dr. Rafael Gilady, testified that his best estimate of the time of death was midnight. He carefully qualified his testimony, however, by saying that the low temperature on March 4 could have speeded rigor mortis and made the time of death somewhat earlier.

Curiously, a *Star-Ledger* article of March 6, the day before Edgar Smith was named as a suspect, indicated that Dr. Gilady had "set the time of death at about 10:00 P.M."

In any event, the jury convicted Smith, made no recommendation for clemency, and the judge sentenced him to die in the electric chair during the week of July 15, 1957. He didn't die. He appealed. He kept on appealing. His appeals delayed the execution, which of course was their purpose.

At last, by happenstance, William F. Buckley, Jr., learned that Edgar Smith had been an avid reader in prison of Buckley's *National Review.* One thing led to another, and before long the columnist and the convict were corresponding at length: some 2,900 pages of writing in all.

In 1971, on the nineteenth appeal of the Bergen County jury's verdict and Judge Arthur J. O'Dea's sentence of death—largely through Buckley's well-meaning intervention and encouragement—a U.S. circuit court judge ordered the State of New Jersey to retry Edgar Smith for the murder of Victoria Zielinski.

No trial took place. Instead, by prearrangement, Smith appeared before Superior Court Judge Morris Pashman and confessed to the murder (as "something I had to do to get free," he later wrote). The judge sentenced him to twenty-five to thirty years, gave him credit for the time already served, and suspended the remainder of his sentence, specifying four years and four months probation.

Buckley's chauffeured limousine picked Smith up as he left Trenton State Prison and whisked him into New York City for the taping of two of Buckley's "Firing Line" television shows.

Smith then turned his attention to writing another book, *Getting Out,* in which he once again ridiculed New Jersey courts and law enforcement officials. He explained away his guilty plea as a mere technicality and assured readers that he would "close the door on the past."

Had he done so, the story would end there. But he didn't. The past came back to haunt him, or rather it came back to haunt, or, more accurately, to terrorize a young woman in Chula Vista, California.

On the afternoon of October 1, 1976, Smith approached Mrs. Lefteriva Ozbun, thirty-three, in the parking lot of a clothing manufacturing plant in Chula Vista, south of San Diego, where she worked. He struck her, taped her hands behind her back, and forced her into his car at knifepoint. She screamed, but no one responded.

As Smith drove away, Mrs. Ozbun began kicking the car's windshield, finally smashing it. Smith tried to restrain her, but she wrenched her hands free of the tape and clutched the wheel of the car. It swerved off the highway, I-5, near the Mexican border. Smith stabbed Mrs. Ozbun in the abdomen. She opened the passenger's door, fell from the car, and stumbled away. Smith roared off in his car, a brown Pontiac. Witnesses described the automobile to police and gave the license-plate number.

A warrant went out for "Death Row" Smith's arrest (the media had by now given him that sobriquet), charging him with kidnapping, armed robbery, and attempted murder. FBI agents caught up with him on October 13 in a fourteenth-floor hotel room in downtown Las Vegas. He surrendered without a struggle, admitting the assault on Lefteriva Ozbun, and then—perhaps to clear the air—also admitting that he had murdered Victoria Zielinski back at the Mahwah sand pit in 1957. Smith, forty-two years old at the time of his arrest in Nevada, said he "recognized that the devil I had been looking at . . . was me."

This time there was no jailhouse lawyering, no journalistic intercession. "Death Row" Smith drew a life sentence.

 # Mama's Little Felony Murderer

---

NEWARK

Wayward Son Robs Café and Murders His Mother

MARCH 18, 1959

For Lee Daniels, Jr., March 18, 1959, was a bad day. It was even worse for his family. Before the day ended his mother lay dead, murdered, in the luncheonette she owned at 214 Waverly Avenue, Newark, and his younger sister, Lorraine, hovered between life and death from a gunshot wound.

Junior Daniels, twenty-five, entered the C&L Sugar Bowl, his mother's café, shortly before 11:00 P.M. He asked for coffee. His sister, twenty-two, working as a waitress at the C&L, refused to serve him. The family members had been arguing among themselves for some time. Mrs. Clara Daniels, fifty-eight, the mother, had ordered Lee out of her house eight weeks earlier, believing he was stealing from her, a good bet in view of the length of his rap sheet. Lorraine sided with her mother.

On this occasion, though, Mrs. Daniels relented and told her daughter to serve Lee the coffee. She did. When Lee finished it, he got up, walked to the front door of the luncheonette, locked it, pulled out a .22-caliber revolver, aimed it at his sister, and asked for the money in the cash register.

Lorraine said no, whereupon he shot her, wounding her critically.

This was too much for Mrs. Daniels to take. She tried to grab her son's arm, yelling, "You won't shoot your own mother!"

But he would. And did. Twice.

She fell to the floor, mortally wounded.

The unruly son fled.

Junior Lee has to be rated a more capable killer than he was a thief, for inexplicably he took no C&L money with him.

His getaway lacked finesse, too. A brother-in-law, William Hynes, heard the shooting from the kitchen of the café and gave chase. Hynes flagged down a passing squad car. The policeman, catching up with Daniels a few blocks from the café, arrested him.

It turned out that Daniels had held up a tavern at 173 Sherman Avenue earlier the same day. He was tried for both crimes, and on July 11, 1959—justice being swifter in those days—received a life term for killing his mother, plus an added ten to fifteen years for the tavern holdup.

Batman in Blairstown

Stanley Marrs, thirty-two, had a criminal record dating back more than a dozen years. His most recent conviction was for assaulting a girlfriend and three teenagers with a baseball bat, an act that earned him the nickname "the Batman." The police alarm on the morning of November 25, 1959, described him as "very dangerous." A kid who knew him said, "He was one of the strongest men I've ever seen."

Marrs was wanted for questioning in connection with the brutal murder of Lester Silverman, a community-minded department store owner in Blairstown. Silverman's wife, Dorothy, found her husband badly beaten in the basement of his store at about 10:30 in the morning. He died before the rescue squad could get him to the hospital.

State Troopers Lester Pagano and James Suydam talked with a witness who told them he had seen the bad-tempered Marrs in the store just before Mrs. Silverman found her dying husband. The troopers went to the tiny village of Johnsonburg, where Marrs rented a room at the inn. Although the suspect wasn't there, they checked his room and found some bloodstained clothing.

They waited. Trooper Suydam called the Blairstown station and, being informed that Silverman had died, was told to return to the scene of the murder. Trooper Pagano, meanwhile, remained at the Johnsonburg Inn, concealed near the door to Marrs's second-floor room.

When Marrs came up the steps, Pagano stepped forward and placed him under arrest. He prodded the strongman down the stairs, into the bar, and asked the bartender or one of the patrons to phone the Blairstown barracks for help. They shook their heads. No one wanted to get involved.

Trooper Pagano decided he should handcuff the suspect. When he tried to do so, Marrs broke loose and made for the porch, where Pagano caught up with him. As they struggled, Marrs pulled a pistol from his jacket and fired twice at point-blank range. The trooper fell, hit in the abdomen.

Rolling into position for firing, Pagano got off five shots at the fleeing suspect. One hit Marrs in the leg, another in the back. Marrs turned and emptied his .32-caliber pistol, then threw the gun at Pagano.

At this moment other troopers arrived at the dusty crossroads and subdued the Johnsonburg strongman, who, partially paralyzed, was taken to Warren Hospital in Phillipsburg. He recovered, was tried, convicted, and sentenced to life imprisonment for the murder of Lester Silverman. He got an additional twenty-one years for shooting Trooper Pagano.

Lester Pagano, twenty-nine, suffering severe abdominal and spinal cord injuries, was taken to Newton Memorial Hospital, where his condition remained critical for quite a while. Paralyzed from the waist down, he seemed destined never to return to duty. But after years of therapy he did return, rejoining his colleagues at the Blairstown barracks.

PART FOUR

A
BLOODSTAINED
DECADE

Murder at the Clarke Estate

NORTH BRUNSWICK

3 Women and Taxi Driver Slain in Doctor's Posh Home

JANUARY 26, 1960

A banner headline in the *Star-Ledger* summarized in screaming black ink what had happened the day before: Four people had been slain for no apparent reason in the luxurious home of a prominent New Brunswick surgeon. The reporters called it "one of the most bizarre crimes in years."

They were right. It was indeed a bizarre crime, so much so that only after two more murders, equally senseless, would an explanation begin to emerge.

The bare facts were these. A little after 11:30 A.M. on January 26, 1960, a red-and-black taxi pulled into the tree-lined 250-foot driveway of Dr. Francis Clarke's three-acre estate off Route 27 in North Brunswick. There were two men in the cab, the driver and a passenger. The driver, Morris Michael, fifty-seven, worked for the 20th Century Taxicab Association in Newark.

Two witnesses observed one man leaving the house at about 12:05 P.M. He drove away in the cab, and he was not the cabbie. The witnesses described this man as perhaps thirty-five years old, handsome, bespectacled, wearing a brown felt hat and a beige, double-breasted overcoat that appeared to be foreign-made.

There were three women in the house at the time the cab arrived. One was Mrs. Edith Clarke, the elderly wife of the doctor. She had recently suffered a stroke and was bedridden. With her were Miss Dorothy Moore, sixty-six, a housekeeper, and Mrs. Cora Thaddies, twenty-nine, a maid.

The Clarkes' daughter, Mrs. Frederic Chapin, also twenty-nine, who had been visiting her parents' home, had gone to town earlier that day to do some shopping and to meet her father. She talked with him briefly at about 11:30 A.M. in his office at 116 New Street, New Brunswick. When she returned to the Clarke estate at 1:15 P.M., she noticed the dining room table was set for lunch. Calling out and receiving no reply, she went upstairs.

In her mother's bedroom on the second floor, Mrs. Chapin found three bodies lying side by side on the bed, all of them bound hand and foot with stockings, neckties, sashes, and leather belts. Each victim had been killed by a single copper-tipped bullet from a .32-caliber weapon.

In a smaller bedroom across the hall Mrs. Chapin found Morris Michael, the taxi driver, who was also bound hand and foot and shot. A sheet covered his body.

At the time of her discovery of the bodies, her father was performing an operation at Saint Peter's General Hospital in New Brunswick. Hospital authorities waited until Dr. Clarke finished the operation before telling him of the tragedy at his home.

Nothing seemed to have been taken from the house. None of Dr. Clarke's patients, nor anyone else, seemed to view revenge as a likely motive. Neither Dr. Clarke nor anyone else connected with the case could identify the man shown in the precisely drawn (and, as it turned out, accurate) sketches of the killer provided by a New York City detective, who based his likenesses on the descriptions provided by the two witnesses.

What possible motive existed for the massacre?

No one could say. The police had few clues and no plausible suspects. On the face of it there was no reason whatever for someone to kill Mrs. Clarke, the housekeeper, the maid, and the unlucky taxi driver.

The investigation stalled.

Then the killer struck again, nearly six months later, on July 10. Incredibly, he used the same .32-caliber pistol. And even more incredibly, he used it to kill two policemen.

For this double murder, unlike the quadruple murder, the police knew the killer's motive: He wanted to avoid answering charges on a series of traffic violations.

The killer was Michael Fekecs, twenty-five, a Hungarian refugee and an all-around nogoodnik. Sid Dorfman in the *Star-Ledger* described him as "darkly handsome" and, somewhat less flatteringly, as "an arrogant and insane mass murderer and thief."

Fekecs's final homicidal folly began when Patrolmen George Dunham and John Lebed of Franklin Township arrested him for driving his Lincoln Continental (Fekecs owned five cars) while his license was revoked. Officers Dunham and Lebed took him in, bail was set at $250, and Fekecs asked to be allowed to go to his apartment at 140 Montgomery Street, Highland Park, to pick up the bail money. Since his Continental had been impounded, the two policemen obligingly drove him there.

A little before 7:00 P.M., a woman who lived in Fekecs's apartment building phoned the Highland Park police to complain that someone had just drilled a hole in her wall.

True enough. It was a .32-caliber hole, and on the other side of the wall the investigating officers found Patrolmen Dunham and Lebed, dead.

The massive manhunt that followed left little room for Fekecs to maneuver or escape. He was soon spotted in the Vauxhall section of Union. Two Union police officers responded. They located him in a wooded area off the Garden State Parkway, and at least five shots were exchanged. Fekecs, presumably realizing it was all over, shot himself in the forehead.

He eventually died from the wound, but only after three and a half months in a coma. The mass murderer fought hard for life, but lost. He never regained consciousness. His Czechoslovakian-made .32-caliber pistol thus claimed its seventh and least-mourned victim.

Who exactly was this Michael Fekecs, and why was he doing these terrible things? There are no satisfactory answers. He was an odd amalgam of nine-to-five factory worker, two-bit thief, heartless swindler, high liver, and, of course, vicious killer.

He held down an eighty-dollar-a-week job at the Westinghouse Electric plant in Edison, but he spent some of his time there proposing robberies to at least one of his co-workers. He approached various friends with similar plans. He conned twelve thousand dollars from the seventy-four-year-old New Brunswick man who had sponsored his entrance into the United States. One way or another the youthful, clean-cut rascal managed to acquire two Lincolns, an Edsel, an MG, and a Jaguar, plus a huge wardrobe and a sizable collection of jazz records.

Why no one thought to question Fekecs early on is unclear. He had once worked briefly as a floor refinisher at the Clarke estate. And only eleven days before the Clarke murders, he told a fellow refugee as they passed the estate in a car, "That would be a good place to rob. He's a rich doctor." (Fekecs's actual take was about three hundred dollars in cash.)

Fekecs died in Elizabeth General Hospital at 1:15 A.M. on November 2, 1960. No one claimed his body.

32 "I Blew My Top"

The parents of Noreen Bernadette Buckley, sixteen, and Margaret Ann Kennedy, fifteen, both of Morris Plains and students at Bayley-Ellard Catholic High School in Madison, knew something was wrong. On the afternoon of Wednesday, June 20, the two girls had taken a bus from Morris Plains to nearby Morristown to do some shopping. They did not return that night, and at 6:45 the next morning their parents reported them missing.

At about 3:00 that afternoon, three teenage boys were driving on the wooded roads of the old Fairburn estate off James Street in Morris Township, south of Morristown. They came upon the badly battered body of a girl. Upon being told what the boys had seen "at the racetrack"—actually, an oval roadway around an abandoned polo field—an aunt of one of them called the police.

The battered and bloody body, fully clothed and lying in the roadway, was that of Noreen Buckley. A police search of the area turned up a second body, that of Meg Kennedy, about an hour later and a few hundred feet away. Both girls were wearing cotton blouses, sneakers, and bobby socks. Both had been savagely beaten. The autopsy report would show that they had died between 8:30 and 9:00 P.M. on Wednesday, June 20. The girls' black shoulder bags and a white scarf were found about sixty yards from Meg Kennedy's body. Nothing seemed to have been taken from the shoulder bags. The police also recovered a bent and bloody jack-handle lug wrench along James Street near Springbrook Road.

Meg Kennedy and Noreen Buckley had last been seen alive at the Colonial Luncheonette on South Street in Morristown. How they had gotten from there to the once-parklike estate of the late president of the Diamond Match Company was not known for certain.

Police, however, were almost immediately alerted by a tipster to look for a 1962 green Ford Fairlane and an eighteen-year-old ex-marine who lived at 23 James Street, Morristown. They found the former leatherneck on Thursday night at the Bertrand Island amusement park on Lake Hopatcong. He was there with his seventeen-year-old girlfriend, taking advantage of the park's "nickel night." Police questioned him for six hours. He denied any involvement with the twin slaying, although he admitted seeing the girls at the Colonial Luncheonette at about 8:00 on Wednesday night. The young man was released but put under surveillance. The last person to talk to him was Detective Sergeant Joseph Logan of the New Jersey State Police.

The investigation continued. It included a thorough examination of the green Ford Fairlane that the youth had been driving on the night of the murders. The car, which belonged to the young man's father, was found to contain bloodstains—but no lug wrench. Whereupon Frank C. Scerbo, the Morris County prosecutor, ordered the slim, bespectacled youth brought in again. This time he was charged with murder.

The name of the alleged killer was James H. Vance, Jr. He had attended Bayley-Ellard but had dropped out to join the Marine Corps. His four-year enlistment had ended after only six months with an honorable discharge; while he was in the marines he was hospitalized for psychiatric treatment. Vance explained the reason for the hospital stay as "nervousness." He knew Meg Kennedy and Noreen Buckley from Bayley-Ellard. Despite the mounting evidence against him, he maintained his innocence. He told a story, easily disproved, about having been beaten up while changing a tire, thus accounting for both the bloodstains in the car and the missing lug wrench. He voluntarily took a lie detector test.

At 6:00 P.M. on Saturday Vance asked to talk privately with Detective Sergeant Logan. He and the trooper talked for hours, a rambling conversation covering everything imaginable. Sometime around 3:00 A.M., said Sergeant Logan in an interview with Campbell Allen of the *Daily Record*, "Out of the blue he blurted out: 'Get your pad and pencil and start writing.' " Vance admitted killing the two girls. His confession, calmly delivered, made the tragedy seem even more senseless than it appeared on the surface.

Vance had met Meg Kennedy and Noreen Buckley in front of the

Colonial Luncheonette. They were waiting for a bus to take them back to Morris Plains. He offered them a ride in his father's car, but instead of driving them home he took them (according to his confession) to take a look at his own wrecked car at the Fairburn estate. He wasn't lying to them about this. The car had really been there, but unbeknown to Vance, the police had towed it away.

Noreen Buckley began to tease him about the phantom car. Vance felt she was calling him a liar. Apparently other students at Bayley-Ellard had taunted him about making up unlikely stories to explain why he had returned so soon from the Marine Corps. This unfair mockery tonight was the last straw. There *was* a wrecked car. He *wasn't* lying.

"I blew my top," the prosecutor later quoted Vance as saying. He certainly did. He opened the trunk of the Fairlane, grabbed the Ford's lug wrench, and hit Noreen with it. Then he hit her some more.

Meg Kennedy, horrified, jumped from the car and ran. But the enraged ex-marine, still clutching the lug wrench, caught her a few hundred feet away from the car and hit her. Then he hit her again and again.

His jacket soaked with blood, Vance slid behind the wheel of his father's Ford and headed back toward Morristown. On the way he flung the lug wrench out the window. When he reached his house, he pried up a floorboard in the attic and stuffed his blood-drenched jacket beneath it.

Next day Jimmy Vance took his date to Bertrand Island. He told her, "We can have some fun." She had no inkling that anything was amiss. "He was talkative, friendly, and a gentleman like always," she said. The girl wore his Marine Corps service ring—although, after his arrest and confession, she returned it to him.

The Morris County prosecutor intended to try Vance for the Margaret Ann Kennedy murder first, apparently reasoning that the second killing, more than the first, showed premeditation, or at least suggested the killer's rational desire to silence an incriminating witness. It was probably a sensible decision, but the court-appointed defense attorney, Charles M. Egan, made an equally sensible one: he decided that Vance had no credible defense.

A trial would have included expert testimony about Vance's psychological state at the time of the murders, and it might have clarified the reason for his Marine Corps hospitalization. Which is to say, a trial might have shed some light on the otherwise inexplicable. But there was no trial. Superior Court Judge Thomas J. Stanton allowed Vance to change his plea from not guilty to no defense, thereby placing himself at the mercy of the court while also eliminating the possibility of a death sentence.

In a fifteen-minute session at the Morris County Courthouse, during which Vance's mother wept, the eighteen-year-old ex-marine received a life sentence for the murder of Margaret Ann Kennedy and a twenty-five-to thirty-year term, to run consecutively, for the murder of Noreen Bernadette Buckley.

Defense attorney Charles M. Egan blamed the murders on "gross stress intolerance," which says something but not much. Egan was well aware of the ambiguity. "What mechanism was operating in Vance that night on June 20," he said, "no one will ever know. I don't think Jimmy knows. Only God knows."

 # The Coppolino Case

This may not have been a murder at all, since the man accused of killing Lieutenant Colonel William E. Farber was tried in New Jersey and found not guilty. The defense had suggested that Farber died of natural causes. But the accused then faced a second murder charge in Florida, where it was alleged he had killed his thirty-two-year-old wife by means of a lethal injection. On that charge, he was tried in the Sunshine State, convicted, and sentenced to life imprisonment.

The man was Dr. Carl Coppolino. His specialty, not coincidentally, was anesthesiology, and his case is among the most famous in New Jersey history.

No one saw anything amiss when Colonel Farber died at his home on Wallace Road in Middletown. Farber, a retired army officer and an insurance executive, had a history of heart trouble. His wife, Marjorie, had fallen in love with Dr. Carl Coppolino, the slim, young, hawk-nosed man across the street. Marjorie and Carl had been having a steamy affair for some time, apparently without the knowledge of either of their spouses.

At any rate, Dr. Coppolino's wife, Carmela, also a doctor, certified the cause of the colonel's death as a heart attack. She relied on Carl's word.

Speaking of heart attacks, Dr. Coppolino had already suffered a few of his own. Indeed, he had abandoned his active practice at the age of thirty because of continuing heart trouble. In 1963, at the time of Colonel Farber's death, he was receiving twenty-two thousand dollars a year in disability benefits.

Carmela continued to practice medicine, and the two of them lived comfortably on his insurance and her income, first in Middletown, later near Sarasota, Florida.

Then, unaccountably, on August 28, 1965, at Long Beach Key, Florida, Dr. Carmela Coppolino, née Musetto, also died. A Florida friend of Carl's, Dr. Juliette Karow, certified the cause of Carmela's death as a coronary occlusion. No autopsy was performed.

Twenty-two days later, Carl Coppolino and Mary Gibson, his former bridge partner and present lover, applied for a marriage license at the Sarasota County Courthouse. Within a week of getting the license, and less than a month after Carmela's death, they were married.

By this time Marjorie Farber was living near Sarasota, too, once again as a neighbor of the Coppolinos.

When Carmela died and Carl promptly married Mary Gibson, Marge Farber decided to go public. She went to the sheriff and county prosecutors in Sarasota and told them she suspected that Carmela Coppolino had died of an injection of succinylcholine chloride. She suspected this, she said, because three years earlier Carl had given her a supply of the same drug for the purpose of doing away with her husband. However, when the drug failed to kill Bill Farber, or so she claimed, Carl obligingly came over to her house and smothered him with a pillow.

Was her story true? Or was it simply the revenge of a scorned woman? Both bodies were exhumed—Colonel Farber's from Arlington National Cemetery, Carmela's from a cemetery in Boonton. Autopsies were performed, whereupon Dr. Carl Coppolino was indicted on murder charges in both New Jersey and Florida.

The New Jersey trial came first, starting on Monday, December 5, 1966, at the Monmouth County Courthouse in Freehold. In essence it pitted Dr. Milton Helpern, New York City's renowned chief medical examiner, against F. Lee Bailey, the dynamic defense attorney from Boston.

Bailey won. Marge Farber, trying to justify or at least explain her admitted part in murdering the colonel, spun a tale of having been hypnotized (clinically, that is) by Carl Coppolino. In fact, Dr. Coppolino did use hypnosis in his practice and had written a book about it, but Marge came across on the witness stand as having been driven more by spite than by a hypnotic trance.

Dr. Helpern thought he had detected manual strangulation in his autopsy, rather than smothering with a pillow. But lawyer Bailey offered telling evidence that the double cricoid fracture observed by Dr. Helpern could have been postmortem, perhaps the result of careless exhumation.

As for the succinylcholine chloride, the very reason Dr. Coppolino chose it—if he did—was because it was untraceable. It would not, and did not, show up in abnormal quantities in the autopsy. Still, there was a nagging fact the jury had to consider: just before each death Dr. Coppolino had asked an old friend, Dr. Edmund Webb, to obtain a supply of the muscle relaxant drug for him. In 1963 it was supposedly for killing the Farber's unruly collie dog. In 1965 it was supposedly for medical research on cats and other small animals.

Marjorie Farber's unconvincing testimony may have prompted a finding of reasonable doubt all by itself. Even her confession of complicity failed to carry the expected impact. On December 14, 1966, after only four and a half hours of deliberation, the Monmouth County jury found the defendant, Dr. Carl Coppolino, not guilty.

He would be less fortunate in Florida, where a puncture wound in Carmela's buttock plus expert testimony that the succinylcholine chloride in her body was not natural but "store-bought," as the testifying doctor put it, led to a verdict of second-degree murder. He was sentenced to life imprisonment.

34 At a Lodi Tavern

LODI

2 Cops Shot in Rt. 46 Tavern
As New York Thugs Celebrate

AUGUST 26, 1963

A raucous celebration had been going on since about midnight at Lodi's Angel Lounge, a square, two-story cinderblock tavern at 501 Baldwin Avenue, about fifty feet back from Route 46. The celebrants were Frank Falco, twenty-five, Thomas ("Rabbi Tom") Trantino, twenty-seven, and Anthony Cassarino, twenty-eight. Earlier in the evening they had successfully burglarized an apartment at 280 Ocean Parkway, Brooklyn.

Joining in the festivities at the Angel Lounge were four married women. One of them, Patricia Miles Falco, nineteen, was the estranged wife of Frank Falco. Another, Patricia Ann McPhail, twenty, shared an Allendale apartment with Mrs. Falco. Also present were Norma Jaconetta, twenty-three, of Paterson, in whose home the burglars were temporarily headquartered, and Sally Vandervliet, nineteen, of Rutherford.

Complaints about noise had sent the police to the tavern several times that evening. By 2:30 A.M. or so, the men had tossed down seven or eight double shots of whiskey, and the decibel level was rising. While Cassarino danced with Sally Vandervliet, Trantino decided to liven things up by firing a few gunshots at the floor. Mrs. McPhail left.

Two Lodi policemen responded to the latest complaint. They were Peter Voto, forty, a detective sergeant with thirteen years on the force, and Gary Tedesco, twenty-two, scheduled to be sworn in as a probationary patrolman that same week.

The officers, dressed in street clothes, found the door to the tavern locked. They knocked loudly and were let in.

"How many times do I have to come here?" Voto asked as he walked Cassarino to the checkroom to get his coat and some identification. He frisked the New York City man but found no weapon.

Tedesco waited in the barroom until his partner came back. As Voto returned, he noticed a towel lying on the bandstand. It covered a pistol, hastily hidden there while the officers were pounding on the door. Voto walked toward it.

Trantino moved in behind him and pressed a pistol to the back of the detective's head. "Strip," he told Voto. When the cop refused, Trantino pistol-whipped him. Voto then removed his coat but would go no further.

Anthony Cassarino, drunk as he was, had seen enough. He was in too much trouble already. He and Falco were being sought in New York City in connection with the July murder of a nineteen-year-old apprentice *Times* pressman at the Vivere Lounge on Second Avenue near Eleventh Street. Seeing no reason to push his luck in New Jersey, Cassarino left the tavern on foot. But trouble dogged him. At 4:45 A.M., after the shootings, he was picked up by police on a street in Hasbrouck Heights.

Meanwhile, back at the Angel Lounge, Frank Falco grabbed Voto's revolver from its holster, and, as the three women watched in horror, Trantino used his own pistol to shoot the sergeant twice in the head and once in the back.

Trantino then turned to Gary Tedesco, who was unarmed, and ordered him to take off his clothes. The young man complied, stripping to his underwear. It did not save him. Frank Falco, perhaps to prove himself the macho equal of Trantino, shot the rookie cop dead. Altogether, fourteen shots were fired in the tavern, including the ones that led to the final phoned-in complaint.

The three women rushed out of the building to Mrs. Jaconetta's car, piled in, and took off with the headlights out. When a Hackensack detective, Frank Fusco, tried to pull the car over to tell the driver to turn them on, a wild chase ensued. The young women were finally stopped on Atlantic Avenue, Hackensack, and held as material witnesses.

The two killers took off on foot. Falco, who lived on Twenty-ninth Street in Astoria, Queens, hailed a passing milk truck and headed toward Orange, where he reportedly kept a room. Trantino, of 346 Fourth Street, Brooklyn, went to Mrs. McPhail's house in Allendale and forced her at gunpoint to drive him across the George Washington Bridge to Washington Heights, where he took a taxi.

A massive interstate manhunt began, pushed, as the *New York Times* put it, "with the grim fervor that often marks the hunt for those who kill policemen."

They found Falco the next day, holed up in New York's Manhattan Hotel, Eighth Avenue and Forty-fourth Street. He was unarmed and sleeping in his underwear when Lieutenant Thomas Quinn, fifty-three, of the NYPD used a passkey to enter Falco's twenty-third-floor room. Quinn put a revolver to the fugitive's throat and woke him up.

The tattooed Falco sprang at Quinn, fought to overpower him, ripped the lieutenant's shirt, hit him with one of the four empty beer bottles on the floor, all the time trying to grab Quinn's service revolver. The two of them crashed over a bedside television set in the struggle. Lieutenant Quinn, still in possession of his weapon, got off six shots at Falco. The second NYPD officer to come through the door (there were six policemen altogether) added three more shots. Seven bullets found their mark. Falco died at the scene.

That left Trantino. Sixteen hours later, neatly dressed and clean-shaven, he walked into Manhattan's East Twenty-second Street police station accompanied by his lawyer, Enid Gerling, who said that her client wanted to surrender.

"For what?" asked Lieutenant Frank Brill at the desk.

"For homicide," she replied.

"What's his name?"

"Trantino."

The lieutenant turned to Detective John Wooton, who was coming down the stairs from the detectives' office. "Here's Trantino," he said. Wooton, surprised, took charge and led the fugitive up the steps, got him placed in a detention cage, and notified the New Jersey authorities.

On February 18, 1964, a jury of seven men and five women found Trantino guilty of murder. They made no recommendation for mercy. Eleven days later Bergen County Judge Joseph W. Marini, the judge who had presided at the trial, sentenced Trantino to die in the electric chair the week of April 5, 1964.

He did not die in the electric chair. In fact, no one died in the New Jersey electric chair after January 1963. In due course Trantino received a life sentence, putting him on a schedule for parole—and leading to a long series of publicized parole denials, as members and friends of the Voto and Tedesco families insisted repeatedly and emotionally that this particular killer not be allowed to go free.

35 Domestic Squabble on River Road

HIGHLAND PARK

Industrial Designer Shoots Wife in 25-Room River Road Mansion

SEPTEMBER 18, 1963

In the jaundiced world of journalism, "Husband Shoots Wife" is scarcely more newsworthy than "Dog Bites Man." For the press to take notice, the spousal killer must be a pillar of the community, a celebrity, or, as in this case, a wealthy businessman living in baronial splendor.

The marriage between sixty-one-year-old Charles Farmer, born Karoly Farkas in Hungary, and his wife, Barbara, fifty, also a native Hungarian, had been on the rocks for some time. He continued to live in their twenty-five-room castlelike mansion (named Merriewold by its former owner, J. Seward Johnson of Johnson & Johnson), located on twelve wooded acres off River Road in Highland Park. The mansion, an Early Norman–style dwelling, had been moved stone by stone from England in 1925.

Farmer ran a prosperous industrial engineering firm, Middlesex Design Company, and did design consulting for major corporations, including nearby Johnson & Johnson. Both the engineering firm and the estate were in his wife's name.

Barbara, an art patron and reputed kook, was staying with a brother in Edison. She had recently filed a suit for separate maintenance and another to evict her husband from the River Road estate. Charles himself, a few weeks earlier, had filed affidavits to have Barbara declared mentally incompetent. He declared that she was a believer in black magic and the occult, an "open and brazen" adulteress with Waylande Gregory—an

The dress Mrs. Mills was wearing. A casual, cigar-smoking detective in the Somerset County prosecutor's office holds up the blood-soaked dress Mrs. Mills was wearing when she was murdered. The stain around the neck came from the victim's throat being cut after she had been shot three times. (Special Collections and Archives, Rutgers University Libraries)

Charlotte Mills at the trial. The daughter of the slain choir singer thought she knew who had killed her mother. The self-proclaimed flapper is shown here arriving for the trial of Mrs. Frances Hall and two alleged accomplices. "Money can buy anything," Charlotte said after the verdict. (Special Collections and Archives, Rutgers University Libraries)

Trooper Robert Coyle. In 1924 the New Jersey State Police had been in existence for just three years. Until December 18, 1924, no trooper had been murdered in the line of duty. On that day Trooper Coyle was shot and killed while detaining a suspect for questioning in a thwarted payroll holdup. (New Jersey State Police Museum)

"NOT GUILTY" IS JURY'S VERDICT IN TRIAL OF MARY MATTIA.

Young Mother Is Freed Of Charge of Murdering Noel Pappalardo, Sea Isle Justice of the Peace, After Two-Day Trial Before Justice Campbell.

WOLVERTON MAKES ELOQUENT PLEA.

"WHAT SHE DID, SHE HAD A RIGHT TO DO," DECLARES CAMDEN ATTORNEY, IN CLAIMING SELF DEFENSE AS MOTIVE— COURT ROOM IN TEARS.

Freedom! No one, perhaps, who has never endured the ordeal of more than four months in a prison cell, waiting in the shadow of a charge of willful murder, can appreciate what it meant to Mrs. Mary J. Mattia, 22-year-old girl mother, of Washington, D. C., when she heard the verdict of "not guilty" pronounced by the jury which heard the evidence in her two-day trial in the Cape May county court this week.

With true stoicism and fortitude Mrs. Mattia sat throughout the trial, rarely crying. Except on the witness stand, she seldom spoke, even to her attorney. The instant the verdict of "not guilty" was pronounced, an exclamation of joy escaped her lips. Sobbing, she thanked the members of the jury for their verdict.

From Shadows To Sunshine

The verdict meant that Mrs. Mattia was freed of the charge of killing Noel Pappalardo, 52-year-old Justice of the Peace at Sea Isle ⸺ ⸺-father of the acr⸺ ⸺nd. - Pappalar⸺ T⸺

had anything to do with Teddy, he would kill her and everyone else in the house."

"Soon afterward he again caressed her and made suggestions. He called her names and made allegations. When Mrs. Margaret Saliba told him that she was with Mary on the boardwalk he called them both liars.

"On the morning of July 3rd Pappalardo followed Mary to her room, kicking and screaming, and he ran out. A minute later he returned and was choking her but she fought so furiously that he again ran from the room.

"Mary then ran into room 5, expecting to see Mrs. Pappalardo and tell her of the occurrences. When she got in the room she heard someone in the hall and, thinking it was Pappalardo again, she rummaged quickly for a gun and found it. She went to her room and laid the gun on the bed. Then she heard some⸺ ⸺ hall again. She opened ⸺ ⸺. Pappala⸺

Sympathetic jury frees Pappalardo's killer. This front-page story in the Cape May County Gazette *of November 20, 1925, makes it clear that the jury, the community, and the reporters all felt that young Mrs. Mattia was justified in shooting the amorous Sea Isle City justice of the peace.*

Trooper Peter W. Gladys. Of the eleven state troopers who have been murdered, ten have been shot. The exception is Trooper Gladys, whose throat was cut on December 28, 1928, by a man he was driving to Hightstown for arraignment on a minor domestic complaint. The killer, David Ware, was executed on May 5, 1929. (New Jersey State Police Museum)

Lindbergh home at night. *Colonel Charles Lindbergh, the "Lone Eagle," and his wife had built this home in rural Hunterdon County to escape the glare of publicity. But after their infant son was kidnapped on the night of March 1, 1932, the house became a beehive of activity, a command post for the investigation. (Newark Public Library, New Jersey Division)*

Union Hotel, Flemington. *Across Main Street from the courthouse where Hauptmann was tried for the murder of the Lindbergh baby stands the Union Hotel, dating from 1878. It was a meeting place during the trial for a host of celebrity journalists, including H. L. Mencken, Walter Winchell, Adela Rogers St. Johns, and Damon Runyon. (Gerald Tomlinson)*

Bruno Richard Hauptmann. *These mug shots were taken in the Bronx after Hauptmann's arrest on the morning of September 19, 1934. Although Hauptmann maintained his innocence to the end, investigators amassed overwhelming circumstantial evidence linking him to the crime, including $14,600 in ransom money found in his garage. (New Jersey State Police Museum)*

New Jersey's electric chair. *Bruno Richard Hauptmann was put to death in this electric chair in the New Jersey State Prison, Trenton, on April 3, 1936. The chair, built by Carl F. Adams, an electrician, was first used on December 11, 1907, to execute Saverio Di Giovanni for a murder in Raritan. (Special Collections and Archives, Rutgers University Libraries)*

Lindbergh exhibit at the State Police Museum. *This impressive display of artifacts in the Lindbergh case features the ladder used in the kidnapping, ransom notes sent to the family, Hauptmann handwriting specimens and comparisons, contemporary photographs and posters, and a video of newsreel footage of the trial. (Gerald Tomlinson)*

SCHULTZ IS SHOT, ONE AIDE KILLED AND 3 WOUNDED

ATTACK IN NEWARK CAFE

Beer Runner and Three Companions Assailed by Two Gunmen.

HIS CONDITION IS GRAVE

He Is Hit in Abdomen by Two Machine Gunners as His Henchmen Return Fire.

LINK TO BROOKLYN KILLING

Witnesses in Broadway Shooting Pick Picture of Stern, Man Sought in Amberg Death.

Gangland bullets felled Arthur (Dutch Schultz) Flegenheimer, notorious former beer-runner, and three companions in a Newark (N. J.) tavern last night, precipitating warfare between racketeering gangs that led to the shooting about an hour and a half later of a Schultz henchman and a companion in this city.

Schultz and the three men with whom he had been poring over account books and papers in a small rear dining room in the Palace Chop House and Tavern, at 12 East Park Street, Newark, were serious-"-... "^·30 P. M. in a "·nwed-off

---

Schultz Out on Bail On Income Tax Charges

Dutch Schultz made the last of his many appearances in court in Newark last Thursday, when his counsel, State Senator John E. Toolan of New Jersey, filed a challenge accusing Federal Judge William Clark of "personal bias and prejudice."

The action resulted in a postponement of a hearing on an application to remove the racketeer to New York to face trial on an indictment charging conspiracy to evade income taxes. Schultz did not appear in court at the time. He was out in $50,000 bail. The postponed hearing was scheduled to come up this week.

Meanwhile, a committee of New Jersey lawyers yesterday undertook to investigate charges of Judge Clark regarding the conduct of the attorneys representing Schultz.

SCHULTZ AIDE SHOT HERE HOUR LATER

Krompier, Lieutenant of the Gangster, Critically Wounded in Broadway Barber Shop.

COMPANION ALSO INJURED

Assailant Opens Door Just as Pair Prepare to Leave and Fires Into Room.

Dutch Schultz shot dead in Newark tavern. This front-page story in the New York Times of October 24, 1935, reports the slaying of a famous gangland figure—J. Edgar Hoover's "Public Enemy Number One"—at the Palace Chop House and Tavern. Also killed were Schultz's aide Abbadabba Berman and two others.

Railroad bridge at Brainards. Trooper Cornelius O'Donnell was fatally shot on this bridge while escorting a suspected ax murderer from a cabin hideout in Martins Creek, Pennsylvania, back to New Jersey. The killer, Ernest Rittenhouse, leapt into the Delaware River and momentarily escaped. This view is from the Pennsylvania side of the river. (Gerald Tomlinson)

Trooper Cornelius O'Donnell.
*Troopers Frank C. Perry and
Cornelius O'Donnell were both shot
in the presence of eyewitnesses on
July 15, 1945, by a man with mental
problems who had killed his twenty-
eight-year-old wife in Orange with an
ax. Perry recovered from his wounds;
O'Donnell did not. (New Jersey State
Police Museum)*

MONDAY, APRIL 21, 1947   Published daily except Sunday, at Press Plaza,
Asbury Park, N. J.

Woman's Strangler Hunted in County

Body Is Crammed In Trunk on Lonely Road, Dog Leash on Neck

BULLETIN

FREEHOLD.—It was learned
here this morning that a woman
in Troy Hill, near Morristown,
had identified a photograph of
the trunk murder victim near
Keyport as her missing sister.
She notified Newark police and
was scheduled to come there
this afternoon.

(Sta. Correspondent)
KEYPORT.—Three mysterious
telephone calls gave authorities a
new line of approach today in their
quest for the identity of the nude
woman whose throat, still bound
by a dog leash, was found in a
trunk abandoned on lonely Bethany road, Raritan township Saturday night.

State police who received the
calls last night, declined to discuss them beyond saying they
were anonymous inquiries concerning the murdered woman.
Hopeful that they might lead at
least to the identity of the victim, officials planned a careful
check, but generally the probe was
directed to the discovery of a
dentist who has extracted six upper teeth from a woman patient
within the last two weeks.

To Query Dentists

Prosecutor J. Victor Carton said
this morning he planned to call
upon the state board of dentistry
to aid the search after receiving
an autopsy report from Dr. Jules
Toren of the Marlboro state hospital.

MURDERED WOMAN FOUND IN TRUNK—State Police Sgt. Fred
Schultz examines the trunk in which the unidentified body of a
woman, about 45, was found on Bethany road in Raritan township, near Keyport, Saturday night. A leash of the type used
for dogs was around her neck. (Press Photo—Cohn)

*"Keyport Trunk Murder" seems
clueless. This front-page story in the
Asbury Park Evening Press is fairly
restrained. The discovery of a nude,
unidentifiable body of a woman in a
steamer trunk blocking a back road in
Monmouth County sparked considerable press attention.*

NORTH
BROAD
STREET

PERRY STREET

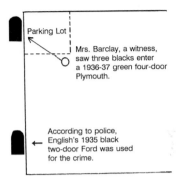

Parking Lot

Cigar salesman Endracher, a witness, saw two light-skinned blacks leave the Horner store and walk north.

Mrs. Barclay, a witness, saw three blacks enter a 1936-37 green four-door Plymouth.

Mrs. Horner said three blacks entered the store. She identified them, but only when told to pick the three from photos of the six defendants.

213 North Broad Street

According to police, English's 1935 black two-door Ford was used for the crime.

Lenox Restaurant

Criminals had stationed a lookout here. Confessions differed. Some said he was McKenzie; others said Thorpe.

ALDEN STREET

Patrolman standing here could offer no useful testimony.

N
↑↓
S

Scene of the "Trenton Six" murder. *The notorious case of the "Trenton Six" began on the morning of January 27, 1948, with the murder of William Horner, an elderly junk dealer, at 213 North Broad Street. Six blacks were charged with the murder. The case became famous worldwide when taken up by the American Communist Party as a supposed example of the United States' judicial railroading of innocent, poorly educated blacks.*

Police closing in on mass killer Unruh. *The body of Maurice Cohen lies on a Camden sidewalk (his wife was killed inside her house) as detectives move in to capture insane twenty-eight-year-old Howard Unruh. The World War II veteran thought his neighbors were talking about him behind his back. He killed thirteen. (Special Collections and Archives, Rutgers University Libraries)*

THE 60 MURDER CASES AND THEIR COUNTIES

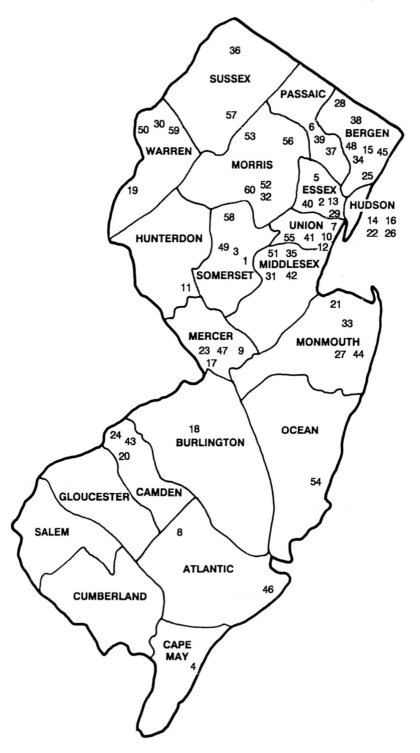

KEY TO THE 60 MURDER CASES AND THEIR COUNTIES

Names shown are those of victims

ATLANTIC
8 Lilliendahl 9-15-27
46 Helfant 2-15-78

BERGEN
15 Redwood 2-6-37
25 Moretti 10-4-51
28 Zielinski 3-4-57
34 Voto-Tedesco 8-26-63
38 Savino et al. 3-21-66
45 Fasching 1-8-75
48 Sherman 12-24-79

BURLINGTON
18 Strouth et al. 4-2-42

CAMDEN
20 McDade 8-15-45
24 Pilarchik, et al. 9-5-49
43 Coxson 6-8-73

CAPE MAY
4 Pappalardo 7-3-25

ESSEX
2 Brigham 12-27-22
5 Daly 9-3-25
13 Schultz 10-23-35
29 Daniels 3-18-59
40 Behrman 4-11-68

HUDSON
14 MacKnight 7-31-36
16 Littlefields 10-16-37
22 Eliops 7-24-47
26 Hummels 7-2-53

HUNTERDON
11 Lindbergh 3-1-32

MERCER
9 Gladys 12-28-28
17 Mytovich-Tonzillo 11-8-38
23 Horner 1-27-48
47 Stockton 12-7-79

Note: Date is that of first murder,
if more than one; or date of abduction

MIDDLESEX
31 Clarke 1-26-60
35 Farmer 9-18-63
42 Foerster 5-2-73
51 Puskases 2-25-82

MONMOUTH
21 Schreil 4-19-47
27 Anderson 11-1-55
33 Farber 7-30-63
44 Zygmaniak 6-20-73

MORRIS
32 Buckley-Kennedy 6-20-62
52 Hoffman 11-23-82
53 Keimel 7-24-84
56 Edwards 11-15-88
60 Reso 4-29-92

OCEAN
54 Marshall 9-7-84

PASSAIC
6 Ullrich 2-17-26
37 Kavanaugh 2-24-66
39 Oliver et al. 6-17-66

SOMERSET
1 Hall-Mills 9-15-22
3 Coyle 12-18-24
49 Tozzi 8-15-81
58 Heikkilas 1-29-91

SUSSEX
36 Hyland 9-5-65
57 Pompelio 2-13-89

UNION
7 Enz 10-14-26
10 Finiello 9-19-30
12 Greenberg-Hassel 4-12-33
41 Lists 11-9-71
55 Powlett 3-14-85

WARREN
19 O'Donnell 7-15-45
30 Silverman 11-25-59
50 Lamonaco 12-21-81
59 Quince 11-23-91

Johnsonburg Inn, home of "Batman." Trooper Lester Pagano arrested Stanley Marrs, a murder suspect, on the second floor of the Johnsonburg Inn and forced him down the stairs. Marrs broke free, pulled a pistol, and shot Pagano, paralyzing him from the waist down. The killer, "Batman," as he was called locally, got life plus twenty-one years. (Gerald Tomlinson)

Stocks close
on the upside

Stocks had their ups and downs in yesterday's trading but when the final bell sounded the upside was in command. The Dow Jones Industrials showed a gain of .77.

See Pages 20 and 21

Newark Star-Ledger

UNION
SOMERSET
EDITION

WEATHER: Cloudy, high near 40; yesterday, high 46 at 3 p.m., low 28 at 5:30 a.m.

VOL. 46, NO. 342   ★★   NEWARK, N. J., WEDNESDAY, JANUARY 27, 1960   Entered as Second-Class Matter Feb. 14, 1922 at the Post Office at Newark, N. J., Under the Act of March 3, 1879   5 CENTS

4 slain in doctor's home

Dr. Francis Clarke's North Brunswick home near Rt. 27, where slaying occurred

3 women, taxi driver shot on Jersey estate

By RICHARD O. SHAFER and JOE CARRAGHER

In one of the most bizarre crimes in years, the luxurious home of a prominent New Brunswick surgeon was turned into a shooting gallery yesterday by a killer who murdered the doctor's invalid wife, two women servants and a Newark taxi driver.

The only clue to the slayer last night was a gardener's story that he saw a man emerge from the house, about 250 feet from Route 27 on a three-acre estate in North Brunswick, and drive off in a taxicab that had arrived with two men in it some time earlier.

On the strength of the gardener's story, police broadcast an alarm for a neatly dressed white man, about 30, weighing 170 to 190 pounds, about 5 feet 10 inches tall, clean-shaven and with thin features, and wearing a grayish-brown overcoat brown felt hat and glasses.

An alarm was also out for the taxicab, owned by the Twentieth Century Cab Co. of Newark.

ROBBERY OR REVENGE?

Police theories about the motive for the massacre of the four victims, each killed by a bullet in the forehead, ranged from robbery to a mad lust for revenge by the slayer against the surgeon for some real or fancied grievance.

Victims of the tragedy were Mrs. Edith Clarke, invalid wife of Dr. Francis Clarke, chief surgeon at St. Peter's Hospital in New Brunswick;

Miss Dorothy R. Morse of

Morris Michael

Mystery surrounds murders at Clarke estate. An eye-catching headline in the Newark Star-Ledger *introduces this story of an apparently senseless multiple murder. Dr. Francis Clarke was operating on a patient in a New Brunswick hospital when the killer struck at the doctor's home. The man would strike again, just as strangely.*

Clarke estate, North Brunswick. *Dr. Francis Clarke's three-acre estate, seen here from the air, where three women were murdered. They included Edith Clarke, his wife. The killer arrived by taxi; the driver of the taxi was also killed. (Special Collections and Archives, Rutgers University Libraries)*

Angel Lounge, Lodi. *This tavern, just off Route 46, was where a pair of drunk and boisterous burglars, Thomas Trantino and Frank Falco, murdered two Lodi policemen, detective sergeant Peter Voto and rookie patrolman Gary Tedesco, who were trying to quiet them down. The date was August 26, 1963.* (Star-Ledger)

List grave marker, Westfield. *This marker in Fairview Cemetery memorializes four of John List's five victims, although not in the precise order of their deaths. Helen was the first to die. The body of his mother, Alma, the second victim, was flown to Michigan for interment. (Gerald Tomlinson)*

Chesimard "Wanted for Escape" poster.
More than a dozen years after the
shootout on the New Jersey Turnpike, the
state police issued this bulletin concerning
Chesimard's escape from the Clinton
Correctional Institution for Women.
Assata Shakur, as she preferred to be
called, was thought to be the "soul" of the
Black Liberation Army. (New Jersey State
Police Museum)

JOANNE DEBORAH BYRON CHESIMARD
AKA: Assata Shakur, Justine Henderson, Joanne Byron, Barbara Odoms, Joanne Chesterman, Joan Davis, Mary Davis
L/K/A: 350 Omega Street, Pittsburgh, Pennsylvania

SEX	Female	SCARS	Round scar, left knee, bullet wounds left shoulder and underside of right arm
RACE	Negro		
AGE	38 years old		
DOB	7/16/47	TATTOOS	Unknown
POB	New York City	S.S. No.	051-38-5131
HEIGHT	5' 6"	S.B.I. No.	336640A
WEIGHT	138 lbs.	F.B.I. No.	11102J7
HAIR	Black	F.P.C. No.	AAAAAA0711AAAAAA0410
COMPLEXION	Medium	BLOOD TYPE	B Positive

ATTENTION: Subject may be dressed in Muslim or men's clothing.

REMARKS - Chesimard escaped from the New Jersey Correctional Institution for Women, Clinton, N.J. with the assistance of numerous members of the REVOLUTIONARY ARMED TASK FORCE. The fugitive was serving a life term, plus 26-33 years consecutive, for the May 2, 1973 murder of a New Jersey State Trooper on the New Jersey Turnpike, East Brunswick, N.J. CHESIMARD is a self proclaimed revolutionary and member of the BLACK LIBERATION ARMY.

NOTIFY

New Jersey State Police
Fugitive Unit
West Trenton, New Jersey 08625
Telephone: (609) 882 - 2000, Ext. 2436

F.B.I./N.J. State Police
Joint Terrorism Task Force
Newark, New Jersey
Telephone: (201) 622 - 5613, Ext. 281

USE EXTREME CAUTION - SUBJECT WILL RESIST ARREST
Subject has numerous fictitious identifications and carries automatic weapons.

New Jersey State Police
Printing Unit

Fugitive Bulletin No. 1
Dated: March 1, 1986 (90)

Car in which Chesimard was riding.
Trooper James M. Harper stopped this
1965 white Pontiac at milepost 83-S on the
New Jersey Turnpike. Joanne Chesimard
opened fire, wounding Trooper Harper in
the shoulder. In the ensuing shootout, in
which twenty to thirty shots were ex-
changed, Trooper Werner Foerster,
Harper's backup, was killed. (Star-Ledger)

The Trenton Times
Home Final

TRENTON, N.J., TUESDAY, APRIL 14, 1981   FOUR SECTIONS, 36 PAGES

Alford convicted of Stockton murder
'A good fight, but I'll be back,' defendant tells prosecutor

By J. STRYKER MEYER
Staff Writer

After deliberating for 3¾ hours, a Mercer County jury found Keith Earl Alford guilty of the brutal murder of Trenton civic activist Emma Jane Stockton, the second murder conviction for the former truck driver in the past six months.

Ms. Stockton's burned and mutilated body was found tied to her bed in her Mill Hill townhouse Dec. 7, 1979. She had been stabbed with a corkscrew, knitting needle, knives and slivers of wood and had been raped.

After the verdict was delivered yesterday by the jury of seven men

and five women, Alford turned to veteran homicide prosecutor Paul M. O'Gara — the man who had also convicted him of the murder of Anna Mae Chicaleski — and said, "I'm coming back. I'm coming back. I thought you lost.

"The Marines always gain ground but can never hold it. It was a good fight, but I'll be back," Alford, an ex-Army paratrooper, said to O'Gara, a former Marine officer.

Alford, 25, then turned and hugged his attorneys, Mercer County Public Defender Theodore V. Fishman and First Assistant Public Defender J. Stewart Husid.

ALFORD IS SERVING a life sentence for the murder of Mrs. Chicaleski, a 67-year-old Hamilton Township grandmother whose badly beaten body was discovered in her house 12 days after Ms. Stockton was killed. Alford will not become eligible for parole for the Chicaleski murder for 25 years.

Now he faces a second life sentence for the Stockton slaying.

Much of the testimony in the Stockton trial centered on the gruesome, blood-spattered scene investigators found when they entered the third-floor bedroom of Ms. Stockton's Mercer Street home and details of

the wounds inflicted on the 37-year-old woman.

In his closing remarks to the jury, O'Gara detailed the prosecution's scenario of Ms. Stockton's last moments alive — and the beginning of the trail of clues which led to Alford's conviction.

"Ms. Stockton was cutting her toenails when she heard Mr. Alford crack the glass on her door ... when he entered the (rear, second floor) door, his bandana fell out of his pocket. He didn't know he didn't have it until he was charged with her murder.

(Continued on Page A6, Col. 3)

KEITH EARL ALFORD

Jury convicts killer of Emma Jane Stockton. The Stockton name is among New Jersey's
most famous. Richard Stockton signed the Declaration of Independence. Robert Stockton
fought in the War of 1812 and served in the U.S. Senate. Emma Jane, a descendent, a
Trenton civic leader, was murdered in Mill Hill.

Trooper Philip Lamonaco. *An eleven-year veteran of the New Jersey State Police, Lamonaco had become something of a legend on Interstate 80 east of the Delaware Water Gap. In 1979 he was named Trooper of the Year. An encounter with terrorist fugitives Thomas Manning and Richard Williams ended his life on December 21, 1981. (New Jersey State Police Museum)*

Lamonaco marker, I-80 westbound. *Trooper Lamonaco, thirty-two at the time of his death, had made more than two hundred criminal arrests in a three-year period on the busy but rural twenty-four-mile stretch of I-80 he patrolled. The press called him "Super Trooper." This marker, east of the murder site, indicates the westbound section of highway named in his honor. (Gerald Tomlinson)*

Bombed-out Puskas home. *Investigators study what is left of the house of Andrew and Patricia Puskas at 182 First Street, Middlesex Borough. On February 25, 1982, the couple died instantly when a bomb explosion destroyed their house. No plausible motive could be established, and the case remains unsolved.* (Star-Ledger)

Mall from which Amie Hoffman was abducted. *Within two weeks in 1982 James Koedatich kidnapped and killed two young women. The first, eighteen-year-old Amie Hoffman, disappeared from this parking lot. The second, Deirdre O'Brien, was kidnapped a few miles away. A later abduction and murder, that of Lisa O'Boyle, also started in this parking lot. (Gerald Tomlinson)*

Where Maria Marshall was murdered. *Investigators were suspicious of Robert O. Marshall's story about pulling into this Oyster Creek picnic area of the Garden State Parkway to check on a tire he thought was going flat. In the isolated spot ("No parking after dark") Marshall's wife Maria was shot and killed; he was slightly injured. (Gerald Tomlinson)*

Robert O. Marshall at his trial. *The Toms River insurance broker concocted a callous, harebrained plan for murdering his wife of twenty years, the mother of his three boys. Marshall's alibi—he had been robbed of some Atlantic City blackjack winnings, he said—unraveled quickly. An unsympathetic jury recommended the death penalty. (Ocean County Observer)*

Funeral of Policewoman Powlett. *Abigail Powlett of the Plainfield Police Department was the first woman officer in New Jersey to die in the line of duty. She was shot suddenly and senselessly after being held hostage by a drifter. Services, attended by family, friends, and fellow officers, were at the Mount Zion Baptist Church in Boonton.* (Star-Ledger)

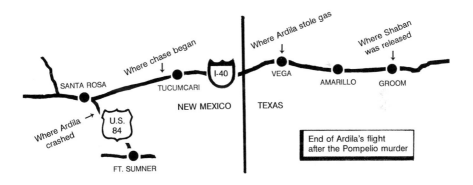

Where chase began

Where Ardila stole gas

Where Shaban was released

I-40

SANTA ROSA

TUCUMCARI

VEGA

AMARILLO

GROOM

NEW MEXICO

TEXAS

Where Ardila crashed

U.S. 84

FT. SUMNER

End of Ardila's flight after the Pompelio murder

Heikkila returning from his Jamaica trip. *After killing his adoptive parents with shotgun shells labeled "Mom" and "Mom and Dad," twenty-year-old Matthew Heikkila fled to Jamaica. He hoped to take his girlfriend with him, but that plan failed. Heikkila is shown here* (center) *entering the Somerset County Courthouse to face murder charges.* (Star-Ledger)

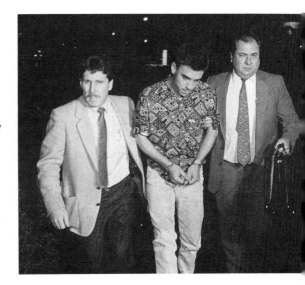

before Judge Molineaux. The prosecution failed to refute the barrage of expertise. Indeed, Farmer had already spent two years and four months after the shooting in the Trenton State Prison for the Criminally Insane, undergoing shock therapy treatments. Farmer claimed he still doubted he had killed his wife, not quite comprehending, he said, "where reality ended and the nightmares began."

 # McAfee's Back-Porch Bombing

> ## McAFEE
> ## Fire Bomb on Back Porch
> ## Kills Sussex Man and Dog
> ### SEPTEMBER 5, 1965

Joseph J. Hyland, forty-eight, an employee of the American Hard Rubber Company in Butler, walked his dog, a German shepherd puppy, every morning at 6:00 A.M. On this particular Sunday morning, though, the dog began whimpering in the kitchen at about 4:00 A.M. Hyland's wife, Ruth, sixty, awoke and asked her husband to take the dog out. He got up, put the dog on a leash, and opened the kitchen door leading to the back porch. Something partially obstructed the swing of the door.

On the porch Hyland saw a jug with a wick burning at the top. Several items (pipe bombs, in fact) were attached to the jug. He called to his wife, "Ruth, come out here. There's something funny going on out here." But before she got there he kicked at the jug—and an ear-splitting explosion rocked the neighborhood. Hyland, engulfed in flames, raced around the house to the front door, where Ruth met him in the foggy darkness and told him to stay outside. Within moments, a neighbor arrived with a blanket and put out the flames. Hyland, with third-degree burns over 90 percent of his body, died six hours later in Franklin Hospital. The German shepherd puppy died at a local animal hospital.

The other people who lived at Sun Valley Estates on Route 517, a mile north of McAfee, could add nothing to what Hyland had told the police before he died—the obstructed door, the glass jug, the burning wick, the kick—and what Ruth, badly shaken, had told them about the whimpering dog, the puzzled call from her husband, the blinding flash, and the thundering explosion. Hyland, a "good, steady worker" at American Hard

Rubber, had no known enemies, no gambling debts, no union conflicts, no neighborhood feuds—nothing to suggest a motive for murder.

An intensive investigation by the state police led nowhere. Hyland, a quiet, unobtrusive machine operator whose death benefited no one, seemed then, and seems now, a highly unlikely victim for one of New Jersey's front-page murders. No motive was ever established. Was Hyland the wrong man, murdered by mistake? That is, was somebody else in Sun Valley Estates the intended victim? Was Hyland's house for some reason the target of arson, and his murder the unexpected consequence of a serious but lesser crime?

No one knows. The case is unsolved, closed. Given the jug and the burning wick (and the unforeseeable 4:00 A.M. appearance of Hyland on the back porch), reckless arson makes more sense than intentional murder. But why? Was it a horrendous prank? Had someone planted a fire bomb out of pique? Not likely. The little pink one-story bungalow on Lincoln Avenue survived the blast, its back porch showing the black burn marks of a flash fire, but nothing more. Its owner and his restless puppy, however, were dead, their deaths mysterious and unavenged.

 # Who Killed Mrs. Kavanaugh?

Slaying of Pretty Young Housewife Leads to Farrago of Murder Charges

FEBRUARY 24, 1966

The Passaic County prosecutor described the case as "bizarre and weird." He might more accurately have called it "tangled and botched."

It began, although no one knew it at the time, when Paul Kavanaugh, twenty-four, reported his wife, Judith, missing. She had dropped him off for work in Garfield, he said, at about 1:00 A.M. on February 24, 1966. Paul Kavanaugh was an independent newspaper distributor (essentially a truck driver) for Matzner Publications, a company that operated twenty-two weekly newspapers in New Jersey and one daily, *Wayne Today*.

Early the next morning the Kavanaughs' family car was found abandoned on Badger Avenue, Newark. It had been torched.

On March 13, about three weeks later, a man exercising his hunting dogs discovered a young woman's body, nearly nude, lying in a wooded gully beside the Garden State Parkway near the Clifton exit, not far from the Kavanaughs' home at 90 Hazel Street. The body, clad only in a black sweater and high-heeled shoes, was that of twenty-one-year-old Judith Kavanaugh. She had been dead for at least two weeks. A source close to the investigation said, "It's definitely murder—a hole was found in her head."

Nothing much seemed to happen after that. Weeks dragged into months, and finally the victim's mother, Mrs. Emily Marchione, began to complain to local newspapers that the investigation had apparently ended and that the killer was going to go free. She offered a thousand-dollar reward for information leading to an arrest. The police cranked up their probe once more, and on December 1, after eight grand jury sessions and sixty-six witnesses, Paul Kavanaugh, the victim's husband, was indicted and arrested for the murder of his wife. The motive? Paul was playing around with another woman, the prosecutor said, "at diverse times and places." That was true enough. But had it led to murder? At first the state said yes, but later, as other evidence (or at least another story) came to light, a different motive for the execution-style slaying emerged. This was not just a case involving "the other woman," it seemed—it was a conspiracy. A big one. Maybe.

Approximately two months before Kavanaugh's indictment, Paterson police had arrested a small-time hoodlum, Gabriel ("Johnny the Walk") DeFranco, forty-two, on a charge of counterfeiting. This arrest, the state would later contend, was more important than it appeared to be, because Johnny the Walk was walking around with a big secret in his keeping, one that could be very damaging to certain people. These people were sufficiently concerned that they took action. On the morning of October 6, 1966, the body of Gabriel DeFranco, his throat slashed from ear to ear, turned up on the front porch of his garden apartment at 297 Fifth Avenue, Paterson.

The DeFranco murder investigation blew the Kavanaugh case wide open—or perhaps blew it apart. No longer was Paul Kavanaugh thought to have killed his wife, a pretty strawberry blonde, because of another woman. Now it was alleged that he wanted her dead to keep her from squealing on him.

Here was the prosecution's new scenario. A local counterfeiting ring numbered among its members both Johnny the Walk DeFranco and Paul Kavanaugh. Among the other alleged members of the team were Harold Matzner, thirty, of Denville, an executive at Matzner Publications; Police Sergeant John C. DeGroot, forty-one, of Clifton; and Vincent Kearney, Jr., twenty-six, a salesman friend of DeFranco's, and a former numbers runner, of Paterson.

When the other four counterfeiters learned of DeFranco's arrest, they feared that the small-time gambler and underworld figure would cut a deal for himself by revealing details of the Kavanaugh murder. What details? Damning ones. Judith Kavanaugh, according to the prosecution, had been killed to keep her from blowing the whistle on her cheating—but, more importantly, counterfeiting—husband. DeFranco had been involved in the murder of Judith Kavanaugh and could (and perhaps would) name the other participants. That was the dangerous prospect facing the killers.

As a consequence, Matzner, DeGroot, and Kearney allegedly converged on the unfortunate DeFranco and, in the early morning hours of October 6, 1966, slit his throat. The killing of Gabriel DeFranco occurred seven months after the murder of Judith Kavanaugh and two months before the indictment of Paul Kavanaugh on "the other woman" murder charge. The two related cases were tried backward, chronologically.

On October 26, 1968, publishing executive Harold Matzner, Clifton detective John DeGroot, and former numbers runner Vincent Kearney, Jr., went on trial in Paterson for the murder of Gabriel DeFranco. Matzner testified that DeFranco was an underworld informant who funneled information about organized crime to his Wayne newspaper chain. On the night of DeFranco's murder, said the publishing executive, he had been attending a meeting at the Hotel Warwick in New York City. The other defendants had pretty fair alibis, too.

Ted Hall, an investigative journalist for the *Herald News* of Passaic, learned from Treasury Department agents that the counterfeiting operation—there really was one, evidently—had not begun until six months after Mrs. Kavanaugh was murdered for allegedly threatening to expose it. The series of articles in which this startling claim was made never appeared in print, however, and Hall was fired from the paper, either for his fearless journalism (Hall's view) or insubordination (his boss's way of looking at it).

In what was until then the longest murder trial in New Jersey history, the prosecution relied on two key witnesses. One was Mrs. Jacqueline Natoli, thirty-one, typically described in the press as "a shapely blonde," and, as she identified herself, a member of the counterfeiting ring and a habitual liar. At the time of the trial, Mrs. Natoli was facing bad-check and fraud charges. The other key witness for the prosecution was Edward G. Lenney, a convicted armed robber, who testified that he had helped to kill DeFranco, in company with Matzner, DeGroot, and Kearney. The sexy Mrs. Natoli and the beefy Mr. Lenney were granted immunity from prosecution for their testimony.

Defense attorneys argued that Gabriel DeFranco was the victim of an underworld execution. The wealthiest of the defendants, Harold Matzner, buttressed this rub-out argument, saying that a gambler-informant had told him, "Danny Palidoro killed DeFranco." (Palidoro, a mob figure, was by then dead and could not respond.)

Confused? So was Superior Court Judge Gordon H. Brown, or so it seemed, when he confided to the jury (bused up to Paterson from New Brunswick because of the extensive and possibly prejudicial pretrial publicity in Paterson), "Where is the truth? Like a vein of gold, it is where you find it."

The jury of eleven men and one woman, after deliberating for about six hours, did not find that vein of gold in the testimony of the shapely lady or the hefty con. It acquitted Harold Matzner, John DeGroot, and Vincent Kearney, Jr., of the murder of Gabriel DeFranco. The spectators cheered and applauded when the not-guilty verdict was announced. This verdict put Sergeant DeGroot in the clear, but it left Matzner and Kearney still facing the charge of having murdered Judith Kavanaugh.

Mrs. Kavanaugh, the prosecution argued in the second trial, had been murdered by Harold Matzner and Vincent Kearney, Jr., and the crime had been observed by others. This trial, like the previous one, relied heavily on the testimony of purported eyewitness Jacqueline Natoli. According to Mrs. Natoli, she, Judith Kavanaugh, Paul Kavanaugh, Harold Matzner, Vincent Kearney, Jr., and Johnny the Walk DeFranco were all crowded into a station wagon outside a Clifton diner. Matzner and Mrs. Kavanaugh began to argue. Matzner slapped Judith, then throttled her, causing her to lose consciousness, while her husband sat by, observing the attack but neither participating nor intervening. After Paul Kavanaugh had been dropped off nearby to ponder this turn of events, the rest of the entourage drove to the Matzner home in Denville, twenty-five miles away, where Mrs. Natoli said she "heard" Kearney shoot the unconscious victim "like an animal" in the woods behind the house. Matzner's wife, Dorothe, was present for this part of the crime and consequently was tried along with the other three.

Matzner claimed he was at a newspaper convention in Chicago on the night of February 24, 1966, when the murder had presumably occurred, and produced hotel registration receipts and a restaurant check to prove it. Mrs. Matzner said she was home in bed. Kearney said he had no idea where he was, but guessed he was probably helping DeFranco count the day's numbers receipts. Kavanaugh said he was delivering newspapers. His wife had driven him to Garfield that night, and he reported her missing the next day. All the defendants denied ever having seen Mrs. Natoli.

The jury, nine men and three women (chosen in Elizabeth and bused in because of the publicity in Paterson), deliberated for less than seven hours before finding the four defendants not guilty. One juror smiled and waved at them as the jury was leaving the courtroom. The relieved defendants smiled back.

"Now I just hope they go out and find the guy who did it," Paul Kavanaugh said.

But the guy who did it was never caught—or at least he, or she, or they were never convicted. The Kavanaugh and DeFranco murders remain unsolved.

"Dr. X" and "Flying Death"

> ORADELL
> ## Girl Dies in Riverdell Hospital After Surgery—Was It Curare?
> MARCH 21, 1966

A medical doctor is assumed to be a healer, not a killer. Yet there is a long, unhappy history of doctors who have used their expertise, along with a presumption of integrity, to commit murder. Sometimes they have gotten away with it.

Take the case of "Dr. X"—Dr. Mario E. Jascalevich, chief of surgery at Riverdell Hospital, 576 Kinderkamack Road, Oradell. A Bergen County jury acquitted him of three counts of murder in October 1978 (the evidence was circumstantial, dated, and medically complex, the apparent motive hard to credit, and the defense attorney an accomplished pro), but a bare recital of the facts—stripped of all the trial's histrionics—leaves a core of strange events and unexplained coincidences that point persuasively to the charming Argentinian doctor as a calculating, if enigmatic, killer.

No one knows for sure where the story begins. One convenient, if melancholy, starting point is the death of Nancy Savino, four, following a successful operation for the removal of lymphatic cysts on her small intestine. Dr. Stanley Harris, the surgeon who performed the operation, reported Nancy's recovery as "smooth and uneventful." At 7:40 A.M. on March 21, 1966, her chart showed her to be sleeping peacefully. At 8:00 A.M. a technician arriving to take a blood sample could not waken her. At 8:15 A.M. Dr. Jascalevich, summoned from a room across the hall, pronounced her dead.

There was no apparent reason for Nancy Savino's death. An autopsy was performed by the Riverdell pathologist. It yielded an inconclusive result—"cause undetermined."

Other recuperating patients, as the doctors at Riverdell could not help noticing, began dying after apparently successful operations. The patients were never Dr. Jascalevich's—with one exception, that of Carl Rohrbeck, seventy-three, on whom Dr. Jascalevich was to operate for the repair of a ventral hernia scar. Inexplicably, he canceled the operation at the last minute, telling Dr. Jay Sklar, Rohrbeck's admitting physician, that he, Dr. Jascalevich, had "a premonition" about operating on the elderly man. When Dr. Sklar objected, Dr. Jascalevich went to the patient's room to have another look. Soon a nurse returned and said, "Dr. Sklar, your Mr. Rohrbeck just died." Dr. Sklar, astonished, went to the patient's room and found that Dr. Jascalevich, while visiting the patient, had started an intravenous feeding tube going. An autopsy yielded inconclusive results.

Rohrbeck's death preceded Nancy Savino's by more than four months. His case, and a number of others, came to light when Dr. Harris and another Riverdell surgeon, Dr. Allan Lans, decided to investigate on their own the growing list of postoperative deaths after Nancy Savino's. Their first serious discussion of the troubling events followed the death on October 23, 1966, of Eileen Shaw, thirty-six, who had just given birth to a healthy child by cesarean section. Dr. Stanley Harris had then done a routine tubal ligation, from which Mrs. Shaw was recovering nicely.

At 8:00 A.M. the next day Dr. Jascalevich visited Mrs. Shaw and changed the bottle on the intravenous feeding apparatus. When the nurse, who was out of the room at the time, returned, she saw that Mrs. Shaw was turning blue, or "cyanotic," as the medical chart stated. The patient was pronounced dead at 9:20 A.M. Again, Dr. Harris was shaken. He had lost eight postoperative patients in less than seven months. None of their deaths could be satisfactorily explained.

While Dr. Harris was in the doctors' lounge the day after Eileen Shaw's death, going over the autopsy report, he expressed his bewilderment to Dr. Lans. Dr. Lans suggested a working lunch at the Colonial Inn in Englewood. There they went over the alarming list of cases that were turning Riverdell Hospital into a deadly terminus for too many patients. They identified eight suspicious deaths. Later, after they went though the hospital records, the number rose to thirteen. But no knew for sure, then or ever, the exact number of patients who expired during intravenous feeding while Dr. Jascalevich bustled in and out of their rooms.

The common elements in the cases were striking. All the patients who died had an IV tube running, which made the introduction of any drug or poison a simple matter. Many of the incidents had occurred around 8:00 A.M. Every one of the deaths came suddenly and unexpectedly. Respiratory arrest was a common factor, often with a notation of "cyanotic." Finally, Dr. Mario E. Jascalevich had been seen in or near some, if not all, of the patients'/victims' rooms just prior to their leavetaking.

Drs. Lans and Harris decided to bring their concerns before the hospital's board of directors, whose members were sufficiently disturbed by the story to go to the Bergen County prosecutor's office. This was unprecedented—doctors, in effect, accusing another doctor of murder, with everyone likely to suffer professionally. But nothing happened, at least not for the public record. The prosecutor investigated but did not ask for an indictment. Dr. Jascalevich quietly resigned from Riverdell, after which the number of unexplained deaths at the hospital plummeted, and life went on—for the survivors.

It might have stayed that way, *would* have stayed that way, except for an anonymous letter a decade later to the *New York Times,* following newspaper reports of a number of similarly suspicious deaths at a Veterans Administration hospital in Michigan. The vaguely worded tip went to Myron Farber, a *Times* investigative reporter who, under the byline M. A. Farber, transformed the sketchy tale about an unnamed chief surgeon at an unnamed New Jersey hospital into one of the biggest murder cases in Garden State history, and earned its writer a Pulitzer Prize nomination for what became known as the "Dr. X" articles. (The Michigan deaths, it turned out, were unrelated to those at Riverdell.)

The first of Farber's long and detailed "Dr. X" articles appeared in the *Times* on January 7 and 8, 1976. The initial headline read, "Evidence of Curare Sought in 9 Deaths." Joseph C. Woodcock, Jr., the Bergen County prosecutor, was about to have three bodies exhumed and checked for the presence (after all these years) of the muscle relaxant curare, medically useful as an anesthetic but lethal if misused. The reason was that back on October 31, 1966, Dr. Harris, suspecting skulduggery, had surreptitiously opened Dr. Jascalevich's locker at Riverdell and discovered, with a shudder of horror, many pharmaceutical boxes and bottles labeled "Tubocurarine—10 c.c."

Tubocurarine is curare, supposedly a traceless instrument of death. South American tribes along the Curary River on the border between Peru and Ecuador mixed the extract from a native climbing vine with various other substances and applied it to the sharpened end of a blow dart or an arrow. These tribes knew from long experience what happened when the projectile pierced the skin or hide of a victim. The result was arrested breathing, followed by death. Curare thus acquired the sobriquet "flying death."

Tubocurarine had been in common use among anesthesiologists for decades (though it would hardly be stored in a personal locker), but it was not commonly used by surgeons. The unexplained postoperative deaths at Riverdell Hospital suddenly looked plainly, if chillingly, explainable.

But why would Dr. Mario E. Jascalevich (not named in the *Times* articles because no indictment had yet been handed down), a respected chief of surgery, be murdering other doctors' patients in this or any other manner? It seemed to make no sense. Dr. Harris's and Dr. Lans's belief, and the prosecution's contention, was that Dr. Jascalevich feared losing a significant amount of income because a few new Riverdell doctors, Dr. Harris among them, were being granted the right to perform surgery, a lucrative privilege that Dr. Jascalevich had previously monopolized.

A curious sidelight is that Dr. Jascalevich had suggested to Dr. Harris, early in their association, that the two of them become partners in a group practice. Dr. Jascalevich had even announced the arrangement in a premature memo to the hospital staff. Dr. Harris, a much younger man, repudiated the memo, causing, it seems safe to speculate, hard feelings on both sides, although little was made of the incident in the trial.

In any event, the exhumations took place, autopsies were performed, many laboratories and many tests sought evidence of curare in the three bodies—and they all found it. Even a lab hired by defense counsel found curare in the remarkably well-preserved body of four-year-old Nancy Savino. It was present in her eye, liver, and lung. Since, according to hospital records, no curare had been administered to any of the patients who died suspiciously, the circumstantial case against Dr. Jascalevich appeared to be airtight.

Dr. Jascalevich never denied having curare bottles in his locker, but he claimed he had been using the muscle relaxant for experiments on dying dogs at the Seton Hall School of Medicine in Jersey City. No credible evidence that he had performed such experiments was ever discovered. Indeed, the people at Seton Hall and at adjacent Pollack Hospital, who should have known about the dogs, could not, or would not, back the doctor's story.

Prosecutor Joseph C. Woodcock seemed to view the murders, terrible and rationally inexplicable as they were, as quite clear-cut and provable. He maintained that "the causes of death attributed on the death certificates [are] a medical impossibility. All nine of these deaths exhibited conditions exactly like a respiratory arrest that could be consistent with curare poisoning. Each of these patients had gone in for a simple operative procedure. All died swiftly."

He assigned the case to Sybil Moses, a young, inexperienced assistant prosecutor. Dr. Jascalevich, on the other hand, fully aware of the trouble he was in, obtained as his defense attorney Raymond A. Brown, regarded by many as the best criminal defense lawyer in New Jersey. "When I die," Brown once said, "I hope they put on my tombstone that I was angry, nasty, and competent." The judge was William J. Arnold, a judicial journeyman, trying his last case before retirement. The indictment named five presumed victims, including Nancy Savino, Carl Rohrbeck, and Frank Biggs, fifty-nine, a patient who had died after a successful gastrectomy.

Ray Brown, by turns clever, abrasive, condescending, and sarcastic, tore apart the prosecution's strong but circumstantial case. The jury, few of whose members were college educated, almost certainly had a hard time understanding the long and complex testimony regarding the scientific tests for curare. While damning in their conclusions, these tests were relatively new and exceedingly convoluted. Brown, with his baggy suit and just-folks manner, was masterful in rebuttal of their findings.

Judge Arnold, by contrast, sometimes dozed in his robes. He was not in command, and prosecutor Sybil Moses, despite her sharp rejoinders to Brown's tactics and comments, could not control the situation on her own. New Jersey, so often the butt of jokes, gained no stature from these proceedings. A reporter for the Miami *Herald* called the trial "a debating society gone berserk." A cheering section for Dr. Jascalevich may or may not have influenced the jury, but it added to the circus atmosphere.

Perhaps the most poignant moment, for anyone who suspected that Dr. Jascalevich might be guilty as charged, came in Raymond Brown's cross-examination of Dr. Allan Lans.

Q: Was [Dr. Jascalevich] a gentle person?

A: Yes.

Q: Kind to people?

A: Most people.

Q: Who was he unkind to. You?

A: No.

Q: Who was he unkind to?

Dr. Lans did not answer right away. After a long pause, he said, "Nancy Savino."

But Raymond Brown had long since won the jury to his side of the contest. He portrayed the doctors at Riverdell as being inept at surgery, jealous of Dr. Jascalevich, and cold-bloodedly out to frame him for their own protection and advancement. He portrayed Myron Farber of the *Times* as a man eager to further his journalistic career and willing to do so at the expense of the truth. He implied that the unexplained deaths at Riverdell had been due to natural causes.

After the longest criminal trial in New Jersey history, Judge Arnold dismissed two of the five counts of murder, leaving the ones involving Nancy Savino, Carl Rohrbeck, and Frank Biggs for the jury to decide. After deliberating a little more than two and a half hours the jury found Dr. Jascalevich not guilty on all three counts. The spectators in the courtroom cheered.

Dr. Jascalevich later settled a long-standing malpractice suit by paying $150,000 to a Jersey City woman who had charged him with negligence in performing pelvic surgery. The Board of Medical Examiners also revoked Dr. Jascalevich's license on the grounds that he had fraudulently altered the plaintiff's operative record.

The small, dapper, bespectacled doctor at that point gave up on the United States and returned to Mar del Plata, Argentina, to continue his medical practice there. In September 1984 he died of a cerebral hemorrhage. He was fifty-seven years old, quite young, to be sure, but still fifty-three years older than Nancy Savino was when she died for no evident reason after a routine and successful operation at Riverdell Hospital.

 # Requiem for a Middleweight

Rubin ("Hurricane") Carter, twenty-nine, had been in trouble with the law since childhood. He had spent time in the Annandale and Jamesburg reformatories and later had served four years in Trenton State Prison for three robberies and assault and battery. While in prison, Carter, a native of Paterson, learned how to box. He was exceptionally good at it, turned pro, and advanced through the ranks. On December 14, 1964, he faced the middleweight champion of the world, Joey Giardello, in a title fight in Philadelphia. Giardello kept the crown by a unanimous decision, but Carter fought well. He and his handlers thought he had won.

Although there was no title rematch, Hurricane Carter continued to fight main events, in Madison Square Garden, London, Paris, and elsewhere. On August 5, 1966—six weeks after the murder for which he was eventually convicted—Carter lost a ten-round decision to Juan Carlos Rivero in Rosario City, Argentina. Internationally known by then, Carter, a flashy dresser and flamboyant personality, was a Paterson celebrity. He gained a reputation as a civil rights activist. Until the night of June 17, 1966, he qualified as a true hometown success story—a kid who had risen from the streets to athletic prominence.

Racial tensions divided working-class Paterson in 1966. Neighborhoods were in transition, and, according to Mayor Frank X. Graves, Jr., there were far too many taverns and too many shootings. One of the shootings occurred early on the evening of June 17 when Frank Conforti, forty-eight, the former owner of Walt's Inn, a bar at 78 Summer Avenue, walked into his old establishment with a twelve-gauge shotgun and shot the new owner, Roy Holloway, forty-eight, twice at point-blank range, killing him instantly. Conforti, who was white, waited in the bar and was arrested and charged with murder. Holloway, who was black, was (significantly or not) the stepfather of one of Hurricane Carter's friends, Edward Rawls. The tragic but unsensational murder of Roy Holloway posed no mystery.

Less than six hours later the main criminal event of the evening took place—and it became a *cause célèbre*. At 2:30 A.M. two black men walked into the Lafayette Grill at 428 East Eighteenth Street, six blocks away from the scene of the earlier shooting. One of the men was carrying a twelve-gauge shotgun, the other a .32-caliber pistol. The bartender, James Oliver, fifty-two, who lived over the bar, saw them coming and responded by throwing a bottle at them. The assailants opened fire. Four people fell in the fusillade. One was bartender James Oliver, struck and killed by a shotgun blast. Another was Frank Nauykas, sixty, a machinist from Cedar Grove, killed by a .32-caliber bullet. A third, Mrs. Hazel Tanis, fifty-one, another patron of the bar, died in a hospital a month later. William Marins, forty-two, was critically wounded by shots to the head and shoulder. He recovered, but lost his left eye. After this murderous barrage, the two gunmen walked out of the tavern. (A small amount of money was taken from the cash register, but not by the killers. More about this later.)

Hurricane Carter and a friend of his, John Artis, twenty, were picked up within ten minutes for questioning. Two Paterson policemen, having learned from witnesses that the gunmen had fled the scene of the crime in a white car, stopped a slow-moving white 1966 Dodge with New York license plates about fourteen blocks from the Lafayette Grill. In it were Hurricane Carter, who had rented the car; his friend, John Artis, who was driving; and a third man, John Royster. There were no weapons in the vehicle, and the officers did not detain the three men.

Not long afterward, however, a more complete description of the car led police to think the white getaway car might well have been Carter's. They began looking for it, and shortly after 3:00 A.M. they spotted the white Dodge about five blocks from the murder scene. Carter and Artis said that for the past forty-five minutes or so they had been at the Nite Spot Cocktail Lounge on Eighteenth Street. After leaving the lounge, they had dropped off John Royster at his home and were now on their way to the apartment of John Artis's girlfriend. This time the police directed Carter and Artis to drive to the Lafayette Grill, where a police van took them to Paterson police headquarters for questioning. The interrogation lasted seventeen hours, after which both men were released. Twelve days later, Carter and Artis, having waived their rights against self-incrimination, testified before a Passaic County grand jury. No indictments were handed down.

Intensive efforts to solve the case, bolstered by the incentive of a $10,500 reward, produced no results. Six weeks passed. Carter fought his losing boxing match in Rosario City, Argentina, in August and returned home.

Then, on the night of October 14, 1966, Hurricane Carter and John Artis were arrested for the murders of James Oliver, Frank Nauykas, and Hazel Tanis. It was Artis's twenty-first birthday. Police said that the boxer and the unemployed laborer had given conflicting statements about their movements on the night of the murder. Indeed they had, but the most conclusive evidence (although some jurors would later dispute this) was the purported eyewitness observations of two men who, at the moment of the murders in the Lafayette Grill, were busy breaking into the Ace Sheet Metal Company, a couple of blocks away. These two worthies were Alfred P. Bello and Arthur D. Bradley, both twenty-three, both with criminal records, and both, it was later claimed by defense attorneys, with something to gain by helping the prosecution prove its case against Carter and Artis.

Be that as it may, an all-white jury of eight men and four women found Hurricane Carter and John Artis guilty of murder in the first degree but rejected the prosecution's request for the death penalty. Carter received two consecutive life sentences and a third life sentence to run concurrently. Artis got three concurrent life sentences, making him eligible for parole in fourteen and a half years.

This was a major murder case all the way, given the involvement of Hurricane Carter, a nationally known sports figure. But on September 26, 1974, seven years after the imprisonment of Carter and Artis, it drew larger headlines than ever before, when the prosecution's two star witnesses, Alfred P. Bello and Arthur D. Bradley, recanted their testimony. They claimed they had been pressured by Passaic County detectives into identifying Carter and Artis as the killers, even though they could make no such positive identification. "All the cops were convinced Carter and Artis did it," Bello said, "and they wanted me to believe it."

Whether Bello and Bradley were lying now—the statute of limitations on perjury having run out—or whether they had been lying in the first place was unclear. But serious doubts had been raised about the convictions. The state public defender called for a new trial, and the New Jersey Supreme Court ordered it unanimously.

While Carter waited for his second trial, the publicity on his behalf escalated. (Artis was awaiting a second trial, too, of course, but he lacked Carter's name recognition.) The Reverend Ralph D. Abernathy, a noted civil rights leader, joined the ex-middleweight contender for a press conference at Clinton State Prison. Muhammad Ali and Candice Bergen expressed support. Bob Dylan recorded a song titled "Hurricane."

Many people believed that without the two supposed eyewitnesses the state's case would fail. But some members of the first jury maintained that the evidence against Carter and Artis was strong enough even without Bello's and Bradley's testimony. Apparently it was, but then again maybe not. In his six days on the witness stand, Bello (not the most reliable of witnesses) renounced his recantation—and once again identified Carter and Artis as the killers. On December 21, 1976, in Passaic County Court, after nine hours of deliberation, following nearly six weeks of testimony, the second jury of eight men and four women (this time including two blacks) convicted Hurricane Carter and John Artis of first-degree murder.

Edward Carter, a cousin of Rubin Carter and a regular spectator at the trial, said to him, "Keep your head high. Look beautiful, man. They can't take that away from you." In this second trial the prosecution suggested a specific motive, which it had not tried to do at the first trial. The killers' intent, according to the state, was to avenge the murder, six hours earlier, of a black man (Roy Holloway) by a white man (Frank Conforti) in Walt's Inn, a few blocks away from the scene of the Eighteenth Street slayings. On the face of it, revenge seemed a definite possibility. The murderers made no effort to rob the bar. (Alfred P. Bello admitted taking sixty-six dollars from the cash register of the Lafayette Grill in the confusion after the murders there.) The two black gunmen—everyone agreed that two black men were the assailants—had begun shooting immediately and indiscriminately upon entering the Lafayette Grill, a white bar.

Nevertheless, it was the racial angle—the gratuitous implication of a motive (gratuitous because the prosecution did not have to specify a motive)—that ultimately got the convictions tossed out. It took a while for this to happen. John Artis was released on parole on December 22, 1981, after serving fourteen and a half years in prison. On August 17, 1982, the New Jersey Supreme Court, by a four-to-three margin, rejected Carter's appeal for a new trial.

Then, on November 7, 1985, Judge H. Lee Sarokin of Federal District

Court in Newark decided that the New Jersey Supreme Court was wrong. There was a constitutional issue at stake, Sarokin said. The prosecution had improperly suggested to the jury that racial revenge was the motive for the murders. Insufficient evidence existed to support such a theory, he believed, and "the insidious and repugnant argument that this heinous crime is to be understood and explained solely because the petitioners are black and the victims are white" would not be allowed to stand.

Judge Sarokin refused to accept "a conviction which rests upon racial stereotypes, fears and prejudices." Sarokin found racial revenge to be "an unacceptable assumption." He wrote, "It would be naive not to recognize that some prejudice, bias and fear lurks in all of us. But to permit a conviction to be urged based upon such factors, or to permit a conviction to stand having utilized such factors, diminishes our fundamental constitutional rights."

It would be revealing to know what motive Judge Sarokin might suggest to account for the triple murder at the Lafayette Grill in those days of Paterson's bitter racial strife.

40 Millburn's Shady Art Dealer

MILLBURN

Art Dealer Facing N.Y. Indictment
Slain in Gallery with Female Partner

APRIL 11, 1968

Richard Behrman, forty-four, knew how to do two things exceedingly well: make a great deal of money and get into a great deal of trouble. At the time of his death Behrman was facing a 519-count larceny indictment in the Bronx—the longest ever obtained there—for a scam involving the sale of late-model used cars. According to Bronx District Attorney Burton Roberts, Richard Behrman and another man, Harold Gelvan, thirty-eight, advertised high-quality used cars at cut-rate prices, then delivered reconditioned taxis or police cars. Or else they delivered cars without titles. Or, worse yet, they delivered nothing at all in exchange for their customers' payments or deposits. Behrman and Gelvan operated under the name of Consolidated Auto Wholesalers, Inc.

This auto sales racket was just one of Behrman's many schemes to waltz off with other people's money. In 1952 he had been released from Sing Sing Prison after serving four years of a five- to ten-year sentence for shipping cartons of old newspapers to foreign importers rather than the hosiery he had sold them. In a second indictment facing him at the time of his murder, he was accused of passing bad checks in the amount of $14,619 to a Manhattan jewelry store. Behrman was also charged, along with two accomplices, with stealing $23,000 from an elderly couple in Darby, Pennsylvania. His alleged accomplices were Major B. Coxson, thirty-nine, and Count Kelly, thirty-five, both of Angora Terrace, Pennsylvania. Coxson, a high-living character who would one day run for mayor of Camden, had ties to Philadelphia mob boss Angelo ("The Docile Don") Bruno.

On the morning of Friday, April 12, 1968, Renwick Mitchell of Philadelphia, a young part-time employee at the Age Galleries, 557 Millburn Avenue, Millburn, arrived for work and found two bodies. One was that of Richard Behrman, a bachelor, recently of Livingston and before that of 969 Park Avenue, Manhattan. At the time of the murder he was living in a room at the gallery. The other body belonged to Behrman's partner, Marilyn Pivnick, a thirty-six-year-old divorced mother of three, of 26 North Derby Road, Springfield.

Behrman, wearing a green sport jacket, black slacks, a white shirt, and a tie, had been shot once in the back of the head. Heavyset and balding, described by a friend as "a well-mannered, cultured man," he was found seated against a wall near the desk in his second-floor office. Mrs. Pivnick, a trim figure in a costly black-and-white knit checked suit, had been shot once in the forehead. Her body was found lying at the foot of the stairs leading to Behrman's office. The murder weapon, believed to be a .32-caliber pistol, was not found. From the positions of the bodies it looked as if Behrman had been shot first and then Pivnick when she came to investigate. Apparently, the two of them had been preparing paintings for an auction. Their gallery, Behrman's peccadillos notwithstanding, was a real business that was sponsoring a show that weekend at the Tamarack Lodge in Ellenville, New York.

Millburn police found themselves without a motive, a murder weapon, or any suspects in the killings. Nothing was missing from the red-carpeted gallery, which Behrman and Pivnick had operated for about three months. The two of them had been conducting art auctions throughout the country, with Behrman, a multitalented man, it would seem, acting as auctioneer.

The case sounds a bit like an episode from the television series "Murder, She Wrote," in which Jessica Fletcher stumbles upon a homicide, sorts out the various possible motives, eliminates the red herrings, and, sad-eyed at the self-defeating foibles of humankind, points the finger at the actual, if unlikely, killer. Unfortunately, Jessica Fletcher was not visiting an old friend in Millburn on the weekend of April 13–14, 1968. The case remains unsolved.

But there is a footnote. Major B. Coxson, one of the two men indicted with Richard Behrman in that $23,000 ripoff of a Pennsylvania couple, was himself murdered more than five years later, on June 8, 1973, in Cherry Hill. The Coxson murder, like that of Behrman, engendered front-page headlines. (See "In a Black Cadillac," page 147.)

PART FIVE

FROM
THE
LISTS
TO
LAMONACO

The Elusive
John List

WESTFIELD

Pious Accountant Executes Family and Disappears Without a Trace

NOVEMBER 9, 1971

"My God, you'd better send help out here. There's been a mass murder. There's bodies all over the place."

"Out here" was 431 Hillside Avenue, Westfield, an imposing nineteen-room white house in a quiet, affluent neighborhood. It was the home of the List family. Five of its six members were still there. They had been dead for a month, murdered by the one missing family member, John Emil List, forty-six. John had thoughtfully left notes explaining almost everything, including why the multiple murders made such good sense. "I didn't want them to go into poverty," he had written. Also, one of his three children, Patricia Marie, sixteen, was beginning to be a bit rebellious. He, being a devoutly religious man and a pillar of the church, feared for her Christian soul.

The bodies of the children were arranged neatly on sleeping bags in the large ballroom. Frederick Michael, thirteen, lay next to Patty, and beside him was John Frederick, fifteen. Their mother, Helen, forty-six, also lay on a sleeping bag, positioned at a T-angle to their heads. A fifth body turned up a little later. It was that of Alma M. List, eighty-four, John's mother. He had left an explanation for her separation from the rest of the family: "P.S. Mother is in the attic. She was too heavy to move."

The bodies were discovered on December 7, 1971, the thirtieth anniversary of the Japanese attack on Pearl Harbor. They had lain in the deserted house for nearly a month in the positions John had placed them. He had planned the whole exploit carefully, sending explanatory notes to anyone who might wonder about the absence of the various Lists—including the absence of John himself. A careful and intelligent accountant, he clearly did not intend to answer to any earthly law for the murder of his family. As the head of the household, failing economically, he thought he had done the right thing, the only possible thing, and he intended to move on, to start over.

By now, of course, the trail was cold. Police located John List's 1963 blue Chevrolet Impala on December 9 in the long-term parking lot at Kennedy International Airport. The parking voucher was dated November 10. List had left a number of identifying cards and papers in the car, showing pretty clearly that no one named John Emil List was going to show up on any manifest of airline passengers—or anywhere else if the killer could help it.

Where had he gone? No one knew at the time. No one knew for the next seventeen and a half years, in fact—not until one of "Robert P. Clark's" favorite television shows, *"America's Most Wanted,"* aired on Sunday evening, May 21, 1989. On that particular night "Bob" missed the program. He and his new wife, Delores, went to a church social instead, so he was unaware that the show was about him, complete with a reenactment, photographs, and a carefully sculpted plaster bust. Three hundred people called the TV program's hotline. One of them, an anonymous caller, said that the thirteen-inch, ten-pound plaster bust of List, fashioned to show what he would probably look like in 1989, bore a distinct resemblance to an accountant in Midlothian, Virginia, a man named Robert P. Clark. Another call came in from Aurora, Colorado, this one not anonymous, and this caller, too, identified the plaster bust of John List as a perfect image of Robert P. Clark, an old acquaintance, an accountant who formerly lived in Aurora but had moved to 13919 Sagewood Trace in the Brandermill development in Midlothian, Virginia.

The FBI moved in to investigate. First they visited Mrs. Delores Clark at her suburban home, a three-bedroom ranch-style house. They showed her the 1971 FBI flier with photos and a description of the fugitive, John Emil List. She sagged. "It could be him," she said weakly.

And it was, although "Bob" denied it vehemently. "I ought to know who I am," he insisted when they picked him up at his place of work. "My name is Robert P. Clark." But if that were the case, then he and John Emil List had identical fingerprints. Even Bob saw the impossibility of that, but he clung to his story. For a long time, too, Delores refused to accept the truth. "I love my husband very deeply," she said, retreating into prayer and seclusion.

Back in suburban Denver and down in suburban Richmond they were also praying for Bob Clark. He had been such a dedicated, upstanding member of the congregation of each church he had joined. He put in a phone call to his most recent boss to apologize for being arrested in the office. He hoped it hadn't caused any inconvenience. He waived extradition to New Jersey because, he claimed, he wanted to clear his name (still Robert P. Clark) with as little delay as possible.

List continued to maintain his fictitious identity until convinced by his New Jersey lawyer, Elijah Miller, that his best defense lay in preventing the introduction of those gruesomely damning, explanatory letters he had left behind at the murder scene. To have any hope of accomplishing this, he would have to admit to being John List, not Bob Clark. On February 16, 1990, the defendant finally acknowledged that, yes, he was John Emil List.

But his five-page letter to Reverend Eugene A. Rehwinkel, pastor of Redeemer Lutheran Church in Westfield, was admitted into evidence anyway. He had left it with the bodies rather than mailing or delivering it, leading Judge William L'E. Wertheimer to conclude that "John Emil List was more interested in escape and anonymity than absolution." Assistant Prosecutor Brian Gillet read the letter to the jury. It was a weird and revealing document:

> After it was all over [List had written on November 9, 1971, carefully composing his letter amidst the carnage] I said some prayers for them all—from the hymn book. That was the least I could do.
> Now for the final arrangements:
> Helen & the children have all agreed that they would prefer to be cremated. Please see to it that the costs are kept low.
> As for me please let me be dropped from the congregation rolls.
> Also I'm sure many will say, "How could anyone do such a horrible thing."—My only answer is it isn't easy.

Elijah Miller had known from the beginning that the defendant could expect little sympathy. The best Miller could do was to try to prove that List was an obsessive-compulsive basket case, his disorder brought about by an overly strict German Lutheran upbringing. The Reverend Mr. Rehwinkel, called as a defense witness, tried to help out his former parishioner, but his well-meaning attempt was unavailing. The last, slim hope for the defense lay in John Emil List's own testimony. He did not present it himself, however. Instead, Dr. Steven Simring, the state's psychiatric expert, read into evidence a lengthy transcript of List's account of the murders.

> At about 9:00 A.M. Helen was having toast and coffee. She may have said, "Good morning." I don't remember. I shot her in the back of the head, and she crumpled forward. Then I went upstairs. I shot my mother in the back of the head.
> I remember seeing Patty in the entranceway, by the washer-dryer. I met her at the door. I came with her, and I shot her in the back of the head.
> Then Freddie, then John. John was different. When he fell, his body had some jerking movements. So I pulled out the .22, and I shot to hit him on the heart. I didn't want him to suffer.

The jury found John Emil List guilty of murder in the first degree. A two-sentence excerpt from the five-page letter to Reverend Rehwinkel convinced them beyond all doubt that the painstaking defendant deserved the maximum penalty rather than conviction on a lesser charge. List had written: "Originally I had planned this for Nov. 1, All Saints' Day. But travel arrangements were delayed." The members of the jury read that passage a number of times. They interpreted it in the only way that seemed possible. They concluded that for John List to change the murder date so as to ensure a clean escape showed premeditation beyond a reasonable doubt.

Judge Wertheimer sentenced the defendant, by then sixty-four years old, to life imprisonment, calling him a man "without remorse and without honor." List took off his glasses and rubbed his eyes.

42 Gun Battle on the Turnpike

EAST BRUNSWICK

State Trooper, Black Militant Die in Gunfire Exchange Near Exit 9

MAY 2, 1973

It looked routine and minor. About half an hour after midnight, a defective taillight on a battered 1965 white Pontiac with Vermont plates attracted the attention of Trooper James M. Harper, twenty-nine, who was on patrol. The trooper flagged down the car, which was headed south on the New Jersey Turnpike in East Brunswick. Following standard procedure, he radioed the stop. Trooper Werner Foerster, thirty-five, responded. But before Foerster reached the scene, Harper approached the car, questioned the driver, and asked the man to get out and stand at the rear of the vehicle. Trooper Harper then went back and began questioning the young woman in the front passenger seat, who gave answers that did not match those of the driver. While she was being questioned, she kept one hand in her purse. A third person, a man, sat quietly in the rear seat of the car during this encounter.

Meanwhile, Trooper Foerster had arrived and approached the driver at the rear of the car. Harper heard the Foerster say, "Jim, look what I found." Glancing back, he saw the trooper holding up an ammo clip. At the same moment, he noticed the movement within the car. The woman, having taken an automatic weapon from her purse, fired at Harper. The bullet tore through the roof of the car and hit the trooper in the shoulder. As Harper retreated behind the troop car, the woman scrambled out of the Pontiac and exchanged fire with him. She edged toward the rear of the car.

While this was going on, Foerster became involved in a struggle with the driver of the Pontiac. Either the man or the woman got possession of Foerster's gun, shot the trooper in the arm, and then killed him with a shot behind the ear. Next, they ran back to their car, got in, and pulled away. Trooper Harper had already begun to stagger to the Turnpike Administration Building, about two hundred yards away, where he reported the incident. Other troopers responded, and within a few minutes one of them, Robert Palentchar, spotted a car parked on the side of the road a few miles south of the crime scene, near Milltown. When he pulled up, he saw a woman, badly wounded, coming out of the woods. He placed her under arrest. A search of the woods revealed the body of a man dead of gunshot wounds.

The dead man was Zayd Malik Shakur (formerly James F. Coston), thirty-two, at one time deputy minister of information for the Black Panther party. The wounded woman—who was destined to become one of the most notorious fugitives in New Jersey history—was Joanne Deborah Chesimard, twenty-five, a member of the Black Liberation Army (BLA), an extremist group that had broken with the Black Panthers. Indeed, Joanne Chesimard, once a student at the City College of New York, was notorious already. New York City police wanted her for questioning in connection with the murder of two New York police officers in Manhattan's East Village. Police also suspected Chesimard of participating in a 1971 bank robbery and in a grenade attack that blew up a patrol car; both of those crimes took place in Queens.

Chesimard, in serious condition with bullet wounds in both arms and a shoulder, was treated and questioned while under heavy guard at Middlesex General Hospital in New Brunswick. On the morning after the murder she was arraigned in her hospital bed, charged with killing Trooper Werner Foerster. A former New York City police official called Chesimard the "soul" of the tiny militant band, most of whose core members had at one time lived in a two-story house at 757 Beck Street in the Bronx. Later they moved to Atlanta and then back north again.

With Chesimard in custody and Shakur dead, state troopers and local police were combing the woods near the spot where the driver of the Pontiac had disappeared. The search continued for thirty-six hours, until Trooper Douglas Osborne and Patrolman Robert Zygmund of East Brunswick came upon a man wearing a white safari jacket, just as in the wanted-poster description. The fugitive was rain-drenched, without shoes, and in a weakened state. He stumbled from the underbrush, saying, "I give up, man." He was thirty-six-year-old Clark E. Squire, most recently of Manhattan, a member of the Black Liberation Army.

The trial of Squire and Chesimard began on October 9, 1973, in the Middlesex County Courthouse, New Brunswick, amid unusually tight security. Delays and a change in venue moved the date to January, the place to Morris County. Late that month Chesimard was discovered to be pregnant, which, along with some finger-pointing among those responsible for security, led to the defendants' being tried separately, Squire first. On March 11 a jury in New Brunswick found the defendant guilty of murdering Werner Foerster. Five days later the presiding judge sentenced Clark E. Squire to life imprisonment.

Chesimard's trial on the murder charge opened on February 15, 1977, with Middlesex County Prosecutor Edward J. Barone saying that the defendant had "executed" Trooper Foerster with his own weapon. Defense attorney William M. Kunstler argued that Chesimard had her hands in the air when the three shots struck her arms and shoulder. He had forensic experts to back him up, but the jury members were inclined to believe Trooper Harper's account of the shooting rather than Joanne Chesimard's story of quiet submission. An all-white jury convicted her of first-degree murder, and Judge Theodore Appleby imposed the mandatory life sentence. Chesimard murmured, "I am ashamed that I have even taken part in this trial." Kunstler fumed that the trial had been "an empty charade."

What came next was a search for the right prison for Joanne Chesimard, whose adopted revolutionary name was Assata Shakur. The state feared, with good reason, that an attempt would be made to free her. Prison officials felt, also with good reason, that the State Reformatory for Women at Clinton lacked adequate security for a prisoner so likely to figure in a liberation attempt. At first they sent her to Yardville, an all-male facility, but that required virtually solitary confinement. Next they shipped her off to the Alderson Federal Correction Institution in rural West Virginia. But ten months later federal authorities closed the maximum security unit at Alderson, and Chesimard/Shakur came back to New Jersey—to the Clinton reformatory.

The breakout came on the afternoon of November 2, 1979. A man with false identification came to visit Shakur in prison. He was allowed in, unsearched. After a short time two more men arrived to visit a different, unidentified prisoner. They were not searched either. In line with prison policy they were driven in a van to South Hall. On the way the two men drew .45-caliber revolvers, forced the driver into the building at gunpoint, and headed straight for the visiting area. On the way they took a woman guard hostage. Shakur was in the visiting area with the first "visitor." A woman guard who should have been in a bulletproof-glass-enclosed station now left it, apparently fearing the men would shoot one of the guards held hostage. All six of them—Shakur, two hostages, three BLA soldiers—got into the van. The driver barreled out through an unfenced section of the prison and drove to the parking lot of a nearby state school for the mentally handicapped, a mile and a half away. Two cars were waiting there, a blue-and-white Lincoln and a blue Mercury Comet. Shakur and her rescuers took off in them, leaving the two guards shaken but unharmed.

Assata Shakur got away and remained away. At some point she took up residence in Cuba. Clearly, there was a story here. You might think her autobiography, published in 1987, while self-serving, as most autobiographies are, would help to clarify the case. Far from it. It begins, "There were lights and sirens. Zayd was dead." What happened prior to that—how Trooper Harper got shot, how Trooper Foerster was killed, why Zayd was dead, how Chesimard herself was wounded—all these critical details are ignored. In 274 pages Shakur adds little if anything to newspaper accounts of the sudden, shattering event that led to her arrest, conviction, escape, and exile. The only thing the book makes clear is that Joanne Chesimard/Assata Shakur considers the BLA's quixotic "do-or-die battle with the pig power structure in amerika" as a noble revolutionary ideal that was shattered, for her personally at least, by a "white racist, prejudiced jury," not to mention, later on, by the "highest kourt in new jersey."

In a Black Cadillac

CHERRY HILL
Ex-Con Loses Mayoralty Bid,
Then Dies in Brutal Massacre

JUNE 8, 1973

Major B. Coxson, forty-four, an aspirant for the top office in Camden's city government, was not a typical mayoral candidate. A close friend and neighbor of boxer Muhammad Ali, he lived in an affluent area of Cherry Hill, had been arrested seventeen times, convicted ten times, and had served nearly two years in the federal penitentiary at Lewisburg, Pennsylvania. When asked about his criminal record during the campaign, Coxson replied with a laugh, "Most politicians start out as officeholders and wind up getting arrested. I aim to reverse that process." It was a clever line, and it almost worked. The "flamboyant entrepreneur," as the *New York Times* called him, ran a distant second in a field of nine.

The campaign attracted national attention, mainly because of the jaunty and personable Coxson. As associate of Angelo Bruno, the Mafia chief of Philadelphia and South Jersey, Major Coxson owned eleven cars—not just ordinary automobiles, either, but Rolls-Royces, Jaguars, Lincoln Continentals, and such. The cars were equipped with all the amenities, including color television sets, telephones, and bulletproof glass. The candidate's costly house in Cherry Hill, at 1146A Barbara Drive, stood on a large, wooded lot. The mayoral hopeful and his thirty-five-year-old girlfriend, Lois Robinson Luby, shared a huge circular waterbed in a correspondingly vast circular master bedroom. Miss Luby's three children by an ex-husband lived with them.

Coxson had once owned the Rolls-Royce Supper Club in Philadelphia, but had sold it to Lillian Reis, "Philadelphia's most notorious showgirl" (the *Times* again). At the time of his murder he had plenty of money but no visible means of support, although there were rumors that he had been involved in narcotics trafficking. In the past he had been a party to various shady deals concerning the sale of automobiles. One of the deals had linked him in a multicount indictment to art dealer Richard Behrman, murdered in Millburn on April 11, 1968, and Harold Gelvan of Consolidated Auto Wholesalers, Inc., of the Bronx and Philadelphia, who testified against Coxson following Behrman's demise. (See "Millburn's Shady Art Dealer," page 135.)

The end came for Major Benjamin Coxson on June 8, 1973, when he was tied hand and foot in his Cherry Hill home and shot once in the back of the head while kneeling beside his waterbed. He was not the only victim. Lois Luby and her daughter, Lita, seventeen, and son Toro, fourteen, were also bound, shot, and left for dead. Lois and Toro survived, but Lita died within a week at the Cherry Hill Medical Center.

Although the assailants intended to leave no witnesses, they failed. The youngest Luby child, thirteen-year-old Lex, bound hand and foot like the others, succeeded in hopping away from the house and crossing to a neighbors' home, alerting them to what was going on, and they called the police. Lex said that four black men in a black Cadillac had come to their house at about 4:00 A.M. They honked the horn, rousing Coxson, who let them in. According to Lex, "he thought they were friends." The five men talked for a while before the violence started.

Within three weeks FBI agents seized a suspect in South Philadelphia. He was Ronald Harvey, thirty-three, who was already in big trouble with the law, being one of seven men under suspicion in the Washington, D.C., murder of seven Hanafi Muslims in January. The killings occurred in a home donated to the sect by pro basketball star Kareem Abdul-Jabbar as their Washington headquarters. It was a messy affair, for among the victims were four children drowned in a bathtub and one child shot to death. The seven suspects, including Harvey, were thought to be members of a rival Black Muslim sect engaged in a sectarian dispute.

Only Ronald Harvey was identified as one of the four men in the black Cadillac on that June morning in Cherry Hill. But he, along with the other six men, would first be standing trial in Washington, D.C., for the murder of the Hanafi Muslims. Harvey's trial in New Jersey for the Coxson and Luby murders would come later, indeed much later.

All seven men indicted and tried in Washington had long police records. The jury convicted five of them, including Ronald Harvey. Coxson's alleged killer received seven life sentences for his role in the Hanafi

Muslim massacre and was hustled off to the federal penitentiary in Atlanta. Given the time he would be serving there, a New Jersey trial for two more murders seemed almost superfluous. Nevertheless, Harvey was returned to New Jersey in due course and tried for the murders of Major B. Coxson and Lita Luba and the near-fatal assaults on Lois Luby and her son Toro.

There had always been a question of motive. Why had the four men come to Major Coxson's home at 4:00 A.M., conversed with him for some time, then tied him up, along with four others in the house, and proceeded to murder two and badly wound two, while the youngest of the prospective victims hopped safely away? Although the prosecution never established a motive for sure, authorities suspected that the opening conversation and the subsequent violence were linked to drug transactions.

Early in the case, Thomas O'Rourke, director of public safety for Cherry Hill, said he doubted that the four men "came to kill." He was inclined to think "they came to talk, but I believe they were not satisfied with the conversation." Who knows? Whatever the motive or situation, they took drastic action. On the fourth anniversary of the Cherry Hill murders, Ronald Harvey drew two more life sentences.

 # Twenty-Gauge Euthanasia

NEPTUNE

Brother Held for Murder in Shotgun Mercy Killing

JUNE 20, 1973

"Close your eyes now. I'm going to shoot you."

Lester Zygmaniak, twenty-three, spoke these words quietly, in a steady voice. Then he leveled the barrel of a twenty-gauge sawed-off shotgun at his brother's head and fired.

George Zygmaniak, twenty-six, married and the father of a three-year-old son, had been paralyzed from the neck down in a motorcycle accident four days earlier. His brother's single shotgun blast did not kill him instantly. George died twenty-seven hours later in the intensive care unit of the Jersey Shore Medical Center, Neptune. He did not have to be transported there. He was there already. There were five other patients in the room with him, along with two stunned hospital employees.

The tragic sequence of events began at a birthday party and Father's Day celebration on Sunday, June 17, 1973, when a friend's motorcycle George Zygmaniak was driving on the family's eighteen-acre farm on Sweetman Lane in Perrineville flipped and pinned him beneath it. The accident broke his neck and caused severe spinal damage. Doctors at the Jersey Shore Medical Center, where he was taken after first being admitted to the Greater Freehold Area Hospital, diagnosed Zygmaniak's paralysis as irreversible.

Dr. Clement H. Kreider, Jr., the neurosurgeon who handled the case, testified that the patient had pleaded with him, "Please don't let me live like this." Dr. Kreider said that George Zygmaniak could not have screamed in pain, however, as his brother claimed, although another patient who was in the intensive care unit at the time maintained he had heard screams over a three-day period and had also heard the patient shout, "I don't want to live—I want to die."

The Zygmaniaks, a close-knit Polish family whose parents had fled the Nazi Holocaust, lived in Perth Amboy before moving to the farm in Millstone Township in western Monmouth County. George was a technician for the Reynolds Aluminum Company in Woodbridge, Lester a construction worker. Their father had died of a heart attack less than a year before the motorcycle crash.

Lester insisted that his brother had begged for death. "Why don't they let me die?" George asked from his bed while he was still able to speak, and Lester pleaded with hospital personnel to "do my brother a favor—let him die."

By the time Lester smuggled in the twenty-gauge single-shot shotgun, just before 11:00 P.M. on Wednesday, June 20, his brother could no longer talk.

"I am here to end your pain, George," Lester said firmly. "Is it all right with you?" His brother nodded.

"God bless you, George. I'm sorry it had to end like this. Close your eyes now. I'm going to shoot you." The point-blank shot entered George Zygmaniak's left temple. Lester stepped back and waited calmly for the police to come and arrest him. Charged with first-degree murder, he was released on twenty-five thousand dollars bail, an unusually low amount for such a serious charge.

Robert I. Ansell, the Asbury Park lawyer representing Lester Zygmaniak, noted that this was a "tragic case involving substantial issues of a very fundamental nature." The plea was temporary insanity. Although the obvious issue was mercy killing, or euthanasia, the defense avoided using those terms. The prosecution, led by Malcolm V. Carton, ascribed no motive to the act other than an attempt to "play God."

The essential facts were undisputed. Lester Zygmaniak had shot and killed his older brother, George. No one doubted that the family, and the younger brother in particular, were under tremendous emotional strain at the time. Lester was deeply upset at the prospect of George being permanently and hopelessly crippled. So was George.

Still, a plea of temporary insanity seldom succeeds.

This time it did. The jury of seven men and five women in Freehold took two hours and thirty-five minutes to reject the first-degree murder count entirely and to acquit Lester Zygmaniak of murder in the second degree by reason of temporary insanity. Since the jury also found that the defendant had regained his sanity, he left court a free man. He returned to Perrineville to start life anew.

45 Shoemaker and Son

```
LEONIA
Demon Shoemaker from Philadelphia
Begins "Mission of Global Massacre"
                            JANUARY 8, 1975
```

When police responded to the urgent phone calls of neighbors of the DeWitt Romaine family at 124 Glenwood Avenue, Leonia, they found one of the more bizarre crime scenes within recent memory. In a second-floor bedroom of the tan stucco house were two naked women, bound, blindfolded, and gagged. Near them lay a two-year-old boy, also naked and bound. Mrs. Romaine's invalid mother was in another upstairs bedroom. Downstairs in the living room a fully dressed man lay in front of the fireplace, tied hand and foot. Near him lay two more women, fully dressed, face down and bound together at the wrists and ankles. All three captives in the living room had coats over their heads. In the basement a young man sat tied to a water pipe, his hands wired together behind his back, his legs also wired and then tied with cord to his hands. His pants and undershorts were pulled down to his ankles. In front of him in a pool of blood lay a fully dressed young woman, dead, stabbed in the back, chest, and neck.

The murder victim, Maria Fasching, twenty-one, of 176 Christie Street, Leonia, was a practical nurse at Hackensack Hospital. Miss Fasching had been in the habit of stopping by the house on Glenwood Avenue to help care for Mrs. Romaine's invalid mother. Although she was bound hand and foot and brutally knifed, the nurse had not been sexually molested.

None of this seemed to make any sense. The house had been robbed, yes, but the lengthy and baroque modus operandi of the neatly dressed older man and his adolescent accomplice, coupled with the apparently sudden, vicious murder of Maria Fasching, looked crazy. It *was* crazy—and that is the gist of the story.

If the killer had been less obsessed with getting rid of his bloodstained shirt, the case would have been much harder to solve. But the killer (who was obsessed in more ways than one) flung his shirt, along with his tie, into a green toolshed in a nearby municipal park as he and the youngster were running hand in hand away from the murder scene. Unhappily for him, the shirt carried the laundry label "Kallinger" on the inside of the collar, a fairly obvious clue, as it turned out, to the identity of its wearer.

On January 17, nine days after the murder, a veritable army of law enforcement officers apprehended Joseph Kallinger, thirty-nine, and his twelve-year-old son, Michael, in their home at 100 East Sterner Street in the Kensington section of northeastern Philadelphia. The arresting party consisted of six officers from the homicide unit of the Philadelphia police, five Pennsylvania state troopers, two police officers from Dumont and one from Baltimore (where the Kallinger duo had made criminal forays), two investigators from the Bergen County prosecutor's office, two detectives from Dumont, and one from Baltimore.

It soon became public knowledge that the Kallinger family was a moral and mental mess. Joseph had been jailed for child abuse on the testimony of three of his children (including Michael), but the three had later changed their stories. One of the children, Joey, had been found dead in an abandoned downtown Philadelphia building (murdered by Joe and Mike, as it turned out, but no one at the time even knew it was a homicide). Joe had once been found dazed and wandering in Hazleton, Pennsylvania, and had been unable to identify himself for a week. Michael had similarly been picked up dazed and wandering in Camden (an elaborate ruse dreamed up by his father to discredit the police, who had begun to suspect that the elder Kallinger was up to no good).

What the police did not know—and would not know until Flora Rheta Schreiber wrote her controversial book titled *The Shoemaker*—was that Joseph Kallinger had a divine mission. Actually, he had received two missions from God, but the first one, to save mankind through meticulous orthopedic research, had failed after roughly forty thousand experiments (his own figures, which can be taken with a barrel of salt). His second mission contradicted his first. God wanted him to massacre mankind, three billion human beings, more or less, one at a time. While carrying out this mission, he would be expected to slash the sexual organs of both males and females. Joseph Kallinger gladly accepted the challenge, but he felt he needed assistance. He went to his son, Michael.

"Mike," he said, "I have a strong desire to kill people, and you're the one to help me."

As Joseph Kallinger later recalled, his twelve-year-old son answered promptly, "Glad to do it, Dad!" The proud father explained to Schreiber, "We had a close, heart-warming, father-and-son relationship."

Their first victim was a shy, teenaged Hispanic boy, chosen at random. Their second victim was Kallinger's son Joey, a year older than Mike, possibly picked because Joseph believed him to be a homosexual. Their third victim was Maria Fasching. Along the way, though, there had been many assaults and robberies, the father and son traveling by bus to various locales to kill people, mostly without success, because of Joseph's seeming ambivalence toward the three-billion-victim project.

Although these two weirdly paired marauders were wanted in a number of jurisdictions, Pennsylvania got them first, putting Joseph on trial for a kinky robbery involving some sexual shenanigans in a Harrisburg suburb. A hanging judge hit him with a thirty- to eighty-year sentence. Michael got psychiatric help.

Kallinger's murder trial in New Jersey came next. The defendant waved, chirped, and moaned his way through much of it. He was either crazy or acting or both. The prosecution branded him "a fraud and a faker." Two defense psychiatrists called him clearly, hopelessly insane, a paranoid-schizophrenic—in laymen's terms, a raving psycho—but the jury had no intention of letting this smirking fiend loll around in a cozy asylum somewhere. They backed up their Pennsylvania peers, found him sane, and convicted him of murder.

Why did he kill Maria Fasching? There is no easily discernible motive. The crime scene looked like a vignette from hell. Picture the circumstances—a male prisoner in the basement with his pants pulled down; a captive female nurse facing him; both of them in the power of Joseph Kallinger, Philadelphia shoemaker, the failed savior of the world, now the designated destroyer of all humankind, called upon by God to murder, emasculate, or sexually mutilate each and every person on earth, but not quite able to do it on his own—needing an agent to help do his work.

What did the shoemaker demand of the nurse? What did he ask that caused Maria Fasching to say, "Kill me. I don't care to live"? Despite the jury's verdict, was Kallinger crazy? Could be.

 # Murder at the Flamingo Motel

Casino gambling was coming to Atlantic City. Resorts International, the first of the big casinos, would open in May 1978. Ever since New Jersey voters approved the 1976 referendum authorizing legalized gambling in Atlantic City, smart operators had been buying real estate on those famous Monopoly-named streets, angling to get in line for lucrative building contracts, or trying in other ways to cash in on what was sure to be a bonanza.

Edwin H. Helfant, a stocky, balding ex-municipal judge from Somers Point, was one of these smart operators. He had bought the Flamingo Motel on Pacific Avenue, was dabbling in law in Atlantic City, and appeared to be living the good life, with a better life to come. Unfortunately for him, he had made an enemy in the mob six years before. Even more unhappily, this enemy had hooked up with a violently ambitious capo who was determined to dethrone the top Philadelphia mob boss, Angelo ("The Docile Don") Bruno.

Back in 1972 Nicholas ("Nick the Blade") Virgilio had been convicted of murder. Facing a twelve- to fifteen-year prison sentence, he got his friend Nicodemo ("Little Nicky") Scarfo to try to fix matters. Scarfo approached ex-Judge Helfant, well known for his helpfulness, who said, sure, but it will cost twelve thousand dollars to get the Superior Court judge to soften the sentence. Scarfo gave the money to Helfant. But Virgilio drew a twelve- to fifteen-year sentence anyway. Scarfo took note; Virgilio vowed revenge.

After serving his time, Nick the Blade Virgilio returned to Atlantic City and took a job as maitre d' in a restaurant. On a snowy February night he outfitted himself with a black ski mask, a snow shovel, and a weapon. Little Nicky Scarfo drove him to the Flamingo Motel, where Helfant and his wife were relaxing at their usual table in the cocktail lounge. Virgilio ambled in and, forsaking the blade of his nickname, pulled out a .22-caliber pistol and pumped five shots into the Flamingo owner's head. No one moved except Virgilio, who walked out and tossed his snow shovel in a snowbank. It would take eight years to solve the case.

But two things were strikingly evident right away. First, this was a mob hit. Second, it was not an Angelo Bruno hit. The Docile Don made it a practice not to shoot public figures in public places. And with legalized gambling coming to Atlantic City, the very last thing he wanted to see was mob violence in the heart of this supposedly mob-free casino city. A renegade mobster was on the loose.

When the history of Little Nicky Scarfo's violent reign came to be written, the late Judge Helfant would have the distinction, if one can call it that, of being the first of Scarfo's twenty-four or so hits. Helfant's death preceded by more than two years the Scarfo murder of Philadelphia's Mr. Big himself, Angelo Bruno. Many of the Scarfo killings took place in the City of Brotherly Love, but not all of them. Philip ("Crazy Phil") Leonetti, for instance, gunned down Vincent Falcone in a house on Decatur Avenue, Margate, while Little Nicky and two others stood by.

Scarfo's thirst for violence had led the Docile Don to exile him from Philadelphia to Atlantic City in 1964, following Nicky's release from a Pennsylvania prison on a manslaughter conviction. It was a true exile, for Atlantic City, once a bustling and prosperous resort, had gone mostly to seed. So had Scarfo. He lived in a nondescript apartment, tended bar, ran a small loan-sharking and bookmaking operation, and went into the adult bookstore business. He showed no promise of becoming a major power in the Mafia.

Then came casino gambling, and Nicky Scarfo's exile became his opportunity. He found himself sitting right in the middle of one of the biggest racketeering booms in mob history. Not only that, he had the boldness to take full advantage of it. If someone stood in his path, that someone bit the dust, usually in Philadelphia. Soon Scarfo, while still living modestly in Atlantic City, adopted the lifestyle of the rich and famous in Fort Lauderdale, Florida, where he owned an expensive hacienda-style house, a Rolls-Royce, and a forty-one-foot cabin cruiser cheerily named *Casablanca Usual Suspects.*

But the good life ended for Little Nicky Scarfo on November 19, 1988, when the federal Racketeering Influenced and Corrupt Organizations Act (RICO) along with some talkative protected witnesses brought convictions on charges of drug dealing, loan sharking, extortion, and murder to Nicodemo Scarfo and sixteen members of his Mafia family. One of those convicted with Scarfo that day was Nicholas Virgilio—for gunning down Judge Edwin H. Helfant more than ten years earlier. Virgilio drew a forty-year prison sentence. Scarfo got enough prison time to keep him off the streets for more than a lifetime.

47

"He Hates His Mother"

TRENTON

Attacker Binds, Tortures, and Kills Descendent of Declaration Signer

DECEMBER 7, 1979

One of America's great crime reporters, the *New York Post*'s Mike Pearl, observed that the most important thing in his job was "to find out what was a story." He looked for certain elements—celebrities, money, babies, violence, sex. "If you get two or three of them at once," he said, "you get a great story."

The murder of Emma Jane Stockton had four of the five elements, lacking only babies. Emma Jane Stockton, thirty-seven, unmarried, was a descendent of Richard Stockton, one of New Jersey's five signers of the Declaration of Independence and the owner of Morven, a magnificent Princeton estate that later became the home of New Jersey's governors. At the time of her death Ms. Stockton served as executive director of the Greater Trenton Symphony Orchestra and was a member of the board of directors of the New Jersey State Museum. Earlier, she had been an associate fashion editor at *Harper's Bazaar* and had worked independently as an interior decorator.

On the night of December 7, 1979, Ms. Stockton, a blonde, heavyset woman, was expected to attend a benefit dinner-dance for a boys' club. Her escort, unable to reach her at the door of her home or by telephone, enlisted a neighbor with a ladder and then flagged down a police car. They discovered the worst—Ms. Stockton's body in a blood-soaked third-floor bedroom, where she had been bound to her bed, tortured, and murdered. She had been stabbed more than forty times with a crochet hook, a screwdriver, a corkscrew, and a knife. Her attacker had also driven wood slivers into her legs. She had lived through this protracted torture, dying of asphyxiation from a crushing blow to her neck and chest.

The murder seemed to be motiveless. Nothing of value was missing from the house. Ms. Stockton had not been raped. Was she simply, horribly, an unwitting victim of gentrification? She had bought her once-grand but deteriorating Mill Hill house for $4,500 at auction and reportedly had put about $70,000 into restoring it as part of the neighborhood renovation occurring on Mercer Street in downtown Trenton. Mill Hill, a tiny residential section in a crime-ridden area two blocks from the center of town, had become what some called "a precious stone in a cheap setting." Trenton's Mayor Arthur J. Holland, who lived in a restored house a few doors away, had encouraged Ms. Stockton's move from Yardley, Pennsylvania. No question about it, though, the neighborhood *was* dangerous. Ms. Stockton had been raped in her Mercer Street house on November 11, less than a month before the murder, by a young black man who had apparently climbed a ladder to a second-floor window. Police doubted that there was any connection between the two crimes. They were wrong. The same man had committed both.

Even so, the killer might have faded back into the anonymity of Trenton's downtown streets except for one thing. He struck again, less than two weeks later, this time in Hamilton Township. His second victim was Anna Mae Chicaleski, sixty-four, raped, beaten, and strangled to death on December 19. This time the killer did steal something—Mrs. Chicaleski's car, which an off-duty Hopewell Township cop spotted parked at the Ewing Bazaar on North Olden Avenue. A young black man, spattered with blood, was getting out of the car. In his pants pockets were Mrs. Chicaleski's credit cards and Social Security card.

The suspect's name was Keith Earl Alford. He was twenty-four years old, an unemployed truck driver whose own mother, it was said, loathed and feared him. The feeling was mutual. "Make no mistake about it," said a woman who had known Alford as a boy, "he hates his mother." Although the case against Alford in the Chicaleski murder was open and shut, authorities were reluctant at first to say how they had tied him almost immediately to the Stockton murder. The explanation, when it came, was simple enough—two of Alford's thumbprints had been found on Ms. Stockton's bedroom telephone.

Convicted of the Chicaleski murder, Alford already faced a life sentence when he went on trial for killing Ms. Stockton. The testimony was chilling. Not only had the burly ex-paratrooper tortured his victim for two hours before murdering her, he had ignited newspapers and magazines and burned her breasts, abdomen, and legs after she died. The jury took three and a half hours to find him guilty. Superior Court Judge Richard Barlow gave him a second life term.

 # A Suicide or Two

---

ELMWOOD PARK

Wife Dies on Christmas Eve; Was It Murder or Suicide?

DECEMBER 24, 1979

In late November of 1979 Nancy Sherman, fifty, filed for divorce from her husband of nine and a half years. She contended that Robert J. Sherman, fifty-nine, chief of detectives of the Englewood Police Department and a twenty-five-year veteran of the force, had twice threatened her with a gun. She changed her will at the time, too, cutting her husband out of it. Nonetheless, the two were still living together in their Elmwood Park home as the holidays approached.

On the afternoon of December 24, Captain Sherman (according to his story) returned home from his tour of duty at about 2:00 P.M., hung his .38-caliber service revolver in a bedroom closet, and went to bed. Two hours later he heard a shot. He ran to the kitchen where he found his wife on the floor, dead of a gunshot wound to the head. The Bergen County prosecutor, Roger Breslin, termed the death "an apparent suicide."

Mrs. Sherman's daughter by a previous marriage—Mrs. Nancy Luginbill, thirty, of Los Osos, California—was having none of that. She quickly filed a civil suit charging her stepfather with shooting her mother. She got a court order blocking cremation or embalming of her mother's body, and she hired a forensic pathologist, Dr. Louis Roh, to perform a second autopsy. Dr. Roh concluded that the angle of the gunshot wound behind Mrs. Sherman's right ear and the apparent distance of the gun from her head (three to four inches) were inconsistent with a finding of suicide. He suspected murder.

Thereupon, Robert J. Sherman hired a pathologist of his own, the respected former chief medical examiner of New York City, Dr. Dominick J. DiMaio. Unhappily for Sherman, Dr. DiMaio found Mrs. Sherman's wound to be "compatible with suicide or homicide." He sharply criticized the Bergen County prosecutor's investigative staff for failing to test immediately for gunpowder residue particles on Nancy Sherman's hands. The presence or absence of such particles would have been strong evidence one way or the other. By the time Dr. DiMaio examined the body, however, it was too late for the test to be useful.

On April 2, 1980, Robert J. Sherman, by then retired from the Englewood Police Department, was indicted for murder. Prosecutor Breslin pointed out that the original autopsy, which had been performed by Dr. Marlene Lengner, an assistant in the Bergen County Medical Examiner's office, had findings essentially the same as Dr. DiMaio's—murder was a possibility, but so was suicide. In the absence of gunshot residue analysis, there seemed no sure way to prove what had happened in the Shermans' kitchen on that fatal afternoon.

The defendant was to be arraigned on April 3. But at about 5:30 A.M. on that day, five hours before his scheduled court appearance, the retired captain took his own life with a snub-nosed .38-caliber revolver, leaving behind two notes in which he denied killing his wife. He wrote, "I cannot go through what is forthcoming today." Mrs. Luginbill, speaking from her home in California, said, "I was shocked to hear about the suicide, but I still believe that he killed her."

One of the notes Sherman left was addressed to "Kosh," his nickname for his first wife, Katherine, who, after Nancy's death, had invited him to stay at her home in Englewood, the place where they had raised their four children. These children stood to inherit the Sherman property—that is, if Mrs. Sherman's death were ruled a suicide. Otherwise, it would go to Mrs. Luginbill. The ex-captain's note to Kosh urged their four children, two sons and two daughters, "to fight for what is theirs." He concluded on a cheery note: "Have fun and remember dear old dad."

 # Fall of a Renaissance Man

SOMERVILLE

Flamboyant "Who's Who" Engineer Beats Woman Neighbor to Death

AUGUST 15, 1981

Exactly what happened in the parking lot of the Richards Fuel Oils company on South Bridge Street, Somerville, was never quite clear. Apparently there was a confrontation between Jean Tozzi, a fifty-one-year-old divorcée, and Tibor Louis DeDobeau, a forty-seven-year-old bachelor. Witnesses observed the two of them arguing in the parking lot. One witness testified he saw the man "carry something on his shoulders," throw it into a car, and speed away.

No physical evidence linked DeDobeau or his car to the apparent kidnapping. But there was no question about the identity of the fully clothed, brutally beaten body of Jean Tozzi, found two days later along a bank of the Raritan River at the foot of South Bridge Street, about a quarter of a mile from the adjacent apartment buildings where Tibor Louis DeDobeau and Jean Tozzi lived.

They knew each other. That was clear. But the Somerset County prosecutor admitted, "We don't really know the extent of the relationship." Both were single. Neither had friends who could clarify the connection between the sexually molested (but neither undressed nor raped) victim and her alleged killer. What the public found fascinating in this bizarre, solved, but still unexplained murder was the contrast between the prim divorcée and the rakish bachelor.

Jean Tozzi, a mother of four, favored pantsuits and wore her hair pinned up in a bun. Recently laid off from a job at a local dry-cleaning shop, she liked to window-shop in downtown Somerville. Her apartment was furnished with a mattress, a card table, and a lawn chair—nothing more.

Mrs. Tozzi was a bit out of the ordinary, to be sure, but Mr. DeDobeau was a real oddball. "He's very intelligent, a businessman, an entrepreneur," said one man who attended his trial. True. A 1968 emigré from Hungary, he ran an engineering placement firm, Deltanova Corporation, out of his South Bridge Street apartment. A biographical sketch of him appeared in the 1981 edition of *Who's Who in the East*. He claimed to be an inventor and to hold important patents in various countries. The Somerset investigation could find no such patents. But with or without patents, DeDobeau had a certain flair. He wore flashy clothes and carried a long, gnarled, Hungarian-made wooden cigarette holder through which he puffed Lucky Strikes, while vowing to have famed trial lawyer F. Lee Bailey defend him. Actually, he got a court-appointed lawyer after trying vainly and ludicrously to act as his own attorney.

The case against him was circumstantial. DeDobeau was good copy for the media. He offered a $10,000 reward for information leading to the arrest of the "true killer." He reexamined his bachelor status and invited women to submit marriage proposals. He described his trial as "boring" inasmuch as no "sexual-related" details were forthcoming. His prowess as a detective, he said, was what led him to poke around at the riverbank site where Tozzi's body had been found—only to be spotted there by a Somerville police officer.

DeDobeau had a blotchy past, despite the *Who's Who* entry. In 1976 he had been convicted of fondling and exposing himself to two preteenaged girls he had lured to the Bridgewater apartment where he was then living. He had run afoul of the Somerville Board of Health for raising pigeons in his apartment and pointedly ignoring a court order to remove them. He had been frisked by the Secret Service "as a socio-politically inclined dissident" when Ronald Reagan made a 1980 campaign stop in Hunterdon County.

None of which proved he had bludgeoned Jean Tozzi to death. But the investigators who had questioned the loose-lipped mechanical engineer had heard enough self-incriminating statements to know that DeDobeau had a "consciousness of guilt." The jury accepted the prosecution's circumstantial evidence against the darkly handsome defendant, finding him guilty, after five hours of deliberation, of kidnapping, aggravated criminal sexual contact, and murder.

While waiting to be sentenced, DeDobeau went on a hunger strike. It lasted four weeks. When he arrived in the courtroom for sentencing, he was a changed man, disheveled and wasted. Deputies brought him in in a wheelchair. He huddled under a heavy gray blanket, his hair uncombed and wild, and began muttering to no one in particular, "Water is the most beautiful thing in the world . . . water is my best friend . . . water is always with you." (He had refused to drink the water in the county jail, claiming it was contaminated.) DeDobeau feigned sleep as Superior Court Judge Michael R. Imbriani pronounced sentence on him—life imprisonment for felony murder, thirty years for kidnapping, and five years for aggravated criminal sexual contact.

He was wheeled away, his destination Trenton State Prison. The next day he broke his hunger strike, asking for cranberry juice and a milkshake.

50 Trooper Lamonaco's Death

> COLUMBIA
>
> ## State Trooper Philip Lamonaco Slain in Shootout on Route 80
>
> DECEMBER 21, 1981

At 4:13 P.M., four days before Christmas, a passing motorist used State Trooper Philip Lamonaco's car radio to alert the Blairstown barracks that a trooper was lying beside a marked state police car on the shoulder of westbound Route 80 just beyond Exit 4A in Columbia, a tiny community in Knowlton Township. Lamonaco, thirty-two, had been struck by nine shots, fatally by one—a nine-millimeter bullet that pierced his left arm, missed his bulletproof vest, and struck his heart. He died at the scene, although the official pronouncement came from Pocono Hospital, East Stroudsburg, Pennsylvania, at 5:28 P.M.

There were several drive-by eyewitnesses to the shootout. Unfortunately (but predictably), these witnesses offered differing accounts of what had happened. Newark's *Star-Ledger*, reporting the murder on December 22, 1981, said: "They [the police] are looking for three men, possibly Hispanics, who were believed to be on foot."

In fact, there were no Hispanics in the 1977 blue Chevrolet Nova with Connecticut plates that Trooper Lamonaco stopped. There were two Caucasians: Thomas Manning, thirty-five, and Richard Williams, thirty-four, both wanted on criminal charges in various northeastern states. These two bushrangers, living an underground existence and taking regular target practice, thought of themselves as "anti-imperialist freedom fighters" and soldiers in the "armed clandestine movement."

The supposed Hispanic lead was a ruse. After killing Trooper Lamonaco, Manning and Williams apparently used CB channel 19 to call in a report of three Hispanics traveling east on Route 46 in a car with the rear window shot out. This trick, intended to throw police off the trail, worked to some extent. The search for the killers was concentrated at first on Routes 46 and 80 eastbound. But not all the searchers headed east.

At about 7:00 P.M. the bullet-riddled Chevy Nova (for Trooper Lamonaco had emptied his six-shot .38-caliber service revolver in the shootout) was found abandoned in the snow on Polkville Road, a dirt road off Route 94 in Knowlton, a couple of miles from the scene of the shooting. Bloodstains in the car evidently came from one of the fugitives who had cut himself on shattered glass after the shootout. These bloodstains—nearly a decade later—would help show conclusively what had happened in the gathering dusk on that isolated stretch of Route 80 near the Delaware Water Gap.

What *had* happened?

Well, Thomas Manning was a family man, with a twenty-six-year-old wife (herself a fugitive from justice) and three young children, one of them born in a Kingston, Pennsylvania, doctor's office a week before the shootout. They had been living for a year or so on a sixty-acre farm in Marshalls Creek, Pennsylvania, across the Delaware River from New Jersey. Manning wanted to buy Christmas presents for his wife and kids, and he and Richard Williams, the peripatetic "armoror" of the revolutionary group, who was then living with the Mannings, took a trip to Budd Lake, to the Trading Post on Route 46, to pick up some gifts. On the way back the pair somehow attracted the attention of Trooper Lamonaco, presumably for a minor traffic violation, since he did not report the Chevy Nova stop to Blairstown.

Manning was the driver; Williams was in the front passenger's seat. (This is the police reconstruction of events, not Manning's story—more about his version later.) Lamonaco may or may not have recognized Manning as a fugitive, but he apparently did confiscate a gun from Manning and place him under arrest. At this point Williams slid out from the passenger's side of the car and began firing his Browning nine-millimeter semiautomatic at Lamonaco over the roof of the car. Manning, unarmed, ran onto the pavement. Williams, still firing, angled toward the rear passenger side of the car, while Lamonaco, also firing, moved toward the front driver's side. They exchanged approximately twenty shots. One of them killed Lamonaco.

With Lamonaco down, Manning and Williams climbed back into the Nova and took off, exiting Route 80 at the Hainesburg Road turnoff. They took a hilly, circuitous route to Hainesburg, reaching Route 94 on the northern edge of town. Driving south on 94 a mile or so, they took a left at Station Road, crossed a couple of narrow bridges, and turned right onto a dirt road toward Polkville. Soon the Nova got stuck in the snow. The pair made several frantic calls from a nearby pay phone, calls that were later traced to two destinations: an old white frame farmhouse on Brushing Mountain Road in Marshalls Creek, Pennsylvania, where Manning, his family, and Williams had been living; and a house in Germansville, Pennsylvania, occupied by Raymond Luc Lavasseur, his wife, Patricia Gros, and their children. Lavasseur was a fellow revolutionary, who police at first assumed was the man in the car with Manning.

The Mannings' house in Marshalls Creek bore little resemblance to the hardscrabble farmer's residence it had once been. Inside, police found terrorist and guerrilla manuals, disguise and survival kits, electronic surveillance equipment, phone-tapping devices, nine-millimeter ammo, shooters' targets, a framed pen-and-pencil drawing of Black Liberation Army fugitive Joanne Chesimard, and family photographs of the Mannings. All these had been left behind—along with a pet dog and a still-blaring radio—which suggested that the occupants had left in a hurry.

They got away, and, despite an intensive manhunt, they slipped the police net for nearly three years. Colonel Clinton L. Pagano, superintendent of the New Jersey State Police, described the investigation by his department as the most intensive since the kidnapping of the Lindbergh baby in 1932. More than a million fliers and photos were sent out, and more than fifty fugitives in other, unrelated cases were apprehended in the course of the manhunt.

And, finally, the effort paid off. On November 4, 1984, federal agents in Ohio stopped a van in Deerfield, southwest of Youngstown, and apprehended Raymond Luc Lavasseur, thirty-eight, and his wife, Patricia Gros, thirty. Also in the van were the couple's three children and a nine-millimeter pistol. The pair surrendered with no more than an angry kick at one of the federal agents. The children were turned over to juvenile authorities. Shortly after this arrest, forty federal and local police surrounded a house on Cleveland's southwest side and captured three more fugitives, the most important of whom was Richard Williams, the presumed trigger man in the fatal encounter on I-80 near the Delaware Water Gap.

Thomas Manning remained at large, having fled with his wife and children from a rented farmhouse in rural New Lyme, Ohio, on the day of the Cleveland raid. In his haste he left behind in a bedroom trunk a nine-millimeter Browning semiautomatic pistol, which ballistics tests revealed was the gun that killed Trooper Lamonaco.

The search went on. It ended at last on April 24, 1985, when ten FBI agents caught up with the elusive Thomas Manning. When apprehended, he was doing nothing more sinister than playing with two of his children (one of them, Jonathan, three, was born after the murder) in the yard of a rented house in Norfolk, Virginia. His wife, Carol Ann, had been arrested ten minutes earlier as she got out of her car at a nearby shopping center. The four Manning children, the oldest of whom was twelve-year-old Jeremy, were placed in the custody of Norfolk's Social Services Department.

Colonel Pagano was pleased. So was Donna Lamonaco, the slain trooper's widow. So was the general public—but questions remained. Who were these family-style revolutionaries who planted bombs in buildings, robbed banks and armored cars, and committed murder if pressed? The answer seemed to lie with the spaced-out counterculture of the 1960s and 1970s, when revolution was chic but unfocused. Manning and Lavasseur were radicalized combat veterans of the Vietnam War. In the mid-1970s they, along with Williams, joined a New England band of prison-reform rebels called the Sam Melville–Jonathan Jackson Unit, named in honor of a convict (Melville) killed in the Attica prison riot of 1971 and a convict (Jackson) killed in a 1970 shootout in San Rafael, California, while trying to kidnap a judge. In time this group, or what was left of it, became the United Freedom Front, whose ultimate goal was to overthrow the government by force and violence. Its short-term goals involved bombing military installations and the offices of companies doing business with South Africa. To finance their efforts, they robbed banks.

The trial of Thomas Manning and Richard Williams began on November 10, 1986, at the Elks Club in Somerville, with Superior Court Judge Michael R. Imbriani presiding. Judge Imbriani had chosen the Elks Club because of the size of its meeting room, explaining that his courtroom was too small to accommodate the press and the public. Defendant Manning was represented by William M. Kunstler, defendant Williams by Lynne F. Stewart. Their opening statements gave a very different picture of the shootout from the one presented by Assistant Attorney General Anthony G. Simonetti, the prosecutor. Kunstler and Stewart based their defense on those phantom Hispanics sought by police in the immediate aftermath of the murder—wait, make that self-defense. Yes, Manning and Williams had gone Christmas shopping in Budd Lake, but Williams had not returned to Marshalls Creek. He had been picked up by friends who whisked him off to Boston for the holidays. Manning started home alone, came upon two Hispanic hitchhikers, picked them up, and drove on toward the Delaware Water Gap. Trooper Lamonaco spotted him near Columbia and, said the defense, recognized him as a wanted terrorist. The trooper then tried to *execute* Manning, claimed the defense counsel, not arrest him. Manning resisted, of course, and, having prudently brought along a nine-millimeter Browning semiautomatic pistol, successfully defended himself by killing Lamonaco. He then drove the Hispanics to the Polkville Road and told them to vamoose.

This scenario had a few holes. A greeting card with Williams's fingerprints on it had been found in the abandoned Nova. Bloodstains were spattered on the inside of the car, and the blood could hardly have been Manning's, according to his story. (Theoretically, the blood might have come from one of the innocent, vanished Hispanics—except that the jury dismissed Manning's whole hitchhiker tale as a whopper.) Still, the state's case *was* largely circumstantial. No eyewitness had pointed to Richard Williams and said, "That's the man," although some of the eyewitness testimony supported the general outline of Simonetti's reconstruction of events.

After five days of deliberation the jury convicted Manning but could not agree on the charge against Williams. A juror later revealed that the vote was seven to five for acquittal. The result was a hung jury—a reasonable-doubt outcome—but one that from the state's viewpoint was intolerable, even though Williams already faced a forty-five-year sentence for several bombings in and around New York City. (Manning had drawn a fifty-three-year sentence from the same judge in Brooklyn and now got an additional twenty-five-year-to-life sentence in New Jersey.) Prosecutor Simonetti said, "I will recommend to the attorney general that we retry the other defendant as soon as logistically and legally possible."

Nearly four years later Richard Williams was tried, convicted, and sentenced to life imprisonment for the murder of Trooper Philip Lamonaco. A recent advance in technology helped the state prove its case. DNA analysis of the blood spatters in the abandoned Nova, using a technique known as polymerase chain reaction (PCR), showed that the "profile genetic markers" in the dried blood were consistent with only one in eight hundred male Caucasians. The markers were not consistent with Manning's DNA, but they did match that of Williams.

PART SIX

GREED, SEX,
AND
MADNESS

 # Bomb Blast in Middlesex

The Middlesex Borough police chief, James Benson, took the phone call from Andrew Puskas, who lived at 182 First Street.

"Two bottles of gasoline [Puskas said], a piece of pipe, and a bunch of wires—I don't know if it's a joke, but if it is a joke, it's a very poor one."

Benson dispatched Patrolman Robert Schwarz to the scene. Schwarz drove past the house and had to back up his patrol car to the right address. As he stepped out of the car, he saw two young children, Scott and Drew Puskas, leaving the house, bundled up on this frigid morning. It was 8:37 A.M.

Then the ranch-style house blew apart. The front door and its frame slammed into the two boys, throwing them violently forward but also protecting them from the force of the blast. The explosion pinned Patrolman Schwarz against his car. Debris flew by—splinters of wood, shards of glass.

Schwarz, though stunned by the blast, ran toward Scott, seven, whose clothing and hair were on fire He wrapped his leather police jacket around the boy. Drew, two years older than Scott, kept trying to go back into the house, but the flames drove him off. Schwarz asked Drew who was in there, and the boy replied, "My mother and father."

Andrew Puskas, thirty-five, had already put the youngest of his three boys, three-year-old Brian, in the family station wagon, before returning to the house when his wife called out to him. Earlier that morning someone had left a two-foot cardboard box, marked "For Andy Puskas," on their front steps. Patricia Puskas, his thirty-five-year-old wife, had opened it as soon as her husband and the children left.

Puskas took one look at the bomb inside the box, ordered Drew and Scott to leave the house, and called the police. He seemed remarkably calm under the circumstances, saying that he would drive the boys to school but that his wife would be there when they arrived.

Patrolmen Schwarz arrived moments later, just in time to see the roof blow off the house and the walls fly outward. He hoped that Mr. and Mrs. Puskas had somehow made it out the back door, but he doubted it.

Andrew and Patricia Puskas were dead. But why? Every possible motive was considered, starting with their possible involvement with drugs, gambling, the mob. These were out of the question. The Puskases were born-again Christians, active in the local Middlesex Bible Chapel, and as clean-living a family as one could imagine. Insurance fraud? A double suicide? Impossible. There was no insurance, no hint of marital or health problems.

Police concluded that the most likely explanation was revenge. But revenge for what? Investigators, perhaps grasping at straws, noted that the Puskases were anti-Catholic. They had distributed comic books that could be viewed as offensive to Catholics. And Andrew had recently shown three anti-Catholic movies to his youth group at the Bible chapel.

Yet police could find no indication that anyone had actually complained about or been offended by these activities. Even if they had been, it would appear to be a wild overreaction to respond with a carefully built, murderously effective pipe bomb—a bomb that might have killed three children in addition to Andrew Puskas and his wife.

Nevertheless, someone did make and deliver the bomb. A neighbor had seen a stranger in a white station wagon, with a large package visible in the back, driving slowly through the neighborhood at about 8:05 A.M. The driver, a man, pulled into either the Puskas driveway or a driveway next door. This seemed to be a solid clue, but it led nowhere.

The investigation, intensive, lengthy, but fruitless, ground to a halt. Police were forced to wait for an unexpected new lead or an equally unlikely deathbed confession. They are still waiting.

A Stalker
at the Mall

CEDAR KNOLLS
18-Year-Old High School Student
Abducted from Mall Found Dead
NOVEMBER 23, 1982

On Thanksgiving Day a couple walking their dog at the Mendham Borough Reservoir in Randolph Township spotted a fully clothed body floating face down in a concrete retention basin. The body was that of Amie Hoffman, an eighteen-year-old cheerleader at Parsippany Hills High School, who had been missing for more than thirty-six hours. She was last seen in the parking lot of the Morris County Mall in Cedar Knolls, where she worked part-time at a clothing shop. On the night of the abduction her mother had gone to look for her daughter, a Korean-born girl adopted thirteen years earlier, and had found Amie's car with the keys in the ignition and Amie's handbag and jacket on the front seat. Nothing had been taken from the handbag, and there were no signs of a struggle.

The five-foot-two-inch-tall high school senior had been stabbed several times in the chest with a knife. The stab wounds, not drowning, were the cause of death. First indications did not suggest a sexual assault, but forensic tests showed there had been one. Police theorized that the murder had occurred at the reservoir at approximately 11:00 P.M., about an hour and twenty minutes after the abduction.

Less than two weeks later, a second murder of a young woman in Morris County sent fear through local residents. The victim was twenty-five-year-old Deirdre O'Brien, a college graduate with an art history major who was working as a waitress at The Library, a restaurant in Cedar Knolls. Her Honda Civic had been forced off winding, wooded

Washington Valley Road not far from her parents' home. A Morris County Parks Department patrolman found the car at 2:10 A.M. on December 5, its lights on, the key in the ignition, and Miss O'Brien's purse on the front seat.

An hour and a half later an agitated trucker at a rest stop on Interstate 80 in Allamuchy called for help on his CB radio. A young woman, bleeding badly, had banged on the door of his truck, awakening him. "Make sure you send an ambulance," he said. Deirdre O'Brien was taken to Hackettstown Community Hospital, where she was pronounced dead on arrival at 5:10 A.M.

Police hesitated to link the two murders, although they noted the similarities. Deirdre O'Brien had died of multiple stab wounds to her chest. As with Amie Hoffman, sexual assault was not suspected at first, but was indicated later by forensic tests. There were important clues in both murders. Indeed, O'Brien had given a description of her killer to the truck driver as she waited for an ambulance. And police had found distinct tire tracks of the perpetrator's car at the scene of the Washington Valley abduction.

On May 12, 1983, James Koedatich, thirty-four, a Morristown handyman, was indicted for the abduction, sexual assault, and murder of Deirdre O'Brien. Koedatich had been in custody since January 18. He was not a model citizen. Released from a Florida prison in August 1982 after serving eleven years of a twenty-year sentence for strangling the person he lived with, he had also strangled a cellmate while in prison, though apparently in self-defense.

While awaiting trial in Warren County for the murder of Deirdre O'Brien, James J. (Jerry) Koedatich was indicted in Morris County for the abduction, sexual assault, and murder of Amie Hoffman. The key to this indictment, as to the prior one, was forensic evidence from Koedatich's 1970 Chevrolet.

A series of legal maneuvers and delays postponed the trial of Koedatich for either murder until October 1984, when he went on trial for the murder of Amie Hoffman in Morris County Superior Court, Judge Arnold M. Stein presiding. The assistant prosecutor, Michael Rubbinaccio, explained how Koedatich had come to the attention of investigators. In January 1983 Koedatich had reported a knife attack on himself, a false story of how he had been forced off the road on Route 24 and attacked. This odd tale made him a suspect in the Hoffman-O'Brien murders and led to his arrest. Three prosecution witnesses gave varying descriptions of the man who had accosted Amie Hoffman in the shopping mall parking lot. Rubbinaccio admitted that the evidence in the case was mainly circumstantial—principally, fibers and microscopic pieces of foam rubber from Hoffman's skirt that matched material found on the carpet and seatcovers of Koedatich's 1970 Chevrolet.

The jury, having deliberated for eleven hours, found the defendant guilty on all five counts, including first-degree murder. In the sentencing phase of the trial the same jury, after four and a half hours of discussion, ordered a sentence of death by lethal injection.

On February 19, 1985, Koedatich went on trial before Superior Court Judge Reginald Stanton in Belvidere for the murder of Deirdre O'Brien. This jury, too, found the defendant guilty, but could not agree unanimously on the death penalty. Koedatich drew life imprisonment with no chance of parole for thirty years. In imposing the sentence Judge Stanton made no secret of his own opinion of James J. Koedatich, calling him "evil, depraved, and dangerous."

The Carnival Killing

Dawn Keimel, eleven, went with several of her friends to the Jefferson Township Rescue Squad's annual carnival at Lakeside Field on Route 15 South, across from the Pathmark supermarket. She apparently argued with one or more of them, and at around 11:00 P.M. she left by herself to walk home through a wooded, exurban area. She lived at 126 Schwartz Boulevard in the Prospect Point section of Jefferson. Taking a shortcut that would bring her out on Espanong Road, about half a mile from Lakeside Field, she would then have another two miles or so to walk to reach her home.

She never made it. Before midnight her parents reported her missing. Police officers, firefighters, and rescue squad volunteers searched for eighteen hours without finding any trace of her. Then a young girl walking down the driveway of her house on Espanong Road saw a body lying partially concealed in a wooded area on the front lawn. It was Dawn Keimel, dead. Her corduroy pants and blouse were in disarray, leading police to believe she had been sexually assaulted. She had died of massive head injuries, evidently caused by being hit several times with a blunt object such as a tire iron or a pipe.

A motorist driving on Espanong Road at about the time Dawn Keimel reached the spot where she died had seen a car parked off the road and had noticed a muscular, athletic-looking black man standing beside it. A suspect who fit that description—blacks being fairly rare in the area— lived in nearby Mount Arlington (or at least gave that as his address on his driver's license) and had lost control of his girlfriend's car, crashing into a ditch on Weldon Road, not far from the murder site, a few minutes after midnight on the night of Dawn Keimel's death.

He was Richard Johnson, twenty-two, originally from Belmar, on the Jersey Shore. As the Morris County *Daily Record* noted, the young man's history was "fraught with trouble." Johnson had been paroled from Rahway State Prison in May after serving three years and eight months of an eight-year sentence for aggravated manslaughter. In 1980, apparently enraged at an obscene gesture by one of a pair of hitchhikers, he had deliberately driven his van into both of them at a Route 35 traffic circle in Wall Township, killing one and injuring the other.

Upon parole, Johnson shared a camping trailer with his Mount Arlington girlfriend at the Mahlon Dickerson Reservation, a sprawling Morris County park on semirural Weldon Road. From the beginning of the investigation the newspapers referred to Johnson as the "prime [and even as the only] suspect." When police tracked him down at his place of employment, the Mayflower Moving company in Morristown, Johnson went voluntarily to the Jefferson police headquarters on Weldon Road north of the Mahlon Dickerson Reservation for questioning.

What happened there over the next nine hours completely blew any case the prosecution might have developed—and almost certainly could have developed—against Richard Johnson. Although the police considered Johnson a suspect from the very beginning, they pretended otherwise. Johnson matched the description given by the passing motorist on Espanong Road, and the suspect's car accident on Weldon Road showed he had been near the scene of the crime at the time it occurred. Yet Johnson was told he was being questioned about a burglary. He was not given a Miranda warning until two hours after the interrogation began— in fact, not until he tried to leave the police station and was told to stay put. When Johnson asked for an attorney, his request was denied. He asked permission to call his mother and was told no.

A few minutes before 9:00 P.M., after nine hours of intensive questioning, much of it by Mark Prach of the Morris County Prosecutor's Office, Johnson made his move. He took a flying leap at the double-paned thermal window in the Jefferson police station, crashed through it to the outdoors, and lit out for the nearby woods. Prach was alone in the room with Johnson at the time of the escape. Police in the station immediately took off after the suspect, but he got away. Johnson's breakout made the front page of the *New York Post* the next morning.

Forty-two hours later at the office of the *Asbury Park Press,* seventy miles away, Richard Johnson, accompanied by his attorney, Charles Moriarty, surrendered to Monmouth County authorities. Johnson's fear of what might happen to him as a fugitive had evidently prompted this highly visible capitulation. Back in Morris County, Prosecutor Lee Trumbull promised that the questioning of Johnson would resume. And so it did, as soon as Johnson was returned in handcuffs and leg shackles to the Jefferson police station. Once more the interrogation was led by the determined Mark Prach. Once more Johnson maintained his innocence. The suspect still had not been charged with murder.

The police were sure they had Dawn Keimel's killer. Under Prach's relentless questioning, Johnson had made a number of incriminating statements. Unfortunately, there were constitutional problems—Fifth and Sixth Amendment problems—stemming from the interrogation. And they were fatal. The defense argued against the admissibility of most of the evidence, claiming clear violations of Johnson's legal rights. The arguments on this matter dragged on; Johnson remained in jail. Two years later Superior Court Judge Daniel R. Coburn found that Prach had engaged in "devious, unsanctioned, and, mostly, unconstitutional conduct" in his questioning of Johnson on July 25 and 27, 1984. Coburn recognized the "tragedy," as he called it, of the prosecution's behavior. But there it was. Most of the apparently damning evidence against Johnson was legally worthless, including any mention of his flight to Asbury Park.

Prosecutor Lee Trumbull put the best possible face on it. Maybe his office could still proceed against Johnson, he said. Meanwhile, an appeal of Coburn's decision would be pursued in the Appellate Division of the Superior Court. The prosecution got no satisfaction there. A three-judge panel, noting "wholesale violations" of the suspect's rights, upheld Judge Coburn's decision. Few who had followed the case were much surprised. Johnson's public defender, James K. Smith, stated that "even with the statements, there wasn't any realistic likelihood of him being convicted. They simply do not have evidence to convict him of anything."

The Morris County Prosecutor's Office eventually reached the same conclusion. In June 1990 Johnson was offered a plea bargain. If he would plead guilty to aggravated manslaughter in the death of Dawn Keimel, he would receive a ten-year sentence. The time he had already spent in jail and prison would count toward the completion of this sentence. (Johnson had accumulated time for a parole violation in his Monmouth County conviction as well as for drug and assault charges while in prison. He was not a model prisoner.)

But he was very nearly free to leave. Yes, Johnson admitted, he had been preparing to break into an unoccupied house on Espanong Road on that carnival night in 1984. He was startled by the presence of Dawn Keimel, who was taking an unforeseeable shortcut at an odd hour and came upon him from behind. Impulsively, he began bashing the eleven-year-old girl with a tire iron. He did not explain the sexual assault that had also occurred.

Although Superior Court Judge Reginald Stanton had little enthusiasm for the plea bargain, he accepted it because "of serious proof problems in the case. If you [Richard Johnson] went to trial," Stanton said, "there is a substantial chance of acquittal, not because you are innocent, but because the state could not prove your guilt."

In March 1993 Richard Johnson completed his ten-year sentence and returned to life on the outside. The state parole board made it a point to advise authorities in Monmouth and Morris counties that the thirty-one-year-old Johnson, the killer of two people in two separate incidents, was back on the street.

54 Blind Faith: A Contract

LACEY TOWNSHIP

Toms River Man Pulls off Parkway; Says Thugs Shot Wife, Slugged Him

SEPTEMBER 7, 1984

Between midnight and 1:00 A.M. Robert O. Marshall, forty-four, and his wife, Maria, forty-two, were returning to their home in Toms River after an evening of gambling in Atlantic City. A couple of miles north of the Barnegat toll plaza on the Garden State Parkway, Marshall decided to check a tire on his 1981 ivory Cadillac Eldorado. He claimed it felt "wishy-washy." Easing his car left off the highway into the Oyster Creek picnic area, a wooded, unlighted spot between the north- and southbound lanes, he made a left turn, passing a "Do Not Enter" sign.

According to Marshall, he stopped, got out of the car, went to look at the tire—"bulging on the bottom like it had lost air"—and became aware of a dark-colored sedan with its headlights off pulling into the picnic area behind him. As he kneeled beside his faulty tire, paying no further attention to the second car, someone came up to him in the darkness and bopped him on the head. He heard Maria cry, "Oh, my God!" (or so he recalled at the trial, although not before that). Then he passed out. When he woke up, his wife lay across the front seat, shot twice in the back. She was dead. About two thousand dollars they had won at blackjack was missing.

That was the story Robert O. Marshall told the state police and others; its exact details varied from time to time. The story had a number of flaws, the most obvious of which was that the tire, although indeed flat, had been neatly slashed on its sidewall. The air would have escaped immediately. The feel in the car would have been bump-bump-bump, not wishy-washy, and the tire would have been quickly chewed up. In other words, this was not a highway-incurred cut—not unless a purposeful and animated knife had been prowling the Garden State Parkway.

There were other difficulties with Rob Marshall's story. Why had the assailant or assailants merely knocked him unconscious but then proceeded to murder Maria, the mild, unthreatening mother of three teenage sons—execute her, really? Why had Marshall taken out $1.5 million in life insurance on his wife with himself as beneficiary? Why had Rob forged Maria's name to a $100,000 home equity loan application? Why had Rob and a woman not his wife been planning to rent a little bungalow on the Shore? Why had Maria hired a private detective to follow her husband's movements? Why, prior to the murder, had Rob been making a series of long-distance telephone calls to Louisiana? Why, after forty-seven-year-old Robert Cumber, identified by police as a suspect in Maria's murder, was arrested in Bossier City, Louisiana, did Rob adjourn to a motel room and consume thirty to forty tranquilizers in an apparent suicide attempt?

State police and Ocean County detectives strongly suspected Robert Marshall's culpability from the outset. But for many weeks Marshall, who owned an apparently thriving (though not thriving enough to cover his mounting debts) insurance and estate-planning business, seemed to assume, against all logic and common sense, that his status in Toms River made him invulnerable to prosecution. According to Joe McGinniss in his book *Blind Faith*, Marshall told a brother-in-law, a lawyer, that "no one could possibly suspect me of any involvement in Maria's death." Why was that? Because "I am, quite simply, far too prominent. I'm much too high up the civic ladder."

The Ocean County prosecutor, Edward J. Turnbach, unawed by Marshall's self-perceived high position in the community, felt certain he had enough evidence to convict the insurance broker of "soliciting another" to kill Maria, his wife of twenty years. On December 19, 1984, Marshall was arrested and charged. That same day Turnbach also announced the arrest of Larry N. Thompson, forty-one, of Fairview-Alpha, Louisiana, a mechanic and short-order cook, the man accused of actually shooting Maria Marshall at the Oyster Creek picnic area.

As it happened, an indicted co-conspirator arrested earlier, Billy Wayne McKinnon, forty-two, of Greenwood, Louisiana, a former deputy sheriff in Shreveport, had angled for a plea bargain and had been promised a greatly reduced sentence in return for telling all he knew. McKinnon unburdened himself in a twenty-five-page written statement so "devastating," according to Superior Court Judge William H. Huber, that it would make a fair trial of Marshall impossible anywhere in New Jersey. Prosecutor Turnbach made no secret of his personal opinion. He believed the defendant "should be tried, convicted, and executed, but that he should receive a fair trial first."

The trial was moved from Toms River in Ocean County to Mays Landing in Atlantic County. It made little difference. The evidence was more than convincing; it was appalling. Rob Marshall had taken out eight separate insurance policies on his wife's life, the last one for $130,000 the day before the murder. He had made twenty-eight phone calls to a hardware store in Caddo Parish, Louisiana, the contact point for the murder contract. All of this was on the record, and there was more. Marshall confessed to having carried on a torrid fourteen-month affair with Mrs. Sarann Kraushaar, a former vice-principal at the Pinelands Regional High School in Tuckerton. He admitted to having pursued other women since Maria's death.

Billy Wayne McKinnon's testimony did not picture Marshall in an appealing light. McKinnon claimed he had suggested to the Toms River insurance broker that a gunshot wound in Marshall's leg or arm would lend credence to his robbery alibi. Rob would have none of it. Not only did Maria's husband want to be struck on the head rather than shot, he wanted to be hit lightly "so as not to become an idiot [or so said McKinnon] for the rest of his life." Prosecutor Kevin W. Kelly called the defendant a "greedy, desperate coward."

It got worse. The prosecution played a forty-minute audio tape made by Marshall twenty days after his wife's murder and marked "to be opened only in the event of my death." This recording, made at the Best Western Leisure Inn in Lakewood, had a special poignancy. It was taped on the night of his suicide attempt (which the prosecution maintained was nothing but a staged event), and it was recorded in the very room, Room 16, where Rob Marshall and Sarann Kraushaar had often rendezvoused. On the tape Marshall admitted virtually everything the prosecution had uncovered—except the conspiracy to murder his wife. Even so, he said, innocent as he was, a jury would be "compelled" to convict him of the crime. Evidently Rob Marshall was beginning to understand that social prominence in Toms River, while satisfying, was no guarantee of absolution.

After playing the tape, the state rested its case.

Taking the witness stand in his own defense, Robert O. Marshall told his bulging-tire tale again. He admitted he had lied when at first he denied his affair with Sarann Kraushaar. He claimed he still loved Maria "terribly," but said, yes, he had persisted in sending his mistress Sarann tape-recorded love messages for some time after Maria's murder.

The prosecution appeared to have an airtight case against Marshall, but the one against his co-defendant, Larry N. Thompson, the alleged triggerman, had some holes. The defense suggested, quite effectively, that Billy Wayne McKinnon, the man who had fingered Thompson in return for a light sentence, was a chronic liar. Might he not have named Thompson simply to save his own skin? Certainly prosecutor Kevin W. Kelly was finding it hard to tie the man from Fairview-Alpha to the Garden State Parkway except through the unpersuasive testimony of Billy Wayne McKinnon.

Superior Court Judge Manuel Greenberg charged the jury on the morning of September 4, 1986. Two days later, after a total of six hours of deliberation, the Mays Landing panel of peers, seven men and five women, found Robert O. Marshall guilty of conspiring to murder his wife and guilty of hiring someone to do it. Prosecutor Kelly spent just ninety seconds arguing for the death penalty, but it was enough. In less than two hours the jury returned again, this time with a recommendation that Marshall be executed. Judge Greenberg said, "It is incumbent on me to pronounce the sentence of death upon you."

Larry N. Thompson was more fortunate. The jury acquitted him of conspiring to murder Maria Marshall and also acquitted him of committing the murder. He and his wife, Wanda, smiled at the cameras and climbed into their silver Dodge van to return to Louisiana.

Robert Cumber, the hardware store clerk in Bossier City, Louisiana, was not so fortunate. Tried in June 1986, after turning down a plea bargain on a charge of committing insurance fraud, he was convicted of conspiracy to commit murder. Cumber, who prosecutors said had "brokered the contract" between Marshall and his wife's killer, but who assuredly had *not* pulled the trigger in the case, drew a life sentence with a mandatory thirty years before parole—faring far worse than the actual murderer.

But who was the actual murderer? Who had fired the two shots into Maria Marshall's back on that dark night at the Oyster Creek picnic area? McKinnon? Thompson? Someone else?

The answer remained a mystery. Perhaps even Rob Marshall didn't know for sure.

Policewoman Powlett's Death

PLAINFIELD

Policewoman Slain by Drifter Who Held Her at Gunpoint

MARCH 14, 1985

At about 9:50 P.M. on March 14, 1985, two Plainfield police officers, Abigail Powlett, thirty-three, and Kimberly Schlough, twenty-seven, responded to a report of "a bunch of shots" at the Meadowbrook Village Apartment complex at 1001 East Front Street. Both women were part of a street crime task force and were in plain clothes.

The two officers got out of their car, and Powlett approached a man in the yard who fit the description of the suspect. The man, Kim Hailey, twenty-six, a drifter whose last known address was 8 Sanford Avenue, Plainfield, somehow overpowered officer Powlett, grabbed her .38-caliber service revolver, and held it to her head. According to Plainfield's acting police chief, John Propsner, Hailey dragged Powlett about 125 feet, then stood over her, straddling her body.

Office Schlough radioed for help. Among the police to arrive at the scene was Lieutenant John Driscoll, who began to negotiate with Hailey. The assailant was truculent but lucid and did not seem to be under the influence of drugs or alcohol. Propsner ordered a sharpshooter to get into position, while the police tried to avoid provoking the gunman—who nonetheless said several times, "I'm going to kill her, and I'm going to go with her."

During the twenty-five-minute standoff, Hailey forced Powlett to get on her knees twice and plead with her fellow officers not to allow her to die. Suddenly, for no apparent reason, Hailey shot Powlett once in the head. The police who had assembled at Meadowbrook Village immediately opened fire, hitting Hailey in the right leg, abdomen, lung, and groin. He fell beside his victim.

Both officer Powlett and her attacker were rushed to Muhlenberg Hospital in Plainfield. Abigail Powlett was pronounced dead at 2:25 A.M. Kim Hailey died about an hour later.

Abigail Powlett was the first woman police officer in New Jersey to die in the line of duty. Her murder raised questions about two-woman patrols. Acting Chief Propsner said the policy permitting such patrols (rare as they were in Plainfield and elsewhere) would not be changed: "Policewomen are police officers," he said, emphasizing that women go through the same training as men and are assumed to have the same capabilities. Mayor Richard L. Taylor called Powlett a "streetwise, popular, proud, and gifted officer." The city had employed women police officers since 1972.

Abigail Powlett, who lived in Fanwood with her two children, Noreen, eleven, and Jayson, ten, was one of 9 women on the 115-officer Plainfield force. She had served for three years, most recently as an undercover officer in the narcotics unit for the prosecutor's office, an assignment for which she had received a commendation.

Funeral services were held at the Mount Zion Baptist Church in Boonton, the hometown of Powlett's mother, Mrs. Frances Burden. Nearly 2,000 policemen and policewomen paid their last respects. A 250-car funeral cortege accompanied the flag-draped oak casket to the Evergreen Cemetery, 65 Martin Luther King Avenue, Morristown. The color guard fired a three-gun salute.

56

By Ninja
Possessed

MONTVILLE

Man in Black Ninja Outfit
Kills First of Five Victims

—NOVEMBER 15, 1988

At about 7:00 P.M. on November 15, 1988, Roy Edwards, forty-three, and his two daughters, ages nine and seven, approached the front door of their rented home at 3 Willard Lane, Montville. They were met by a strange sight. A tall, thin man in a black ninja jumpsuit, black mask, black combat boots, and surgical gloves sprang from behind some front-yard shrubbery and forced them inside at gunpoint. Inside the house the ninja intruder demanded money. He seemed to know that Roy Edwards, a Jamaican who was employed as the registrar at the Wilfred Beauty Academy in Newark, had started a sideline business of selling rare coins from his home.

The intruder, a light-skinned black man who wore glasses, proceeded to handcuff, gag, and blindfold Edwards and his daughters and took them to the upstairs master bedroom, where he sexually assaulted the girls. After about an hour and a quarter, Edwards's wife, Irene, forty-three, returned home from her work as a registered nurse in Paterson. Having difficulty opening the front door, she sensed that something was amiss. Suddenly, the door opened, and the ninja assailant hit her on the head with a blunt object, probably the .22-caliber handgun he was carrying.

The man took her first to the master bedroom, where she, too, was handcuffed, gagged, and blindfolded. He then took her to another up-stairs room and demanded money. She told him the only money she had was in her purse. He took seven hundred dollars or so from the purse, after which he assaulted her. His repeated sexual attacks on the girls and later their mother, along with beatings of their father and insistent demands for money, continued over nearly a four-hour period.

At about 11:00 P.M. Roy Edwards, seeing his chance, or so he thought, ran from the master bedroom and raced down the stairs. The gunman gave chase, catching his prey in the family room, but Edwards managed to break free and burst through a sliding screen door at the back of the house. The gunman followed and fired; the bullet hit Edwards in the back of the neck, killing him. A pair of cheap, nonpolice handcuffs still bound the victim's hands behind his back.

At this point Irene Edwards smashed an upstairs window and began screaming, "Help me! Somebody's attacking my husband!" A man who was walking his dog nearby phoned the Montville police. By the time they arrived, the ninja killer was gone.

An intensive investigation failed to locate the bespectacled man in black. Police viewed the case as an attempted coin robbery accompanied by sexual and other physical brutality. Detectives tried to link Edwards with his killer but found no connection. The bizarre ninja costume the killer wore while he terrorized the Edwards family was a point of interest but not in itself much of a lead.

Three years later, on October 9 and 10, 1991, the ninja killer struck again—this time in public and this time with a frighteningly expanded arsenal that included two machine guns, hand grenades, homemade bombs, and a samurai sword. He apparently intended to kill a sizable number of people, perhaps as many as thirty, but he was stopped at four.

This time there was no mystery about his identity, even though he began his rampage in ninja-warrior garb, a gas mask, and a bulletproof vest. He was Joseph M. Harris, thirty-five, an ascetic-looking unemployed Paterson resident who had been dismissed a year and a half earlier from his job as a mail clerk at the Ridgewood Post Office. That was two months after his supervisor, Carol Ott, thirty, had filed a harassment complaint against him with the Ridgewood police.

Carol Ott and her boyfriend, Cornelius Kasten, thirty-six, were the first to die. They shared a Talsman Court home in Wayne, which was Harris's initial stop. At about 11:30 P.M. on Wednesday, October 9, Harris broke into their residence and shot Kasten, apparently without warning, as he watched TV in the basement. Harris then went upstairs, where, after a furious struggle, he slashed Ott to death with a samurai sword in her living room. At the time of her death Carol Ott was the night supervisor at the post office in Ridgewood; Cornelius Kasten was the owner of Bergen Express Trucking Company of Lyndhurst.

Joseph M. Harris had just begun his campaign of revenge against the U.S. Postal Service. In his view there were plenty of other people at the downtown Ridgewood post office who, like Carol Ott, deserved to die. He went to Ridgewood, armed and ready to greet the shift beginning at 3:00 A.M. At about 2:15 A.M. a Postal Service driver, Marcello Collado, arrived to make a delivery, and Harris took a potshot at him. It missed. The driver noticed that the gunman was wearing a gas mask. Shortly thereafter the ninja-dressed marauder shot and killed two mail handlers when they showed up early for work: Joseph VanderPaauw, fifty-nine, of Prospect Park, and Donald McNaught, sixty-three, of Pompton Lakes.

Collado, the mail driver, reported his brush with death to the Ridgewood police. Two police officers went immediately to the post office, where Harris confronted them. The ninja killer lit and tossed what looked like a pipe bomb or a stick of dynamite at one of the officers. Both retreated to wait for backup. Twenty seconds later they heard a blast inside the building.

When Carol Ott did not arrive for work by 3:00 A.M., the Ridgewood police phoned the Wayne police, asking them to check her home. Meanwhile, other postal workers were kept at a safe distance from the building as police tried unsuccessfully to reach Harris by phone.

At 6:30 A.M., seventeen Bergen County SWAT-team officers entered the post office through an observation gallery, a kind of catwalk for supervisors to oversee their workers. By then they knew that Carol Ott and Cornelius Kasten had been murdered. A hostage negotiator talked to Harris, first through a bullhorn, then face to face. There were no hostages in the building, only the two murdered men in a basement lavatory, but the SWAT team didn't know that at the beginning.

After about twenty minutes Harris surrendered meekly and was taken in handcuffs and foot shackles to the Bergen County Courthouse in Hackensack. Police then checked the post office, the Ott-Kasten home, and Harris's apartment for possible booby traps. None were found at the post office, which suffered minimal damage, or the Talsman Court home, but Harris's apartment in Paterson was another matter. Bomb experts defused a battery-run explosive device set to go off when the door to his room was opened.

Inside Harris's apartment police found, among other things, pairs of cheap handcuffs of the kind used in Edwards's slaying. They also discovered that Harris had invested and lost ten thousand dollars in a business deal with Roy Edwards. The handcuffs, the failed business venture, and, most of all, the ninja costuming convinced Montville police that their case was now solved. In the Montville assault Harris's only weapon had been a .22-caliber Ruger Mark II—the same gun that killed Kasten, in fact—but by the time of his Wayne-Ridgewood rampage he had added a nine-millimeter Uzi and a nine-millimeter MAC10.

Joseph Harris was first tried in Morristown for the murder of Roy Edwards. Morris Country Assistant Prosecutor Thomas Critchley announced that his office would seek the death penalty. Defense lawyer Joel Harris (no relation to the defendant) tried to show that Harris's life was as cursed as the defendant thought it was. Born in the Clinton State Reformatory for Women to a mother whose five children were all fathered by different men, Harris was raised by a great-aunt. As he grew older Harris came to believe that a ninja spirit inhabited his body, helping him deal with betrayal and sorrow.

The jury weighed the evidence and convicted Joseph Harris of murdering Roy Edwards. A week later the same panel, while recognizing some mitigating factors, recommended that he be executed. Superior Court Judge Herbert Friend pronounced the death sentence. Harris still faced trial for committing the two murders in Wayne and two in Ridgewood.

An Ill-Fated Party in Sparta

When Lance Montie, seventeen, a senior at Sparta High School, invited some friends to his parents' Sparta Commons townhouse condominium at 101 Wagon Wheel Road for a party starting at 5:30 P.M. on Saturday, February 11, 1989, he set in motion a chain of events that made national headlines and left one youngster dead and a number of lives in tatters.

The party was unsupervised. With his parents away on a weekend business trip, Montie, a newcomer to Sparta High School, took the opportunity to invite ten young people to his parents' home. Six of them left before 11:00 P.M., leaving Montie and three others in the townhouse. One of the others was Michael Ardila, nineteen, of Wantage, a graduate of Verona High School in Essex County and unemployed at the time. Another was Donna Shaban, seventeen, a Sparta High School senior, former cheerleader, and Ardila's girlfriend. Ardila and Shaban had become acquainted at a Narcotics Anonymous session about a month earlier. The third person was Anthony Pompelio, seventeen, a senior and formerly a wrestler for the Sparta High School team. He was the son of Roxbury's municipal attorney.

Montie and the others stayed overnight at the two-story townhouse. Although investigators at first found no evidence of drug use, it soon came to light that cocaine had been shared that night by Monte, Ardila, and Shaban. And despite an attempt to get rid of some liquor bottles, there were signs of alcohol consumption, apparently vodka, beer, and wine coolers. Lance Montie, according to his testimony, went to sleep in an upstairs bedroom and did not awaken until about 11:00 Sunday morning. Downstairs in the foyer he found Anthony Pompelio's body, stabbed seven times in the head, neck, and torso. He called the police. The stabbing, it turned out, had occurred at around 7:30 that morning. Tony was dead. Mike Ardila and Donna Shaban were gone. Also missing was a 1988 maroon Jeep Cherokee belonging to Tony Pompelio's father.

The general outline of what had happened soon became clear. Donna Shaban phoned her mother on Sunday to say she was with Ardila and that he would kill her if she revealed their whereabouts. Later in the day she called a friend with the same message. Police issued an all-points bulletin and a nationwide alert for Michael Ardila as the prime suspect in the murder of Anthony Pompelio. But the main search focused on Sussex County and nearby counties in New Jersey, New York, and Pennsylvania.

Ardila had taken some money from the Montie home, but not much. By the time he and Shaban reached Texas he was out of cash and needed gas for the Cherokee. A trucker on Interstate 40 in tiny Groom, Texas, fifty miles east of Amarillo, saw Donna Shaban being pushed or thrown from the Jeep Cherokee at milepost 124, or so he thought. (In fact, she had apparently asked Ardila to let her out on the highway, and he had done so.) The trucker drove Shaban to Texas Red's Truck Stop in Groom, where Jerry Gaines, a Carson County sheriff's deputy, questioned her about what had happened. At first he found her story hard to believe, but a phone call to the Sparta police confirmed the essential truth of what she said.

Meanwhile, Ardila had stopped for gas at the Parker Self-Serve station off Interstate 40 near Amarillo. He tried to pay for it with a credit card issued to Anthony Pompelio's father's law firm. When it failed to clear the electronic checking system, Ardila sauntered out to his car, trying to act casual, and took off in a hurry. The gas station attendant phoned the Amarillo police to report the theft of gasoline and then called Exxon regarding the suspicious credit card.

Within minutes the New Mexico State Police were alerted, and within the hour they spotted the maroon Jeep Cherokee near Tucumcari, speeding west on Interstate 40. When Ardila, reaching speeds up to ninety-five miles per hour, crashed through a roadblock east of Santa Rosa, police opened fire and gave chase. Ardila careened left onto U.S. Highway 84, heading south. The driver of the lead patrol car, getting permission to ram the Cherokee, did so, causing the Jeep to veer off the highway and flip onto its roof. That ended the chase and the fugitive's eighteen-hundred-mile flight. Police arrested Ardila, who spent the night in the Guadalupe County Jail in Santa Rosa. (Shaban spent the same night in protective custody in the Carson County Jail in Panhandle, Texas.)

Extradited to New Jersey, Michael Ardila was arraigned on four counts: knowing and purposeful murder, first-degree kidnapping, possession of a knife with the intent to use it, and theft of a motor vehicle. At the Sussex County Courthouse in Newton, Superior Court Judge N. Peter Conforti set bail at $750,000. The question on most people's minds was not so much "Did Ardila do it?" as "Why?" The single eyewitness to the murder, Donna Shaban, would presumably answer that question at the trial.

Testimony in the case began on September 12, 1990. Of the three survivors of the murder scene, Lance Montie was the first to testify, Donna Shaban next, and Michael Ardila not at all. Montie said that Shaban and Ardila had gone to New York City on the afternoon of the party to buy cocaine. They returned with a gram and a half, all of which Montie, Shaban, and Ardila used during the night. Montie and Ardila also drank a fair amount of vodka. The last thing Montie remembered seeing early the next morning was the clock on the VCR. It read 3:00 A.M. The first thing he remembered being aware of after that was the phone ringing at about 11:00 A.M. It was a friend calling his mother. When Montie, walking downstairs, saw the bloodstains on the wall and carpet, Pompelio's body lying face-down on the floor, and a bloody, four-inch, folding hunting knife on the arm of a chair, he panicked. He knocked the knife to the floor "because I didn't want to look at it."

Donna Shaban's testimony added some details to the picture of the party. According to her story, Ardila, sitting in a loveseat downstairs, knife in hand, ordered her to undress. He then took his own clothes off, sexually assaulted her, and cut her leg. She began crying and calling for Pompelio, who, like Montie, was sleeping upstairs.

When Pompelio awoke and started to come down, Ardila hid behind the staircase and stabbed him in the back, then in the shoulder. He continued stabbing Pompelio, finally slitting his throat. Shaban's memory of all this was rather sketchy, and her response to many questions at the trial was that she didn't remember. She had been under a great deal of stress, she said, and after the murder there had been "a bunch of people badgering me." (She evidently meant the police.)

Donna Shaban's affair with Mike Ardila was definitely over by the time of the trial. Although she acknowledged they had had sex on their first date and frequently thereafter, she testified that she had never loved him and had not agreed to have sex on the morning of the murder. From

the witness stand she made her feelings emphatic: "You are a bastard
. . . You killed someone . . . You're going to die."

He wasn't going to die, because the murder was not tried as a capital
punishment case. Jurors were told to ignore Shaban's outburst. Ardila's
attorney, Jack Hoffinger, said that her accusation of sexual assault was a
pure fabrication, "absolutely false." He pointed out that Donna Shaban
had kept a travel diary of her flight with Ardila, in which she had written,
among other things, "We have been on the run 24 hours." Hoffinger
suggested that her story of being a hostage was implausible. The defense
attorney called no witnesses. He based his case solely on Donna Shaban's
credibility.

The jury of seven men and five women agreed in part with the defense
attorney. But only in part. They acquitted Ardila of sexual assault and
kidnapping—but they found him guilty of knowing and purposeful murder. Donna Shaban's narrative of the events leading up to the murder and
the events afterward did not convince the jury. But her description of
Mike Ardila stabbing Tony Pompelio in the back, chasing him around the
house while continuing to stab him, trapping him against the closed front
door, and slashing his throat registered as horrifyingly true.

On November 15, 1990, Superior Court Judge Donald Collester passed
sentence. "What Michael Ardila did," Collester said, "was the cruelest of
crimes, and he must endure the cruelest of penalties. When Michael
Ardila killed Tony Pompelio, he showed no mercy, and he can expect no
mercy from me." Judge Collester sentenced Ardila to life imprisonment,
with a minimum term of thirty years before being eligible for parole. It
was the maximum penalty he could impose.

58 Heikkila's Night Out

BERNARDS TOWNSHIP
Heikkila Murders Adoptive Parents, Then Treats His Girlfriend to Dinner
JANUARY 29, 1991

Dr. Richard Heikkila, forty-eight, a neurology professor at the Robert Wood Johnson Medical School in Piscataway, enjoyed an international reputation for his groundbreaking research into Parkinson's disease. His wife, Dawn, forty-six, was a real estate agent with Burgdorff Realtors in Basking Ridge. Their younger son, Joshua, nineteen, a freshman at Dartmouth College, had been valedictorian of the class of 1990 at Ridge High School. This family of high achievers lived comfortably on Goltra Drive in Bernards Township.

Oh, yes. There was one other Heikkila—Matthew, twenty, the adopted son of Richard and Dawn—who did not quite live up to the standards of the rest of the family. Neighbors and friends remembered Matthew's adoptive parents as "caring and thoughtful." Nobody ever described Matthew that way, certainly not after the horrific events of January 29, 1991.

Matthew Heikkila had been a problem for some time. An unremarkable, mediocre student, in contrast to his popular, brilliant brother, Matthew disliked Joshua intensely, believing that his parents favored their natural son over him. When the two were in elementary school, their parents attended classes to learn how to cope with Matthew, who felt unloved despite their best efforts to treat both boys the same.

Matt's psychiatric problems became more pronounced after his graduation from high school. In November 1989, at the age of nineteen, he became engaged to a girl from Ecuador. When he went to Ecuador to meet her parents, they quickly called off the engagement upon learning that Heikkila's real age was five years less than the twenty-four he claimed. Depressed, Matt resorted to painkillers and Valium, wound up in a Quito hospital, and had to be shipped home. His concerned parents checked him into Overlook Hospital in Summit, but he checked himself out.

Soon afterward he bought a handgun. He needed it, he said, because a drug dealer from Colombia was planning to kill him. In fact, he phoned police on December 3, 1989, with the news that someone was about to kill him. His father overheard the call and asked Matthew about it. Matt, in no mood to explain, pointed the loaded gun at his father and said, "If you're not quiet, I'll put a bullet through your head."

This was a step too far. His parents reported the incident, and police charged Matthew Heikkila with making terroristic threats. Richard and Dawn Heikkila, who wanted their son to receive treatment, not punishment, refused to testify at the grand jury hearing. The jury returned an indictment anyway. Attempts by his parents to get it dismissed proved futile, and in July 1990, in a nonjury trial, Superior Court Judge Michael R. Imbriani found Heikkila not guilty of the criminal charge by reason of insanity. Released to the custody of his parents, he was warned to stay away from guns, alcohol, and drugs.

Between the time of Matthew's 1989 threat against his father and the judge's verdict of not guilty, Heikkila's parents twice committed him to the Carrier Foundation, a private psychiatric hospital in Belle Mead, once from December 4 through 30, then again from January 8 through 22. Although at home Matt seemed to be deeply troubled, he functioned quite well socially. Handsome and flirtatious, he easily attracted girlfriends, at least two of whom (besides his Ecuadorian ex-fiancée) came to regret their involvement with him. During this period he was taking Proxilin, a psychotropic drug intended for the management of schizophrenia.

Heikkila began dating a nineteen-year-old girl from Long Branch in late 1990. After about three months she became pregnant. A week or so later Matt told her he had fallen in love with someone else, but he urged her to have the baby anyway. In January 1991, while dating his new girlfriend, Matt took a recently purchased double-barreled twenty-gauge shotgun to Long Branch and asked his former girlfriend to marry him. She declined. He pointed the gun at her head and said he would kill her if she revealed their relationship. (After Heikkila's arrest, she had an abortion.)

Matthew's new girlfriend, Marta Morales of Union City, attended the College of Saint Elizabeth in Convent Station. He had met her in October when the two of them were working at the nearby Madison Hotel. She would be celebrating her twentieth birthday on January 29, 1991, and Matthew decided to make it a special occasion. He would take her to dinner at a fine New York City restaurant. To do so, he needed a car and a credit card or two. (His sketchy job history, marred by accusations of theft, had not made him financially independent or credit worthy.)

He took out a box of shotgun shells, marked one shell "Mom," another "Mom and Dad," and phoned his parents to come home because he had a surprise for them. Mrs. Heikkila arrived first. According to a letter Matthew later sent to New York City's Channel 5, his mother, who had come upstairs to meet him, began crying when she saw the shotgun. He told her to walk down the hall to the family room where they could talk. Following close behind, he shot her unawares, nearly blowing her head off with a slug from the shell labeled "Mom." He took her credit cards and the keys to her Audi. Dr. Heikkila got home about forty-five minutes later. As he started down the basement stairs in search of his wife, whom Matthew said he had tied up there, Matt shot him in the head from behind with a slug from the shell labeled "Mom and Dad." Matthew took his father's credit cards, then put the shotgun in a kitchen cabinet and left to meet his date.

Marta Morales noticed a couple of bloodstains on Matthew's shirt when he picked her up. He dismissed them as coming from a bite by the family cat. They dined in Manhattan at Windows on the World, atop the World Trade Center. There, Matthew used his father's credit card to pay for the meal. While driving back to Bernards Township, Matt promised Marta a surprise for her birthday. At the Heikkila family home he immediately handcuffed her—a surprise all right, but an unwelcome one—and began to talk about killing her and killing himself. He escorted her down the hall to see his mother's body, saying he had to do away with his parents because "they didn't love me" and "they knew too much." In one of the many letters he wrote he complained that they "just got in my way." Heikkila made clear that the promised surprise he had in store for Marta Morales was to murder her.

During the night Morales, handcuffed throughout the ordeal, succeeded in convincing Matthew to flee the country rather than kill her or himself. She would go with him, she said. He considered various destinations, decided on Jamaica, packed his bags, and made airline reservations for the two of them by phone. Marta told him she had to stop at her home in Union City to pick up her passport. As soon as her mother saw Marta and Matthew, she knew something was wrong. She refused to let her daughter go with him. Matthew went on alone, flying from Newark to Montego Bay without being intercepted.

Although he had not covered his tracks very well, it took Jamaican police six days to find him. He did not stay at a major hotel, but instead checked into Miss Mary's Place, a small bed-and-breakfast hideaway on the beach at Negril. He was finally spotted by a traffic cop who had arrested him following a motorcycle accident on a previous visit to the island. (On that occasion Mrs. Heikkila had phoned to criticize the police treatment of her adopted son.)

On February 15, 1991, a Somerset County grand jury indicted Matthew Heikkila on capital murder charges. The only question seemed to be whether he was insane at the time he killed his parents and kidnapped Marta Morales. The trial began on November 12, 1992. The presiding judge was Michael R. Imbriani, the same judge who had found Matthew Heikkila not guilty by reason of insanity a year earlier on a charge of threatening to shoot his father. This time a jury of nine men and three women took five hours to find the defendant guilty on all twelve counts of the indictment. The jury spent another five hours in the penalty phase of the trial before deciding against a death sentence.

During the penalty phase, Matthew Heikkila took the opportunity to blame Judge Imbriani and the judicial system for his plight. "If you had followed through on my treatment plan," he told the judge, "I would still have my family." This rebuke sounded hollow but not really surprising to Somerset County Prosecutor Nicholas L. Bissell, Jr., who countered, "That's all he's ever done is blame other people." Heikkila had unkind words for his deceased parents, too, to which Judge Imbriani replied, "Your parents showered you with an abundance of love and tried with all the energy and ability they possessed to guide you into a life of happiness and accomplishment."

The convicted killer, unapologetic, snapped, "Sentence me and get me out of here."

Judge Imbriani sentenced Heikkila to sixty years in prison without parole.

 # The Family Says, "Die!"

ALLAMUCHY

Family and Friends Join Forces to Gun Down Abusive NJIT Cop

NOVEMBER 23, 1991

Revell Quince, forty-three, a sergeant on the police force of the New Jersey Institute of Technology (NJIT), had a solid reputation as a cop. His colleagues viewed him as strict but fair. A 1967 graduate of Orange High School and a 1973 graduate of the State Police Academy, Quince was responsible for the training of new recruits and for instruction on the use of weapons. The twenty-four-member NJIT police force along with thirty-eight other security officers shared responsibility for protecting the central Newark campus of the nine-thousand-student engineering school.

Although well liked by his fellow officers, Sergeant Quince was not popular with everyone. That became abundantly clear on the night of November 23, 1991, when Quince, returning home from work, reached his rural residence on the Johnsonburg Road in Allamuchy. At about 11:20 P.M. that Saturday the tough, stocky police sergeant approached the front door of his house. The entrance was brightly lit, as always. Shots rang out. Quince, hit in the back, spun and began firing his nine-millimeter semiautomatic service pistol into the darkness in the direction from which the shots had come. Two more bullets struck him, one in the chest, another in the shoulder. His son Chistopher, eighteen, came out the front door to help his father. A shot, apparently from Quince's gun, struck him in the right foot.

Sergeant Quince fell, badly wounded. He died an hour later at Hackettstown Community Hospital. Christopher was admitted in fair condition. He would recover.

The bullets that hit Revell Quince came from a high-powered rifle fired from across the road. It looked very much like an assassination, and it was.

Three days after the shooting five people were arrested and charged. One was William Quince, twenty, the victim's son by his first wife. William lived in the family's house in Allamuchy, knew there was a plot afoot to kill his father and said nothing about it, but did not take part in the actual murder. Another was Cynthia Gregory, twenty-two, Quince's stepdaughter, a cashier at a Chester supermarket, who also lived in the house. She was a bona fide conspirator, agreeing to provide alibis—and she was also the primary reason for the murder plot. Police learned that Cynthia Gregory had been sexually and physically abused by her stepfather for many years.

Donald Lucas, twenty-four, a foreman at the Midas Muffler shop on Route 46 in Washington Township, was Cynthia Gregory's boyfriend. He said Cynthia told him that the only way they could be together and happy was if Quince were "totally out of our lives." That may well have been true, because Donald Lucas also claimed he had been threatened and attacked by people acting on Quince's orders. Sergeant Quince evidently liked Donald Lucas no better than Lucas liked him.

The actual triggerman, however, was Jeffrey Lucas, eighteen, unemployed at the time of the killing. He lived with his brother Donald and their mother in a small house in Knowlton Township near the Delaware River. Jeffrey's only connection with the Quinces was through his older brother, whom, according to Donald, "he thought he had to do something to protect." What he did was to dress all in black, take up a position on a ridge some distance from the Quince home, aim a .308 Mauser rifle with a telescopic sight at the targeted cop, and fire the fatal shots. (An earlier, similar effort to kill Quince had failed when the rifle misfired.)

Brian Bastedo, twenty-four, of Mount Bethel, Pennsylvania, the fifth conspirator, had a motive similar to Donald Lucas's. Bastedo had been dating another stepdaughter of Revell Quince, who, like Cynthia Gregory, had allegedly been sexually abused. Jeffrey Lucas, the sniper, and Brian Bastedo, the driver of the getaway car, were communicating by means of walkie-talkies on the night of the murder as they waited for Quince to arrive home. Bastedo, like Donald Lucas, claimed to have been the target of Revell Quince's threats and physical attacks.

In a plea-bargain arrangement, Jeffrey Lucas, Brian Bastedo, and Donald Lucas drew the longest sentences, three to five years each. (Donald Lucas, one of the planners of this none-too-perfect crime, had purchased the walkie-talkies and had helped dispose of the rifle and shells in the Paulinskill River after the shooting.) William Quince and Cynthia Gregory, both of whom had lived with the abusive sergeant but had participated less directly in his murder, received lighter sentences.

The Lucases' and Bastedo's sentences were increased somewhat at the insistence of Warren County Prosecutor John O'Reilly. There had been local criticism of the leniency of the plea-bargain punishments meted out. One of those who objected was Dick Kramer of Hackettstown, whose daughter had been murdered and who had subsequently founded the group Voices for Victims, Inc. Said Kramer, as quoted in the May 21, 1993, issue of the *Star-Ledger*:

"I don't doubt that Quince was a creep, but where do these three guys get off taking control? It's murder and they should serve time. You can't walk around killing people just because you don't like what they do."

Saga of the Failed Yuppies

Exxon Executive Disappears; Authorities Fear Kidnapping

APRIL 29, 1992

Although he had the use of a company limousine, Sidney J. Reso, fifty-seven, president of Exxon International, was in the habit of driving his own car the short distance from his home to work at his company headquarters in Florham Park. Reso, who was raised in New Orleans but had moved many times in his corporate career, lived in a $680,000 French colonial home on a wooded, five-acre estate on Jonathan Smith Road in Morris Township. His wife of thirty-seven years, Patricia, said goodbye to him at 7:30 on the morning of April 29, 1992.

At about 8:45 A.M. a neighbor and good friend of the family noticed Reso's car, its engine idling, at the end of the driveway some two hundred feet from the house. The neighbor phoned Mrs. Reso, but she was taking a shower and could not come to the phone. The neighbor then called Exxon officials. By the time they phoned her, Patricia Reso had received the neighbor's message on her answering machine and had gone outside to check. She found her husband's briefcase and topcoat on the back seat of his car. Foul play seemed certain. A neighbor, interviewed later that morning, said, "We're all just heartsick, and we're sitting here praying for Sid."

Details of the ransom demand were not released until later. The FBI received a letter not long after the abduction, however, asking for $18.5 million in used $100 bills to secure the safe return of Reso—and to spare other Exxon executives a similar fate. The money was to be put into a number of Eddie Bauer laundry bags. The kidnappers also specified that the FBI provide them with a cellular telephone number to use in future communications. This request was apparently based on the incorrect belief that calls to a cellular phone are harder to trace than regular phone calls. The FBI quickly erected an array of antennae on the tallest office building in Headquarters Plaza, Morristown, and awaited further word. Exxon transferred $25 million to a Morristown bank.

More messages, some by phone, some by letter, arrived from the kidnappers over the next few weeks. Authorities noted that their contents included details unknown to the general public. Some phone messages were prerecorded and the voices were disguised, but the FBI could tell that one speaker was male, the other female. A phone message from the kidnappers that purported to contain Reso's own spoken words was diagnosed by his relatives as a fake. It turned out, however, that Reso had in fact recorded two short messages of ransom instructions, presumably on May 1. One, monitored by the FBI, went to Exxon officials that night. The other was phoned in on the evening of May 3.

On Mother's Day and Father's Day Patricia Reso made public appeals to the kidnappers to release her husband. Her pleas brought no reply, other than the letter that finally named the ransom day. Two phone calls, one a man's voice, one a woman's, arrived at the FBI's task force headquarters in Morristown on June 16, directing agents to pick up a letter at the Morris County Sheriff's Labor Assistance Program mailbox in Morris Township. The letter spelled out the handling of the ransom money and alerted the FBI to be ready to make the drop two days later. On June 18, as promised, instructions began arriving in a sequence of phone calls and written notes. Authorities, as they were directed, spent the next few hours skipping from one Morris County or Somerset County location to another—Gladstone, Morristown, Mendham, Chester, Peapack.

Once again the kidnappers were less clever than they thought. Law enforcement officials had been given time to stake out a great many pay phones throughout northern New Jersey, knowing that all the previous messages had come from pay phones. At about 10:40 P.M. a man called the FBI from a pay phone in the Chester Mall and gave agents further instructions. As luck and near-saturation coverage would have it, a surveillance team noticed a sandy-haired, burly man wearing latex gloves making a call from that particular pay phone at that very time. When the man left the booth, he removed his latex gloves, got into an Oldsmobile Cutlass Ciera with New Jersey plates, and took off. Agents began to track him from that point. A check of the license number revealed that the car he was driving was registered to Bette's Rent-a-Car on Mountain Avenue in Hackettstown.

While agents followed the rented Olds from Chester, another surveillance team near the pay phones at the Somerset Hills Elks Club in Gladstone noticed a woman in a white Mercedes parked nearby. Agents, suspicious of her actions, also began to track her. The time was approximately 11:15 P.M. Meanwhile, the Olds headed south to the train station at Far Hills, where the driver, at about 11:50 P.M., may have spotted the FBI agents following him. He sped away, but soon came to a police roadblock, unrelated to the Reso case, which evidently spooked him. He made a quick U-turn and headed toward Hackettstown to get rid of the rented car. Apparently he made a phone call along the way, because another driver, taking a different route, arrived minutes after he did at the Hackettstown rental car agency. FBI agents, detectives from the Morris County prosecutor's office, and Morris Township police converged on both cars and arrested the drivers.

The two suspects were Arthur D. Seale, forty-five, and his wife, Irene (Jackie) Seale, also forty-five, of Changewater, Lebanon Township. In the white Mercedes that Irene Seale was driving, agents and detectives found four laundry bags similar to the ones requested by the kidnappers. They also found two pairs of latex gloves, a set of license plates, a roll of quarters, and a briefcase. Inside the briefcase were three .38-caliber bullets and a 1985 directory of Exxon executives with their home addresses.

The Seales had been living for the past two and a half years at the home of Arthur Seale's parents on Musconetcong River Road in Changewater, about two and a half miles from Route 31. A welcoming sign at the entrance to the secluded rural residence read "The Seales of Possom Hollow." When the press began arriving, the sign came down. In searching the Seales' house soon after the arrests, FBI agents found a key to a self-storage unit at Secure Storage in Washington Township. They also found handwritten telephone and telex numbers of banks in Zurich and Karachi, a book about Pakistan, and another book titled *The Secret Money Market: Inside the Dark World of Tax Evasion, Financial Fraud, Insider Trading, Money Laundering and Capital Flight.*

What they did not find was Sidney J. Reso. The storage room in Washington Township was empty. Although the Seales were saying nothing to authorities at this point, Jackie did whisper to her husband, "I love you," at their arraignment before U.S. Magistrate Donald Haneke in federal court in Newark. On June 25, 1992, a U.S. grand jury in Newark indicted Arthur and Irene Seale on six counts of kidnapping, conspiracy, and extortion. The search for Sidney J. Reso went on.

In the aftermath of the two arrests, authorities began looking for possible accomplices to the kidnapping. One reason for this was that agents reported having seen a second person, not Mrs. Seale, in Arthur Seale's rented Olds at the Chester Mall. Another reason, apparently, was the common-sense inference that someone must have been guarding Reso while the Seales flitted about northern New Jersey trying to get their hands on those bagfuls of ransom money.

Before Reso's fate became known, authorities learned a great deal about their suspects. Arthur and Irene Seale were, according to those who knew them, the "ultimate yuppies." Arthur Seale, an ex-Hillside policeman, twice suspended and often reprimanded, had left on partial disability worth $13,000 a year and had gone to work for Exxon in the corporation's security department. He stayed there for ten years, rising to a management position with responsibility for security and facilities. He was making something over $60,000 a year when he accepted a buyout package in 1987 during a restructuring of the company. For the three years prior to her husband's leaving Exxon, Jackie Seale worked in public relations for a winery in Lebanon Township. The couple were parents of a teenage son and daughter.

After selling the home they had bought in Chester many years earlier and adding their profit on the deal to the Exxon buyout package, Arthur and Irene Seale headed south in a pair of matching his-and-hers Mercedes-Benz automobiles. They had approximately $350,000 with which to start a new life in Hilton Head, South Carolina. The Seales went first class all the way, buying an expensive thirty-eight-foot French-made sloop that neither of them knew how to sail, enrolling their children in a private school, and purchasing a $400,000 waterfront home in the exclusive Gull Point section of Sea Pines Plantation, Hilton Head. They went into business, acquiring an established outdoor furniture and interior decorating business called Insiders. The Seales, living well beyond their means, loved Hilton Head. "They had it all here," said a South Carolina business associate. "Big house, new boat, nice cars, friends."

Within two years they were broke. Actually, they were worse than broke. They were deeply and apparently irreversibly in debt. They left Hilton Head, the same business associate said, "literally in the middle of the night, owing hundreds of thousands of dollars." The Seales relocated in Vail, Colorado, moving into a luxury townhouse overlooking the Vail Golf Course and taking part-time jobs. Their daughter ran away from home three times in their brief stay at the upscale resort. Once again the family left town hastily, leaving their creditors in the lurch. Tapped out and disheartened, they returned to New Jersey, to the Lebanon Township home of Arthur Seale's parents. It was quite a comedown.

Now the Seales, not merely destitute, were facing the prospect of life imprisonment. Jackie cracked. Within a day of the June 25 indictment, Irene Seale, through her court-appointed lawyer, sought to cut a plea-bargain deal with the feds in return for her cooperation, thus avoiding the possibility of a life sentence. She would reveal Reso's whereabouts, she said, and explain what had happened to him. The bargain was made. Jackie Reso talked. Her story was more gruesome perhaps than the plea-bargain agreement anticipated.

First, the FBI wanted to know where to find Sidney J. Reso. Jackie Seale had the answer. He was in the Pine Barrens. She led investigators to a remote site in Bass River State Park off Exit 58 of the Garden State Parkway, directing them onto a dirt road and then leading them three quarters of a mile on foot down an overgrown path in a piney wooded area. After a twelve-hour search of the locale by forty officers, aided by Buffy, the state police's German shepherd search dog, they found Reso's badly decomposed remains in a shallow, makeshift grave. Investigators who located the body found it hard to believe that the Seales alone could have carried Reso that far into the underbrush, but Jackie insisted they had.

Next, the FBI wanted to know how Reso had come to this unhappy end. The story Irene Seale told was one of astonishing callousness, making the abduction sound more like an act of sadism or revenge than simply one of greed. U.S. Attorney Michael Chertoff, the federal prosecutor, called the crime "unique in its cruelty." On a number of mornings prior to the crime, and also on the morning of it, Jackie Seale jogged in the exclusive Morris Township neighborhood, scouting the area, preparing for the kidnapping. Just before 7:30 on the morning of April 29, she passed the Reso home and doubled back, going past the house again on her way to a rented van waiting nearby. She took the wheel of the van. Arthur Seale, masked, .45-caliber pistol in hand, stepped out and stationed himself at the end of the Resos' two-hundred-foot driveway. When Reso got out of his car to pick up the morning newspaper, the muscular Seale overpowered him and wrestled him into the back of the unmarked van, which Jackie had by then driven alongside Reso's car.

Reso continued to resist, more violently than before, some speculated later, when he saw the coffinlike wooden box awaiting him inside the van. Arthur Seale, still struggling with Reso, shot the Exxon executive in the left arm. The bullet entered behind Reso's wrist, passed through his forearm, and exited near his elbow. Sidney Reso had suffered a heart attack three years earlier, but the kidnappers were unaware of this fact. Seale, now in control, shoved his wounded victim into the box, handcuffed him, bound his ankles, taped his mouth and eyes with duct tape, and locked the box.

Irene Seale drove the rented van west to the Secure Storage facility on Lincoln Avenue in Washington Township, about a ten-minute drive from the Seales' home in Changewater. There the Seales had rented a twenty-foot-square storage room in which to house their victim. Once they had dragged the box inside the unventilated room, the Seales made a pass at treating Reso's gunshot wound with peroxide and gauze bandages. After that they left him, bound, gagged, and locked in the box. The Seales returned twice a day, according to Jackie, to give him water, juice, and crushed vitamins.

Sidney J. Reso, thus treated, died on May 3, the fifth day of captivity, probably from heart failure or complications arising from the untreated gunshot wound. When the Seales arrived to find him dead, they removed his body from the box, wrapped it in plastic sheets, and tied it with ropes. Taking the empty, homemade box back to their Changewater home, Arthur Seale dismantled it and burned the pieces in the back yard, tossing the ashes into the Musconetcong River. Jackie, meanwhile, prepared a Sunday dinner for the two of them, which they ate, authorities said, while Reso's body lay in the storage room awaiting disposal.

Up to this point, for reasons unexplained, the Seales seem to have made only vague ransom demands. But twelve hours or so after Reso died they finally sat down to spell out their price for his safe return: $18.5 million.

By that time the body of Sidney J. Reso had been transported in the trunk of a rented Chevrolet Lumina to what the Seales hoped would be its last resting place—a twenty-four-inch-deep grave in the sandy soil of the Pine Barrens. The kidnapping had turned into felony murder. All that remained—no small task—was to collect the ransom money and flee to Pakistan, a country without an extradition treaty with the United States.

Next began the two-month sequence of sporadic messages and arrangements that ultimately resulted in the cat-and-mouse chase on the back roads of northwestern New Jersey. The elaborate chase lasted four hours and ended with the arrest of the Seales in Hackettstown.

Irene Seale's plea bargain, in which she agreed to testify against her husband at his federal trial, led to the dismissal of a string of charges against her: kidnapping, conspiracy to kidnap, use of the mails for ransom demands and threats, and interstate travel in aid of extortion. She pleaded guilty to extortion and conspiracy, carrying a maximum prison term of forty years. One stipulation of her plea bargain was that she be sent to a prison near one or both of her children.

The day before Arthur D. Seale was scheduled to go on trial in Trenton, he pleaded guilty to the seventeen-count federal indictment against him. There was no plea bargain. Judge Garrett E. Brown, Jr., imposed a ninety-five-year prison term on him, the maximum federal sentence allowed. A few hours later, on the state charges, Superior Court Judge Reginald Stanton sentenced Seale to a life term for felony murder plus a separate thirty-year sentence for kidnapping. The federal and state sentences were to run consecutively, which meant, as the *Star-Ledger* headlined it, that "Reso's killer has no hope of gaining parole."

On November 13, 1992, Arthur D. Seale appeared with Barbara Walters on the ABC television program "20/20." He told of his remorse at Reso's unexpected death. He said that he and Jackie only wanted to live "as middle-class Americans." In fact, they "had developed plans to basically give away bags full of money and . . . fund charitable organizations." He said, "There hasn't been a day since this incident happened that I haven't cried over Sidney Reso."

Before this interview was aired, U.S. Attorney Chertoff held a press conference and, visibly angry, countered it by disclosing details of the barbaric treatment Reso had suffered at the hands of his captors. He called Seale's treatment of his victim "heinous, cruel, brutal, and degrading." Referring to the man who would soon appear on TV to tell of his compassion and remorse, Chertoff added, "A little part of me wishes we could put him in a box."

Source Notes and Commentary

Although the murder cases in this book were covered by many New Jersey newspapers, the most accessible index for finding their dates is *The New York Times Index, 1922–1993*. Some of the murders in the book were not covered by the *New York Times,* however, or by the second principal source consulted, the *(Newark) Star-Ledger.* Others were reported for a while and then dropped. Local daily newspapers, whether noted here or not, may contain articles on the murders, and the dates will generally be the same as those for the larger papers.

Part One / From Hall-Mills to Lindbergh

1 Under a Crab Apple Tree

William Kunstler's *The Minister and the Choir Singer* (1964) is a thorough and readable account of the Hall-Mills case. Reviewers expressed differing opinions about the author's proposed Ku Klux Klan solution. Rex Stout, writing in the *New York Times Book Review,* found Kunstler's reasoning and conclusions plausible. But a *Times* reader, J. N. Bernstein of Paterson, who had himself written extensively on the case, dismissed Stout's review and Kunstler's solution of the mystery as "balderdash." Extensive coverage of the case in the *New York Times* began with page-one articles on September 17, 18, 19, and 20, 1922. A review of the case seventy years later appeared in the *Star-Ledger* of September 13, 1992. A mystery novel with a plot based on the Hall-Mills affair is Anthony Abbott's *About the Murder of the Clergyman's Mistress* (1931).

2 The Brigham Murder

The account here is based on articles that appeared in the *New York Times* on December 27 and 28, 1922, January 4, 5, 6, 7, 8, 25, and 31, 1923, and February 10 and 17, 1923.

3 Trooper Coyle at the Quarry
Leo J. Coakley's *Jersey Troopers* (1971) contains a brief account of Trooper Coyle's murder. Contemporary accounts of the crime and trial can be found in the *New York Times* and in New Jersey dailies for December 19, 20, and 21, 1924, and February 11, March 31, and April 2 and 3, 1925.

4 Sea Isle's Indiscreet Squire
Most of the information about this case comes from two long articles in the weekly *Cape May County Gazette,* July 10 and November 20, 1925.

5 A Crazy Rich Kid
The Mary Daly kidnapping was front-page news in the *New York Times* for a full week: September 5, 6, 7, 8, 9, 10, and 11, 1925. Extensive accounts also appeared in the *Elizabeth Daily Journal* and many other New Jersey newspapers starting on September 5, 1925. Later stories on the case in the *New York Times* and elsewhere are dated September 18, 19, 22, 25, 30, October 9, and November 17, 1925, and May 18 and November 17, 1926.

6 Shootout at the French Hill Inn
This story of the Prohibition era is told in considerable detail in Coakley's *Jersey Troopers.* First reports of the shootout appeared in the daily newspapers of February 18, 1926.

7 The Mail Truck Blitz
A seven-man, two-automobile, daytime robbery in which a submachine gun was used resulted in major press coverage. The *New York Times* gave the story a front-page, three-column, three-line headline on October 15, 1926, and again on October 16. The complexity of the case and the number of perpetrators generated news stories for years, long after the early accounts of October 15, 16, 17, 1926, and November 1, 2, 3, and 4, 1926. Further developments were reported in the *New York Times* on February 16, 1927, March 16, 1927, April 12 and 13, 1927, and December 14, 1927. In 1928 there were stories on January 29 and May 9; in 1929, on January 29, February 1 and 10, and October 5; in 1930, on March 27; and in 1931, on February 3 and April 12.

8 Dr. Lilliendahl's Death
The account here is based on articles that appeared in the *New York Times* on September 16 and 29, 1927, October 3 and 12, 1927, November 28, 1927, December 7 and 9, 1927, and January 7, 1928.

9 An Arrest Gone Bad
Coakley's *Jersey Troopers* outlines the murder. Specific details can be found in the Morristown *Daily Record* of December 29 and 31, 1928, and February 7, 1929.

10 Murder of a Prohibition Agent

An inside look at the problems posed by Prohibition in New Jersey is provided by Ira L. Reeves's *Ol' Rum River: Revelations of a Prohibition Administrator* (1931). The murder of John G. Finiello received extensive coverage in the (Jersey City) *Jersey Journal, Elizabeth Daily Journal, Newark Evening News, New York Times,* and other newspapers. The key dates are September 20, 21, and October 1 and 3, 1930. Later stories appeared in the *Times* on July 7, 1931, July 29 and 30, 1932, November 29, 1933, and February 2, 1934.

11 America's Crime of the Century

Newspaper and magazine coverage of the Lindbergh case was incessant and exhaustive, and many books have been written on the subject; the account in this book is based mainly on Jim Fisher's *The Lindbergh Case* (1987). In most people's minds, this was *the* New Jersey murder. It inspired Agatha Christie's fictional *Murder on the Orient Express* (1934). It gave rise to a number of excellent nonfiction efforts, the best of which so far is Fisher's. Among the others worth reading are John F. Condon's *Jafsie Tells All!* (1936); J. Vreeland Haring's *The Hand of Hauptmann: The Handwriting Expert Tells the Story of the Lindbergh Case* (1937); George Waller's *Kidnap: The Story of the Lindbergh Case* (1961); and Sidney Whipple's *The Trial of Bruno Richard Hauptmann* (1937). The most plausible of the books attempting to exonerate Hauptmann is Anthony Scaduto's *Scapegoat: The Lonesome Death of Bruno Richard Hauptmann* (1976). The Lindbergh case was reported in all major newspapers, starting on March 2, 1932 (the day after the abduction), and continuing through, and after, April 4, 1936 (the day after the execution of Hauptmann).

Part Two / Gang Wars and World War II

12 The Greenberg-Hassel Rubout

As with the gang murder of John P. Enz, it took a long time to sort out the people and details of this mob hit. The first accounts appeared in the *New York Times* and New Jersey dailies on April 13, 14, and 15, 1933. More news on the "beer inquiry" and Waxey Gordon surfaced on May 12, 13, and 23, 1933. After a three-year hiatus, the indictment of Frankie Carbo and details about his alleged involvement with the Greenberg-Hassel murder appeared on January 18, 19, and 28, 1936. Other Carbo stories made the *New York Times* on August 21, 1940, September 23, 1941, November 21, 1947, and October 6 and 31, 1959. A *New York Times* obituary of November 11, 1976, summed up Carbo's criminal activities, including his alleged murder of gangster Mickey Duffy in Atlantic City in 1931.

13 Killing the Dutchman

One of the better true-crime books about a specific New Jersey murder is Paul Sann's *Kill the Dutchman!: The Story of Dutch Schultz* (1971), which provides a comprehensive picture of Arthur Flegenheimer and his violent death. The first newspaper accounts of the mob hit are dated October 24, 1935. E. L. Doctorow's *Billy Bathgate: A Novel* (1989) offers a fictional look at Dutch Schultz and his era through the eyes of Billy, an ambitious fifteen-year-old from Bathgate Avenue in the Bronx. Young Billy, while learning the ways of gangsterism as a trainee in the Schultz mob, falls in love with the Dutchman's latest lady love, with ensuing complications.

14 Willful Gladys Took an Ax

The *Elizabeth Daily Journal,* (Jersey City) *Jersey Journal, Newark Evening News,* and *New York Times* contain detailed accounts of the MacKnight murder. Key dates are August 1 and 2, 1936, and May 18, 19, 28, and June 4, 1937.

15 Death of a Union Boss

"Sandhogs' Leader in Strike Is Slain at Home in Jersey" read the front-page headline in the *New York Times* on February 20, 1937. Extensive (frequently page-one) coverage continued on February 21, 23, 27, and 28, 1937, March 9 and 10, 1937, and October 26, 1937.

16 Who Murdered the Littlefields?

The *Elizabeth Daily Journal, Newark Evening News,* and *New York Times,* along with many other newspapers, gave thorough coverage to this bizarre Maine-based case. First reports appeared on October 17, 18, and 19, 1937. Other important dates are December 3, 1937, June 25, 1938, and August 3, 4, 6, 9, 13, and 14, 1938.

17 The Duck Island Murders

The *Trenton Evening Times* of November 9, 1938, October 2, 1939, and November 17, 1940, reported the murders as they occurred. The long-awaited break in this early serial-killer case became front-page news on January 31 and February 8, 1944. A concise account of the case, which the New Jersey State Police played a part in solving, can be found in Coakley's *Jersey Troopers.*

18 Ambush at Fort Dix

This deadly incident was reported in the *New York Times* for three days—April 3, 4, and 5, 1942—and then disappeared. The narrative in this book is based on a report of the Summary Court, Office of the Provost Marshal, Fort Dix, dated May 28, 1942. The report is contained in the General Correspondence, 1939–1947, Records of the Office of the Inspector General (Record Group 159), and was obtained from the Suitland Reference Branch of the National Archives.

19 First His Wife, Then a Trooper
Accounts of Trooper O'Donnell's death can be found in the Newark *Star-Ledger* and *Morristown Daily Record* of July 17 and 18, 1945. Details of the case and its outcome are in Coakley's *Jersey Troopers.*

20 "It's All Over"
This minor but poignant story appeared in the Newark *Star-Ledger* on August 20, 22, and 23, 1945.

Part Three / Silent-Generation Murders

21 The Keyport Trunk Murder
The *Asbury Park Evening Press,* the Newark *Star-Ledger,* the *New York Times,* and no doubt many other newspapers followed the confusing developments in this less-than-meets-the-eye case. Early accounts are dated April 20, 21, 22, and 24, 1947. Misidentifications were reported on May 15 and 16, 1947. The truth emerged on July 9 and 13, 1947.

22 Drowning His Sorrow
Much of the information in this account is from the August 7, 1947, issue of *The Observer,* a North Arlington weekly newspaper. The key date for the *New York Times* and other dailies is July 26, 1947.

23 Case of the Trenton Six
The intricacies of this *cause célèbre* are explained at length in Claire Neikind's two-part article, "The Case of the Trenton Six," published in *The Reporter* on May 1, 1951, and May 29, 1951. Later events in the trial and its aftermath are covered in the (Trenton) *Evening Times,* the *New York Times,* and many other newspapers, dated June 12 and 15, 1951, November 25 and December 31, 1952, and February 21 and August 12, 1953. A twentieth-anniversary summation of the case can be found in the *Evening Times* of January 26, 1968.

24 Unruh's Bloody Rampage
A much publicized mass murder, the Unruh case was reported in the *New York Times* on September 7, 8, 9, 10, 11, 13, 14, 18, and 23, 1949, and October 8 and 12, 1949. A summary of the case with a photograph of Unruh being arrested appears in Carl Sifakis's *Encyclopedia of American Crime* (1982).

25 R.I.P. Willie Moretti
Mark A. Stuart's *Gangster #2: Longy Zwillman, the Man Who Invented Organized Crime* explains the background and circumstances of mobster Moretti's murder. Relevant *New York Times* articles on the hit are dated October 5, 6, 7, 8, 9, 10, 1951, November 28, 1951, and December 22, 1951.

26 Bayonne's Morro Castle *Killer*
Hal Burton's *The Morro Castle* (1973) explores at length the life and mind of radioman and killer George White Rogers. The first accounts of the Hummel murders appeared in the *Elizabeth Daily Journal, Newark Evening News,* Newark *Star-Ledger, New York Times,* and other newspapers on July 3, 1953. The opening of the Rogers trial was reported on May 18, 1954, and the conviction and sentencing of Rogers on September 25, 1954.

27 The Avenging Motel Owner
Three articles in the Newark *Star-Ledger* of November 3, 1955, tell this story from start to finish. A retelling based on state police records can be found in Coakley's *Jersey Troopers.*

28 Death Row's Edgar Smith
The account here is based on articles that appeared in the *New York Times* and Newark *Star-Ledger* on March 6, 7, 9, 1957, May 29, 1957, June 5, 1957, May 20, 1959, October 8, 9, 14, and 21, 1976, and November 4, 1976. An updating and summary of the Zielinski murder and Ozbun assault can be found in the Newark *Star-Ledger* of September 24, 1992. Edgar Smith's *Brief Against Death* (1968) was written with the encouragement of columnist William F. Buckley, Jr. Smith followed this bestseller with two more books: an autobiographical novel, *A Reasonable Doubt* (1970), and *Getting Out* (1973). Ronald A. Calissi attempted to set the record straight in *Counterpoint: The Edgar Smith Case* (1972).

29 Mama's Little Felony Murderer
This case was front-page news in the *New York Times* and Newark *Star-Ledger* of March 19, 1959. Later developments were reported on March 20, 1959, and July 11, 1959.

30 Batman in Blairstown
Coakley's *Jersey Troopers* outlines the case. Further details can be found in the Newark *Star-Ledger* of November 26, 1959.

Part Four / A Bloodstained Decade

31 Murder at the Clarke Estate
Newspapers throughout the state gave page-one coverage to this strange quadruple slaying. The account here is based primarily on articles in the Newark *Star-Ledger* and *New York Times,* dated January 27, 1960, February 4, 1960, July 11, 13, 14, 16, and 26, 1960, and November 2 and 3, 1960.

32 "I Blew My Top"

Extensive coverage of the Buckley-Kennedy murders appeared in the Morristown *Daily Record* and Newark *Star-Ledger* on June 22, 23, 25, 26, 27, 29, and 30, 1962, July 10, 1962, and September 15, 1962.

33 The Coppolino Case

Paul Holmes's *The Trials of Dr. Coppolino* (1968) suggests that Coppolino was innocent of the Farber murder. So does defense attorney F. Lee Bailey's *The Defense Never Rests* (1971). The well-known mystery writer John D. MacDonald attended the Florida trial of Coppolino and produced a noncommittal book about it, *No Deadly Drug* (1968). Dr. Coppolino, too, wrote a book about his Florida experiences, *The Crime That Never Was* (1980). Both the New Jersey and Florida trials were widely reported in the media. The key *New York Times* dates for the Farber case are July 22, 1966, and December 5, 15, and 16, 1966.

34 At a Lodi Tavern

This case, which the New Jersey attorney general's office as recently as 1992 termed "one of the worst crimes in modern New Jersey criminal history," kept resurfacing in the news because of parole hearings for convicted killer Thomas Trantino. The original story can be traced in the Newark *Star-Ledger, New York Times,* and other newspapers of August 27 and 29, 1963, and February 19 and 29, 1964. Parole-hearing articles in the *Star-Ledger* on September 26, 1990, and November 22, 1990, dealt with Trantino's fifth try for freedom.

35 Domestic Squabble on River Road

Most of the information on this case comes from the New Brunswick *Daily Home News* of September 19, 20, 21, 22, and 24, 1963; and the Newark *Star-Ledger* of January 5, 1966, November 22, 1966, and October 18, 1967.

36 McAfee's Back-Porch Bombing

The inexplicable and unsolved bombing of the Hyland home attracted brief press attention on September 6 and 7, 1965. The account here is based on articles in the Newark *Star-Ledger* and the *New York Times*.

37 Who Killed Mrs. Kavanaugh?

The murder of Mrs. Kavanaugh was the opening event in a bizarre and confusing multimurder case that remains unsolved. An almost Lindbergh-like succession of news stories appeared in New Jersey and New York newspapers for more than half a decade. The account here comes from an array of articles, of which the following are among the more significant. *Star-Ledger*: March 14, 1966, December 1 and 2, 1966, October 12, 1967, October 26, 1968, February 6 and 7, 1969, and November 23, 1971. *New York Times*: December 1 and 2, 1966, October 12, 13, and 28, 1967, October 26, 1968, and December 31, 1968,

February 4, 6, 7, 1969, and October 22, 1969, February 23, 1970, and November 23, 1971.

38 "Dr. X" and "Flying Death"

The articles in the *New York Times* on January 7 and 8, written by Myron Farber, are striking examples of investigative journalism. Farber later wrote a book, *"Somebody Is Lying": The Story of Dr. X* (1982), a persuasive argument that the somebody who was lying was Dr. Jascalevich, né "X." Presenting the same conclusion from a different perspective is Matthew L. Lifflander in *Final Treatment: The File on Dr. X* (1979). The exhaustive newspaper coverage of the case began with Farber's first two *Times* articles, followed by stories (some under other bylines) on May 20, 1976, February 16, 1978, October 25, 1978, November 28, 1978, December 3, 1981, and April 3, 1985 (obituary). The *Star-Ledger* front-page piece on October 25, 1978, was also used in writing this account.

39 Requiem for a Middleweight

News stories on the Joey Giardello-Rubin ("Hurricane") Carter middleweight title fight, December 15, 1964, are useful background reading. Giardello retained his title on a unanimous decision, but not everyone agreed with the officials, especially Carter. The unsuccessful challenger was disgusted, according to the *New York Times* and the *Star-Ledger,* thinking he had won the match, nine rounds to six, and should have become the new champion. On June 18, 1966, newspapers reported that Carter and his friend John Artis were being questioned in connection with the murders at the Lafayette Grill in Paterson, but were not suspects. A different story emerged on October 16, 1966, when Carter and Artis were arrested and charged with the triple murder. A great many news articles thereafter in the *New York Times, Star-Ledger,* and other newspapers dealt with the case. Some important dates are May 22, 1967, June 30, 1967, September 27 and 28, 1974, October 30, 1974, March 18, 1976, December 22, 1976, November 8, 1985, January 12, 1988, and February 20, 1988. An article about Carter's testimony concerning habeas corpus appeared in the *Star-Ledger* of May 21, 1993. Hurricane Carter's autobiography, *The Sixteenth Round: From Number 1 Contender to #45472* (1974), received generally positive reviews, although, as the *New York Times Book Review* critic notes, the author is "often annoyingly evasive."

40 Millburn's Shady Art Dealer

This double murder in affluent Millburn was reported in the *New York Times* and northern New Jersey newspapers on April 13, 14, and 15, 1968.

Part Five / From the Lists to Lamonaco

41 The Elusive John List

Two excellent books dealing with this case are Timothy B. Benford and James P. Johnson's *Righteous Carnage: The List Murders* (1991) and Mary S. Ryzuk's *Thou Shalt Not Kill* (1990). Early newspaper accounts of the murders appeared on December 9, 10, 12, and 17, 1971. The *New York Times* did a one-year update on December 6, 1972, and a five-year update on November 7, 1976. The case burst into the headlines again with the finding, arrest, trial, and conviction of fugitive John List: June 2, 3, 7, 9, 1989, July 10 and 11, 1989, January 24, 1990, February 16, 1990, April 13, 1990, and May 2, 1990.

42 Gun Battle on the Turnpike

The *Star-Ledger* covered the murder of Trooper Werner Foerster and the continuing story of Joanne Chesimard extensively, as did the *New York Times* and many other newspapers, starting on May 3 and 4, 1973, and continuing on October 9, 1973, January 29, 1974, March 16, 1974, December 3, 1976, January 5, 1977, February 16, 1977, March 26, 1977, March 31, 1978, April 8, 1978, and November 3, 1979. An update on fugitive Chesimard appeared in the *Star-Ledger* of February 24, 1992. Under her preferred name of Assata Shakur, Chesimard wrote *Assata: An Autobiography* (1987), a somewhat disorganized book that offers insight into her radicalization but no useful information on the murder.

43 In a Black Cadillac

The *Philadelphia Inquirer* and *Camden Courier Post* were among the newspapers detailing the life and death of Major Coxson. Key dates are June 9, 10, 14, 29, 1973, July 4, 1973, August 22, 1973, September 8, 1973, and June 2 and 9, 1977. Accounts of this case contain references to the Behrman murder in Millburn, since Coxson and Behrman had business dealings.

44 Twenty-Gauge Euthanasia

A debate over mercy killing was spurred by this unhappy affair, reported in the *Star-Ledger, Asbury Park Press, New York Times,* and other papers on June 23, 24, 25, 26, 29, 1973, and November 2, 3, and 6, 1973.

45 Shoemaker and Son

Flora Rheta Schreiber's *The Shoemaker: The Anatomy of a Psychotic* (1983) describes Joseph Kallinger's crimes in precise and often horrifying detail. The (Bergen/Hackensack) *Record,* the *Star-Ledger,* and the *New York Times* were among the newspapers giving extensive coverage to the case on January 9, 10, 11, 19, 1975, February 21, 1975, and October 13, 1976.

46 Murder at the Flamingo Hotel
George Anastasia's *Blood and Honor: Inside the Scarfo Mob—The Mob's Most Violent Family* (1991) portrays the mob background against which Judge Helfant's murder was set. Accounts in the February 17 and 22, 1978, issues of the (Atlantic City) *Press* and the *New York Times* contain contemporaneous stories.

47 "He Hates His Mother"
The *Trenton Times* and the *Trentonian* gave extensive coverage to this shocking murder in the Mill Hill section in stories dated December 9 and 10, 1979, February 9, 1980, April 16, 1980, April 14, 1981, and May 15, 1981. The *New York Times* carried a feature on the murder in its December 22, 1979, issue.

48 A Suicide or Two
The *New York Times* and the (Bergen/Hackensack) *Record* reported this case at length. Key dates: January 3, 5, 9, and 11, 1980, April 3, 4, 6, and 21, 1980, and May 2, 1980.

49 Fall of a Renaissance Man
Much of the information about this case comes from articles in the Bridgewater *Courier-News* of September 4, 1981, November 10, 1981, and February 3 and 5, 1983, and the *Somerset Messenger-Gazette* of February 3, 1983. *Star-Ledger* stories of September 4, 1981, and February 3, 1983, also dealt with the murder.

50 Trooper Lamonaco's Death
The January 1982 issue of *New Jersey Monthly* featured a piece called "82 People to Watch in '82." One of those to watch was Trooper Philip Lamonaco. But by New Year's Day 1982 Trooper Lamonaco had already been killed in a shootout on Route 80 West. The murder was first reported on the front page of the *New York Times, Star-Ledger,* and other newspapers on December 22, 1981. Countless news stories followed, the critical dates of which are January 9 and 20, 1982, November 5 and 8, 1984, April 25, 27, and 28, 1985, November 11, 1986, January 19 and 20, 1987, and December 6 and 14, 1991. Reports on the Lamonaco family's invasion-of-privacy lawsuit against CBS appeared on May 7, 1993. *Reader's Digest* published an excellent article on the Lamonaco murder, "Search for a Terrorist Gang" by Henry Hurt, in its December 1985 issue.

Part Six / Greed, Sex, and Madness

51 Bomb Blast in Middlesex
The account here is based on articles in the *Star-Ledger* on February 26, 27, and 28, 1982, and a ten-year update on the unsolved case that appeared on February 23, 1992.

52 A Stalker at the Mall
The *New York Times, Star-Ledger,* and *Daily Record* devoted considerable space to the Amie Hoffman and subsequent Deirdre O'Brien murders. Because of the legal maneuverings by defense counsel for convicted killer James Koedatich and the publicity given the victims' rights movement, of which James O'Brien, Deirdre's father, was a leader, this case remained in the news for years. Among the key dates: November 26, 27, and 28, 1982, December 1, 7, and 9, 1982, May 13, 1983, December 16, 1983, October 14, 17, and 30, 1984, February 20, 1985, May 2 and 4, 1985, and July 27, 1990. An article about James O'Brien and the victims' rights movement appeared in the *New York Times* of March 2, 1989, and the *Star-Ledger* of April 26, 1993.

53 The Carnival Killing
Dawn Keimel's murder, its investigation, the aborted prosecution, and the early release of the killer are covered in the *Daily Record* and *Star-Ledger* on July 26, 27, 28, 29, 30, and 31, 1984, November 4 and 6, 1986, June 17, 1987, June 5, 1990, and March 28, 1993.

54 Blind Faith: A Contract
Probably more people have read Joe McGinniss's *Blind Faith* (1989) about the Maria Marshall murder than have read any other single book about a New Jersey murder. Yet the McGinniss book, although intriguing to read, has scant research value because of the author's pervasive novelizing and invented dialogue. The main newspaper accounts are dated September 8, 1984, October 1, 15, 18, 23, 1984, December 20, 1984, January 20, 1985, July 17, 1985, January 13, 1986, February 9, 16, 23, 26, and 27, 1986, March 2, 4, 6, 9, 1986, and September 18, 1986. A feature about Toms River and McGinniss's peculiar portrayal of the community appeared in the *New York Times* of March 29, 1989.

55 Policewoman Powlett's Death
Accounts of this apparently pointless murder can be found in the *Star-Ledger, New York Times,* and other newspapers on March 15, 16, 17, 18, and 20, 1985.

56 By Ninja Possessed
This two-part case—a slaying in Montville Township followed three years later by the murders of four Ridgewood post office employees—received major press coverage. The Montville murder was reported in the *Star-Ledger, Daily Record,* and elsewhere on November 17 and 18, 1988. After the investigation had stalled, four new murders by a Ninja-clad marauder made headlines on October 11 and 12, 1991, December 3 and 12, 1991, June 13 and July 31, 1992, April 11, 1993, May 27 and 29, 1993, and June 26, 1993.

57 An Ill-Fated Party in Sparta

Accounts of Anthony Pompelio's murder and the apprehension of his killer appeared in the *New York Times,* New York *Daily News, Star-Ledger, Daily Record, Sparta Independent,* and elsewhere. Reports of the Pompelio murder and the killer's flight are dated February 14, 15, 16, 17, and 18, 1989. Accounts of the trial and its aftermath are dated September 4, 5, 13, 14, 15, 17, 18, 19, 20, 25, 26, 27, and 28, 1990, October 5, 1990, and November 16, 1990. A victims' rights article profiling Richard Pompelio, Anthony's father and founder of the New Jersey Crime Victims' Law Center, was published in the *Star-Ledger* of May 3, 1992.

58 Heikkila's Night Out

The murder of his adoptive parents by Matthew Heikkila received extensive coverage in all major northern New Jersey newspapers, including the *Courier-News, Home News, News Tribune,* and *Daily Record.* The account in this book is based primarily on articles that appeared in the *Star-Ledger* on the following dates: January 31, 1991, February 1, 2, 3, 5, and 16, 1991, June 6, 1992, September 11, 1992, November 13, 17, and 29, 1992, December 5, 1992, January 12, 14, 15, 1993, and February 26, 1993.

59 The Family Says, "Die!"

This carefully planned but easily solved murder was covered in the *Star-Ledger* and other northern New Jersey newspapers on November 25, 26, 27, and 28, 1991, January 14, 1993, February 9, 1993, April 14 and 18, 1993, and May 21, 1993.

60 Saga of the Failed Yuppies

Few New Jersey cases in recent decades have received more media attention than the kidnapping and death in captivity of Exxon executive Sidney J. Reso. Because of the corporate prominence of the victim, even the *Wall Street Journal,* not noted for its coverage of capital crimes, reported on the case on July 1, 1992. The principal sources for the account here were the *Star-Ledger* and *New York Times,* dated May 1, 1992, June 20, 21, 23, 26, 28, 29, and 30, 1992, July 1, 5, and 7, 1992, September 6, 9, 16, 20, 1992, November 13 and 18, 1992, December 1 and 13, 1992, January 23, 1993, April 30, 1993, and May 23, 1993.

Bibliography

Books

The following books proved helpful in researching the murders in this book. It should be noted that there are a number of books, not included here, that deal with other New Jersey murders, such as Peter Maas's *In a Child's Name* (1990), about the murder of a young woman in Manalapan by her dentist husband, and Michael Kaplan's *Buried Mistakes* (1992), concerning another wife murder, this one in the parking lot of the Willowbrook Mall in Wayne.

Alix, Ernest Kahlar. *Ransom Kidnapping in America/1874–1974: The Creation of a Capital Crime.* Carbondale: Southern Illinois University Press, 1978.

Anastasia, George. *Blood and Honor: Inside the Scarfo Mob—The Mafia's Most Violent Family.* New York: William Morrow, 1991.

Baden, Michael M., M.D., with Judith Adler Hennessee. *Unnatural Death: Confessions of a Medical Examiner.* New York: Random House, 1989.

Bailey, F. Lee, with Harvey Aronson. *The Defense Never Rests.* New York: Stein and Day, 1971.

Benford, Timothy B., and James P. Johnson. *Righteous Carnage: The List Murders.* New York: Charles Scribner's Sons, 1991.

Burton, Hal. *The Morro Castle.* New York: The Viking Press, 1973.

Calissi, Ronald E. *Counterpoint: The Edgar Smith Case.* Hackensack, N.J.: Manor Book Company, 1972.

Carter, Rubin ("Hurricane"). *The Sixteenth Round: From Number 1 Contender to #45472.* New York: The Viking Press, 1974.

Coakley, Leo J. *Jersey Troopers.* New Brunswick, N.J.: Rutgers University Press, 1971.

Condon, John F. *Jafsie Tells All!* New York: Jonathan Lee, 1936.

Demaris, Ovid. *The Boardwalk Jungle.* New York: Bantam Books, 1986.

Farber, Myron. *"Somebody Is Lying": The Story of Dr. X.* Garden City, N.Y.: Doubleday, 1982.

Fisher, Jim. *The Lindbergh Case.* New Brunswick, N.J.: Rutgers University Press, 1987.

Haring, J. Vreeland. *The Hand of Hauptmann: The Handwriting Expert Tells the Story of the Lindbergh Case.* Plainfield, N.J.: Hamer Publishing Company, 1937.

Holmes, Paul. *The Trials of Dr. Coppolino.* New York: New American Library, 1968.

Kennedy, Ludovic. *The Airman and the Carpenter: The Lindbergh Kidnapping and the Framing of Richard Hauptmann.* New York: Viking, 1985.

Kunstler, William. *The Hall-Mills Murder Case.* New Brunswick, N.J.: Rutgers University Press, 1964.

Lifflander, Matthew L. *Final Treatment: The File on Dr. X.* New York: W. W. Norton, 1979.

Luckett, Perry. *Charles A. Lindbergh: A Bio-bibliography.* Westport, Conn.: Greenwood, 1986.

McGinniss, Joe. *Blind Faith.* New York: G. P. Putnam's Sons, 1989.

Milton, Joyce. *Loss of Eden: A Biography of Charles and Anne Morrow Lindbergh.* New York: HarperCollins, 1993.

Nash, Jay Robert. *Bloodletters and Badmen.* 3 vols. New York: Warner Books, 1973, 1975.

Reeves, Colonel Ira L. *Ol' Rum River: Revelations of a Prohibition Administrator.* Chicago: Thomas S. Rockwell, 1931.

Ryzuk, Mary S. *Thou Shalt Not Kill.* New York: Popular Library, 1990.

Salerno, Joseph, and Stephen J. Rivele. *The Plumber: The True Story of How One Good Man Helped Destroy the Entire Philadelphia Mafia.* New York: Knightsbridge, 1990.

Sann, Paul. *Kill the Dutchman!: The Story of Dutch Schultz.* New Rochelle, N.Y.: Arlington House, 1971.

Scaduto, Anthony. *Scapegoat, the Lonesome Death of Bruno Richard Hauptmann.* New York: G. P. Putnam's Sons, 1976.

Schreiber, Flora Rheta. *The Shoemaker: The Anatomy of a Psychotic.* New York: Simon and Schuster, 1983.

Shakur, Assata. *Assata: An Autobiography.* Westport, Conn.: Lawrence Hill, 1987.

Sharkey, Joe. *Death Sentence: The Inside Story of the John List Murders.* New York: Signet, 1990.

Sifakis, Carl. *The Encyclopedia of American Crime.* New York: Facts on File, 1982.

Stuart, Mark A. *Gangster #2: Longy Zwillman, the Man Who Invented Organized Crime.* Secaucus, N.J.: Lyle Stuart, 1985.

Waller, George. *Kidnap: The Story of the Lindbergh Case.* New York: Dial Press, 1961.

Whipple, Sidney B. *The Trial of Bruno Richard Hauptmann.* Garden City, N.Y.: Doubleday, 1937.

Newspapers

This book is based primarily on newspaper accounts. Of the papers listed, the two most frequently used were the Newark *Star-Ledger* and the *New York Times*, although for a few cases I relied mainly on local coverage. Some of the newspapers have had differing names over time (the *Star-Ledger* was formerly the *Newark Star-Ledger*, for example), and several are now defunct. The following list includes the current names of surviving newspapers.

Asbury Park Evening Press
(Atlantic City-Pleasantville) *The Press*
(Bridgewater) *Courier-News*
(Camden-Cherry Hill) *Courier-Post*
Cape May County Gazette
(Elizabeth) *Daily Journal*
(Hackensack) *Record*
(Jersey City) *Jersey Journal*
(Morristown-Parsippany) *Daily Record*
(New Brunswick) *The Home News*
(New York) *Daily News*
Newark Evening News
(Newark) *Star-Ledger*
(Newton) *New Jersey Herald*
New York Times
(North Arlington) *Observer*
(Passaic) *North Jersey Herald & News*
(Philadelphia) *Inquirer*
(Somerville) *Somerset Messenger-Gazette*
(Toms River) *Ocean County Observer*
(Trenton) *Times*
(Trenton) *Trentonian*

Index

About the Author

Gerald Tomlinson is a graduate of Marietta College and, for many years, was an editor in trade and text publishing. He is the author of *On a Field of Black* and coeditor of *The New Jersey Book of Lists*. Many of his stories have appeared in *Ellery Queen's Mystery Magazine*.